CITIZENS TO LORDS

CITIZENS
TO LORDS

A Social History of Western Political Thought
From Antiquity to the Middle Ages

ELLEN MEIKSINS WOOD

VERSO
London • New York

First published by Verso 2008
Copyright © Ellen Meiksins Wood 2008
All rights reserved

1 3 5 7 9 10 8 6 4 2

Verso
UK: 6 Meard Street, London W1F 0EG
USA: 180 Varick Street, New York, NY 10014–4606
www.versobooks.com

Verso is the imprint of New Left Books

ISBN-13: 978–1–84467–243–1

British Library Cataloguing in Publication Data
A catalogue record for this book is available from the British Library

Library of Congress Cataloging-in-Publication Data
A catalog record for this book is available from the Library of Congress

Typeset in Sabon by Hewer Text UK Ltd, Edinburgh
Printed in the USA by Maple Vail

In memory of
Neal Wood

CONTENTS

ACKNOWLEDGEMENTS

As so often before, I am particularly grateful to George Comninel, who read the whole manuscript and made his customarily generous and insightful suggestions. My thanks also to Paul Cartledge, Janet Coleman and Gordon Schochet, who read parts of the manuscript and made useful comments but cannot, of course, be held responsible for any failures on my part to take good advice. Perry Anderson kindly agreed to my last-minute request for a quick reading of the whole text and made some very helpful suggestions. And special thanks to Ed Broadbent, who brilliantly played the role of every writer's dream audience, the intelligent general reader. I owe a great deal to his keenly critical eye, together with his unfailing support and encouragement.

My greatest debt is to Neal Wood. Many years ago, we decided that one day we would write a social history of political theory together. Somehow we never got around to it. There were always other projects to embark on and complete. Yet when, after his death, I set out to do it on my own, he remained in a sense the co-author. It was he who first introduced me to the history of political thought; it was he who coined the phrase, the 'social history of political theory'; and this project would have been inconceivable without his rich body of work in the field and his example of scholarly integrity combined with passionate engagement.

1

THE SOCIAL HISTORY
OF POLITICAL THEORY

What is Political Theory?

Every complex civilization with a state and organized leadership is bound to generate reflection on the relations between leader and led, rulers and subjects, command and obedience. Whether it takes the form of systematic philosophy, poetry, parable or proverb, in oral traditions or in the written word, we can call it political thought. But the subject of this book is one very particular mode of political thinking that emerged in the very particular historical conditions of ancient Greece and developed over two millennia in what we now call Europe and its colonial outposts.[1]

For better or worse, the Greeks invented their own distinctive mode of political *theory*, a systematic and analytical interrogation of political principles, full of laboriously constructed definitions and adversarial argumentation, applying critical reason to questioning the very foundations and legitimacy of traditional moral rules and the principles of political right. While there have been many other ways of thinking about politics in the Western world, what we think of as the classics

---

1 'Political' thought, in any of its forms, assumes the existence of political organization. For the purposes of this book, I shall call that form of organization the 'state', defining it broadly enough to encompass a wide variety of forms, from the polis and the ancient bureaucratic kingdom to the modern nation state – although throughout this book, we shall often have occasion to take note of the differences among various types of state. The state, then, is a 'complex of institutions by means of which the power of the society is organized on a basis superior to kinship' – an organization of power that entails a claim 'to paramountcy in the application of naked force to social problems' and consists of 'formal, specialized instruments of coercion' (Morton Fried, *The Evolution of Political Society*, New York: Random House, 1968, pp. 229–30). The state embraces less inclusive institutions – households, clans, kinship groups, etc. – and performs common social functions that such institutions cannot carry out.

of Western political thought, ancient and modern, belong to the
tradition of political *theory* established by the Greeks.

Other ancient civilizations in many ways more advanced than the
Greeks – in everything from agricultural techniques to commerce,
navigation, and every conceivable craft or high art – produced vast
literatures on every human practice, as well as speculations about the
origins of life and the formation of the universe. But, in general, the
political order was not treated as an object of systematic critical
speculation.

We can, for example, contrast the ancient Greek mode of political
speculation about principles of political order with the philosophy of
ethical precept, aphorism, advice and example produced by the far
more complex and advanced civilization of China, which had its own
rich and varied tradition of political thought. Confucian philosophy,
for instance, takes the form of aphorisms on appropriate conduct,
proverbial sayings and exemplary anecdotes, conveying its political
lessons not by means of argumentation but by subtle allusions with
complex layers of meaning. Another civilization more advanced than
classical Greece, India, produced a Hindu tradition of political thought
lacking the kind of analytical and theoretical speculation that characterized Indian works of moral philosophy, logic and epistemology,
expressing its commitment to existing political arrangements in didactic
form without systematic argumentation. We can also contrast classical
political philosophy to the earlier Homeric poetry of heroic ideals,
models and examples or even to the political poetry of Solon, on the
eve of the classical polis.

The tradition of political theory as we know it in the West can be
traced back to ancient Greek philosophers – notably, Protagoras,
Socrates, Plato and Aristotle – and it has produced a series of 'canonical' thinkers whose names have become familiar even to those who
have never read their work: St Augustine, St Thomas Aquinas,
Machiavelli, Hobbes, Locke, Rousseau, Hegel, Mill, and so on. The
writings of these thinkers are extremely varied, but they do have certain
things in common. Although they often analyze the state as it is, their
principal enterprise is criticism and prescription. They all have some
conception of what constitutes the right and proper ordering of society
and government. What is conceived as 'right' is often based on some
conception of justice and the morally good life, but it may also derive
from practical reflections about what is required to maintain peace,
security and material well-being.

Some political theorists offer blueprints for an ideally just state.
Others specify reforms of existing government and proposals for

guiding public policy. For all of them, the central questions have to do with who should govern and how, or what form of government is best; and they generally agree that it is not enough to ask and answer questions about the best form of government: we must also critically explore the grounds on which such judgments are made. Underlying such questions is always some conception of human nature, those qualities in human beings that must be nurtured or controlled in order to achieve a right and proper social order. Political theorists have outlined their human ideals and asked what kind of social and political arrangements are required to realize this vision of humanity. And when questions such as these are asked, others may not be far off: why and under what conditions ought we to obey those who govern us, and are we ever entitled to disobey or rebel?

These may seem obvious questions, but the very idea of asking them, the very idea that the principles of government or the obligation to obey authority are proper subjects for systematic reflection and the application of critical reason, cannot be taken for granted. Political theory represents as important a cultural milestone as does systematic philosophical or scientific reflection on the nature of matter, the earth and heavenly bodies. If anything, the invention of political theory is harder to explain than is the emergence of natural philosophy and science.

In what follows, we shall explore the historical conditions in which political theory was invented and how it developed in specific historical contexts, always keeping in mind that the classics of political theory were written in response to particular historical circumstances. The periods of greatest creativity in political theory have tended to be those historical moments when social and political conflict has erupted in particularly urgent ways, with far-reaching consequences; but even in calmer times, the questions addressed by political theorists have presented themselves in historically specific ways.

This means several things. Political theorists may speak to us through the centuries. As commentators on the human condition, they may have something to say for all times. But they are, like all human beings, historical creatures; and we shall have a much richer understanding of what they have to say, and even how it might shed light on our own historical moment, when we have some idea of why they said it, to whom they said it, with whom they were debating (explicitly or implicitly), how their immediate world looked to them, and what they believed should be changed or preserved. This is not simply a matter of biographical detail or even historical 'background'. To

understand what political theorists are saying requires knowing what
questions they are trying to answer, and those questions confront them
not simply as philosophical abstractions but as specific problems posed
by specific historical conditions, in the context of specific practical
activities, social relations, pressing issues, grievances and conflicts.

The History of Political Theory

This understanding of political theory as a historical product has not
always prevailed among scholars who write about the history of political
thought; and it probably still needs to be justified, not least against the
charge that by historicizing the great works of political theory we
demean and trivialize them, denying them any meaning and significance
beyond their own historical moment. I shall try to explain and defend
my reasons for proceeding as I do, but that requires, first, a sketch of
how the history of political thought has been studied in the recent past.

In the 1960s and 70s, at a time of revival for the study of political
theory, academic specialists used to debate endlessly about the nature
and fate of their discipline. But in general political theorists, especially
in American universities, were expected to embrace the division of
political studies into the 'empirical' and the 'normative'. In one camp
was the *real* political science, claiming to deal scientifically with the
facts of political life as they are, and in the other was 'theory', confined
to the ivory tower of political philosophy and reflecting not on what
is but on what *ought to be*.

This barren division of the discipline undoubtedly owed much to
the culture of the Cold War, which generally encouraged the withdrawal
of academics from trenchant social criticism. At any rate, political
science lost much of its critical edge. The object of study for this so-
called 'science' was not creative human action but rather political
'behaviour', which could, it was claimed, be comprehended by quantitative methods appropriate to the involuntary motions of material
bodies, atoms or plants.

This view of political science was certainly challenged by some
political theorists, notably Sheldon Wolin, whose *Politics and Vision*
eloquently asserted the importance of creative vision in political analysis.[2]
But at least for a time, many political theorists seemed happy enough

2 *Politics and Vision: Continuity and Innovation in Western Political Thought* was
first published in 1960. The most recent expanded edition was published by Princeton
University Press in 2006.

to accept the place assigned to them by the ultra-empiricist 'behaviouralists' then dominant in US political science departments. It seemed especially congenial to the disciples of Leo Strauss, who formed an unholy alliance with the behaviouralists, each faction agreeing to respect the inviolability of the other's territory.[3] The empiricists would leave the philosophers in peace to spin their intricate conceptual webs, while the 'normative' theorists would never cast a critical eye at their empirical colleagues' political analysis. The Straussian attack on 'historicism' was directed against other theorists, in self-proclaimed defence of universal and absolute truths against the relativism of modernity; and, although they would later emerge as influential ideologues of neoconservatism and as something like philosophical mentors to the regime of George W. Bush, Straussian political theorists of an earlier generation were on the whole content to pursue their reactionary and antimodernist (if not antidemocratic) political agenda on the philosophical plane – except when they ventured completely outside the walls of the academy to write speeches for right-wing politicians. Their 'empiricist' colleagues seem to have understood that Straussians, with their esoteric, even cabalistic philosophical preoccupations, represented no challenge to the shallowness and vacuity of 'empirical' political science.

---

3 This is not the place to engage in the debate about Leo Strauss's own political views. The issue here is his approach to the study of political theory. Born in Germany in 1899, Strauss emigrated to the US in 1937 and, especially after his appointment to the faculty at the University of Chicago in 1949, exerted a great influence on the study of political theory in North America, producing a school of interpretation which would be carried on by his disciples and their students. The Straussian approach to political theory begins from the premise that political philosophers, who are concerned with truth and knowledge rather than mere opinion, have been compelled throughout the history of the canon to disguise their ideas, in order not to be persecuted as subversives. They have therefore, according to Straussians, adopted an 'esoteric' mode of writing, which obliges scholarly interpreters to read between the lines. This compulsion, the Straussians seem to suggest, has been aggravated by the onset of modernity, and particularly mass democracy, which (whatever other virtues they may or may not have) are inevitably dominated by opinion and, apparently, hostility to truth and knowledge. Straussians regard themselves as a privileged and exclusive fraternity in their access to the true meaning of political philosophy, taking enormous liberties of interpretation, which stray from the literal text in ways few other scholars would allow themselves. This approach tends, needless to say, to limit the possibilities of debate between Straussians and those outside the fraternity, since other interpretations of texts can be ruled out *a priori* as blind to hidden 'esoteric' meanings. However much Straussians may have denigrated 'empirical' political science, their method has reinforced the enclosure of 'normative' political theory in its own solipsistic domain.

Yet Straussians were not alone in accepting the neat division between empirical and normative, or between theory and practice. At least, there was a widespread view that grubbing around in the realities of politics, while all right for some, was not what political theorists should do. The groundbreaking work of the Canadian political theorist, C.B. Macpherson, who had introduced a different approach to the study of political theory by situating seventeenth-century English thinkers in the historical context of what he called a 'possessive market society', proved to be little more than a detour from the mainstream of Anglo-American scholarship.[4] Scholars who studied and taught the history of political thought, the 'classics' of the Western 'canon', did not always subscribe to the Straussian variety of anti-historicism; but they were often even more averse to history. Many treated the 'greats' as pure minds floating free above the political fray; and any attempt to plant these thinkers on firm historical ground, any attempt to treat them as living and breathing historical beings passionately engaged in the politics of their own time and place, would be dismissed as trivialization, demeaning great men and reducing them to mere publicists, pamphleteers and propagandists.[5]

What distinguished real political philosophy from simple 'ideology', according to this view, was that it rose above political struggle and partisanship. It tackled universal and perennial problems, seeking principles of social order and human development valid for all human beings in all times and places. The questions raised by true political philosophers are, it was argued, intrinsically transhistorical: what does it mean to be truly human? What kind of society permits the full development of that humanity? What are the universal principles of right order for individuals and societies?

It seems not to have occurred to proponents of this view that even such 'universal' questions could be asked and answered in ways that served certain immediate political interests rather than others, or that these questions and answers might even be intended as passionately partisan. For instance, the human ideals espoused by philosophers can tell us much about their social and political commitments and where

4 *The Political Theory of Possessive Individualism: Hobbes to Locke*, was published by Oxford University Press in 1962, but Macpherson had already published articles in the 1950s applying his contextual approach. Although I have disagreements with him and regard his ideal-type 'possessive market society' as a rather ahistorical abstraction, there can be little doubt that he broke important new ground.

5 See, for instance, Dante Germino, *Beyond Ideology: The Revival of Political Theory* (New York: Harper and Row, 1967).

they stand in the conflicts of their day. The failure to acknowledge this meant that these scholars saw little benefit in trying to understand the classics by situating them in their author's time and place. The contextualization of political thought or the 'sociology of knowledge' might tell us something about the ideas and motivations of lesser mortals and ideologues, but it could tell us nothing worth knowing about a great philosopher, a genius like Plato.

This almost naïve ahistoricism was bound to produce a reaction, and a very different school of thought emerged, which has since overtaken its rivals. What has come to be called the Cambridge School appears, at least on the face of it, to go to the other extreme by radically historicizing the works, great and small, of political theory and denying them any wider meaning beyond the very local moment of their creation. The most effective exponent of this approach, Quentin Skinner, in the introduction to his classic text, *The Foundations of Modern Political Thought*, gives an account of his method that seems directly antithetical to the dichotomies on which the ahistorical approach was based, against the sharp distinction between political philosophy and ideology and the facile opposition of 'empirical' to 'normative'. In fact, argues Skinner, we can best understand the history of political theory by treating it essentially as the history of ideologies, and this requires a detailed contextualization. 'For I take it that political life itself sets the main problems for the political theorist, causing a certain range of issues to appear problematic, and a corresponding range of questions to become the leading subjects of debate.'[6]

The principal benefit of this approach, Skinner writes, is that it equips us 'with a way of gaining greater insight into its author's meaning than we can ever hope to achieve simply from reading the text itself "over and over again" as the exponents of the "textualist" approach have characteristically proposed.'[7] But there is also another advantage:

> It will now be evident why I wish to maintain that, if the history of political theory were to be written essentially as a history of ideologies, one outcome might be a clearer understanding of the links between political theory and practice. For it now appears that, in recovering the terms of the normative vocabulary available to any

---

6 Quentin Skinner, *The Foundations of Modern Political Thought, Volume I: The Renaissance* (Cambridge: Cambridge University Press, 1978), p. xi.

7 *Ibid.*, p. xiii.

given agent for the description of his political behaviour, we are at the same time indicating one of the constraints upon his behaviour itself. This suggests that, in order to explain why such an agent acts as he does, we are bound to make some reference to this vocabulary, since it evidently figures as one of the determinants of his action. This in turn suggests that, if we were to focus our histories on the study of these vocabularies, we might be able to illustrate the exact ways in which the explanation of political behaviour depends upon the study of political thought.

Skinner then proceeded to construct a history of Western political thought in the Renaissance and the age of Reformation, especially the notion of the *state* as it acquired its modern meaning, by exploring the political vocabularies available to political thinkers and actors and the specific sets of questions that history had put on their agenda. His main strategy, here as elsewhere in his work, was to cast his net more widely than historians of political thought have customarily done, considering not just the leading theorists but, as he put it, 'the more general social and intellectual matrix out of which their works arose'.[8] He looked not only at the work of the greats but also at more 'ephemeral contemporary contributions to social and political thought', as a means of gaining access to the available vocabularies and the prevailing assumptions about political society that were shaping debate in specific times and places.

Skinner's approach has certain very clear strengths; and other members of the Cambridge School have also applied these principles, often very effectively, to the analysis of specific thinkers or 'traditions of discourse', especially those of early modern England. The proposition that the political questions addressed by political theorists, including the great ones, are thrown up by real political life and are shaped by the historical conditions in which they arise seems hardly more *nor* less than good common sense.

But much depends on what the Cambridge School regards as a relevant *context,* and it soon becomes clear that contextualization has a different meaning than might be inferred from Skinner's reference to the 'social and intellectual matrix'. It turns out that the 'social' matrix has little to do with 'society', the economy, or even the polity. The social context is itself intellectual, or at least the 'social' is defined by, and only by, existing vocabularies. The 'political life' that sets the agenda for theory is essentially a language game. In the end, to contex-

---

8 *Ibid.*, p. x.

tualize a text is to situate it among other texts, among a range of vocabularies, discourses and ideological paradigms at various levels of formality, from the classics of political thought down to ephemeral screeds or political speeches. What emerges from Skinner's assault on purely textual histories or the abstract history of ideas is yet another kind of textual history, yet another history of ideas – certainly more sophisticated and comprehensive than what went before, but hardly less limited to disembodied texts.

A catalogue of what is missing from Skinner's comprehensive history of political ideas from 1300 to 1600 reveals quite starkly the limits of his 'contexts'. Skinner is dealing with a period marked by major social and economic developments, which loomed very large in the theory and practice of European political thinkers and actors. Yet there is in his book no substantive consideration of agriculture, the aristocracy and peasantry, land distribution and tenure, the social division of labour, social protest and conflict, population, urbanization, trade, commerce, manufacture, and the burgher class.[9]

It is true that the other major founding figure of the Cambridge School, J.G.A. Pocock, is, on the face of it, more interested in economic developments and what appear to be material factors, like the 'discovery' (in Pocock's words) of capital and the emergence of 'commercial society' in eighteenth-century Britain. Yet his account of this 'sudden and traumatic discovery' is, in its way, even more divorced from historical processes than Skinner's account of the state.[10] The critical moment for Pocock is the foundation of the Bank of England, which, he argues, brought about a complete transformation of property, the transformation of its structure and morality, with 'spectacular abruptness' in the mid-1690s; and it was accompanied by sudden changes in the psychology of politics. But in this argument, the Bank of England, and indeed commercial society, seem to have no history at all. They suddenly emerge full-grown, as if the transformations of property and social relations in the sixteenth and seventeenth centuries and the formation of English agrarian capitalism, or the distinctively English banking system associated with the development of capitalist property which preceded the foundation of the national bank, had no bearing on their consolidation in the commercial capitalism of the eighteenth century.

---

9 See Neal Wood, *John Locke and Agrarian Capitalism* (Berkeley and Los Angeles: University of California Press, 1984) p. 11.

10 J.G.A. Pocock, *Virtue, Commerce, and History* (Cambridge: Cambridge University Press, 1985), p. 108. An elaboration of this argument on Pocock and 'commercial society' will have to await another volume devoted to the relevant period.

Such a strikingly ahistorical account is possible only because, for Pocock perhaps even more than for Skinner, history has little to do with social processes, and historical transformations are manifest only as visible shifts in the languages of politics. Changes in discourse that represent the culmination and consolidation of a social transformation are presented as its origin and cause.

So, what purports to be the *history* of political thought, for both Pocock and Skinner, is curiously ahistorical, not only in its failure to grapple with what on any reckoning were decisive historical developments in the relevant periods but also in its lack of *process*. Characteristically, history for the Cambridge School is a series of disconnected, very local and particular episodes, such as specific political controversies in specific times and places, which have no apparent relation to more inclusive social developments or to any historical process, large or small.[11]

This emphasis on the local and particular does not, however, preclude consideration of larger spans of time and space. The 'traditions of discourse' that are the stuff of the Cambridge School embrace long periods, sometimes whole centuries or even more. A tradition may cross national boundaries and even continents. It may be a particular literary genre fairly limited in time and geographic scope, like the 'mirror-for-princes' literature, which Skinner very effectively explores to analyze the work of Machiavelli; or, notably in the case of John Pocock, it may be the discourse of 'commercial society' which characterized the eighteenth century, or the tradition of 'civic humanism', which had a longer life and a wider scope. But whatever its duration or spatial reach, the tradition of discourse plays a role in analyzing political theory hardly different from the role played by particular episodes (which are themselves an interplay of discourses), like the Engagement Controversy in which Skinner situates Hobbes, or the Exclusion Crisis which others have invoked in the analysis of Locke. In both cases, contexts are texts; and at neither end of the Cambridge historical spectrum, from the very local episode to the long and widespread tradition of discourse, do we see any sign of historical movement, any sense of the dynamic connection between one historical moment and another or between the political episode and the social

---

11 For a critical discussion of Skinner's 'atomized' and 'episodic' treatment of history, see Cary Nederman, 'Quentin Skinner's State: Historical Method and Traditions of Discourse', *Canadian Journal of Political Science*, Vol. 18, No. 2, June 1985, pp. 339–52.

processes that underlie it. In effect, long historical processes are themselves converted into momentary political episodes.

In its conception of history, the Cambridge School has something
essential in common with more fashionable 'postmodernist' trends.
Discourse is for both the constitutive, indeed the only, practice of social
life; and history is dissolved into contingency. Both respond to 'grand
narratives' not by critically examining their virtues and vices but by
discarding historical processes altogether.

The Social History of Political Theory

The 'social history of political theory', which is the subject of this
book, starts from the premise that the great political thinkers of the
past were passionately engaged in the issues of their time and place.[12]
This was so even when they addressed these issues from an elevated
philosophical vantage point, in conversation with other philosophers
in other times and places, and even, or especially, when they sought
to translate their reflections into universal and timeless principles. Often
their engagements took the form of partisan adherence to a specific
and identifiable political cause, or even fairly transparent expressions
of particular interests, the interests of a particular party or class. But
their ideological commitments could also be expressed in a larger
vision of the good society and human ideals.

At the same time, the great political thinkers are not party hacks
or propagandists. Political theory is certainly an exercise in persuasion,
but its tools are reasoned discourse and argumentation, in a genuine
search for some kind of truth. Yet if the 'greats' are different from
lesser political thinkers and actors, they are no less human and no less
steeped in history. When Plato explored the concept of justice in the
Republic, or when he outlined the different levels of knowledge, he
was certainly opening large philosophical questions and he was
certainly in search of universal and transcendent truths. But his questions, no less than his answers, were (as I shall argue in a subsequent
chapter) driven by his critical engagement with Athenian democracy.

To acknowledge the humanity and historic engagement of political
thinkers is surely not to demean them or deny them their greatness.
In any case, without subjecting ideas to critical historical scrutiny, it

---

12 For a discussion of the term 'social history of political theory', see Neal Wood,
'The Social History of Political Theory', *Political Theory*, Vol. 6 No. 3, August 1978,
pp. 345–67.

is impossible to assess their claims to universality or transcendent truth. The intention here is certainly to explore the ideas of the most important political thinkers; but these thinkers will always be treated as living and engaged human beings, immersed not only in the rich intellectual heritage of received ideas bequeathed by their philosophical predecessors, nor simply against the background of the available vocabularies specific to their time and place, but also in the context of the social and political processes that shaped their immediate world.

This social history of political theory, in its conception of historical contexts, proceeds from certain fundamental premises, which belong to the tradition of 'historical materialism': human beings enter into relations with each other and with nature to guarantee their own survival and social reproduction. To understand the social practices and cultural products of any time and place, we need to know something about those conditions of survival and social reproduction, something about the specific ways in which people gain access to the material conditions of life, about how some people gain access to the labour of others, about the relations between people who produce and those who appropriate what others produce, about the forms of property that emerge from these social relations, and about how these relations are expressed in political domination, as well as resistance and struggle.

This is certainly not to say that a theorist's ideas can be predicted or 'read off' from his or her social position or class. The point is simply that the questions confronting any political thinker, however eternal and universal those questions may seem, are posed to them in specific historical forms. The Cambridge School agrees that, in order to understand the answers offered by political theorists, we must know something about the questions they are trying to answer and that different historical settings pose different sets of questions. But, for the social history of political theory, these questions are posed not only by explicit political controversies, and not only at the level of philosophy or high politics, but also by the social pressures and tensions that shape human interactions outside the political arena and beyond the world of texts.

This approach differs from that of the Cambridge School both in the scope of what is regarded as a 'context' and in the effort to apprehend historical *processes*. Ideological episodes like the Engagement Controversy or the Exclusion Crisis may tell us something about a thinker like Hobbes or Locke; but unless we explore how these thinkers situated themselves in the larger historical processes that were shaping their world, it is hard to see how we are to distinguish the great theorists from ephemeral publicists.

Long-term developments in social relations, property forms and state-formation do episodically erupt into specific political-ideological controversies; and it is undoubtedly true that political theory tends to flourish at moments like this, when history intrudes most dramatically into the dialogue among texts or traditions of discourse. But a major thinker like John Locke, while he was certainly responding to specific and momentary political controversies, was raising larger fundamental questions about social relations, property and the state generated by larger social transformations and structural tensions – in particular, developments that we associate with the 'rise of capitalism'. Locke did not, needless to say, know that he was observing the development of what we call capitalism; but he was dealing with problems posed by its characteristic transformations of property, class relations and the state. To divorce him from this larger social context is to impoverish his work and its capacity to illuminate its own historical moment, let alone the 'human condition' in general.

If different historical experiences give rise to different sets of problems, it follows that these divergences will also be observable in various 'traditions of discourse'. It is not, for instance, enough to talk about a Western or European historical experience, defined by a common cultural and philosophical inheritance. We must also look for differences among the various patterns of property relations and the various processes of state-formation that distinguished one European society from another and produced different patterns of theoretical interrogation, different sets of questions for political thinkers to address.

The diversity of 'discourses' does not simply express personal or even national idiosyncrasies of intellectual style among political philosophers engaged in dialogue with one another across geographical and chronological boundaries. To the extent that political philosophers are indeed reflecting not only upon philosophical traditions but upon the problems set by political life, their 'discourses' are diverse in large part because the political problems they confront are diverse. The problem of the state, for instance, has presented itself historically in different guises even to such close neighbours as the English and the French.[13]

Even the 'perennial questions' have appeared in various shapes. What appears as a salient issue will vary according to the nature of the

---

13 I have discussed these differences at some length in *The Pristine Culture of Capitalism: A Historical Essay on Old Regimes and Modern States* (London: Verso, 1992).

principal contenders, the competing social forces at work, the conflicting interests at stake. The configuration of problems arising from a
struggle such as the one in early modern England between 'improving'
landlords and commoners dependent on the preservation of common
and waste land will differ from those at issue in France among peasants,
seigneurs, and a tax-hungry state. Even within the same historical or
national configuration, what appears as a problem to the commoner
or peasant will not necessarily appear so to the gentleman-farmer, the
seigneur, or the royal office-holder. We need not reduce the great
political thinkers to 'prize-fighters' for this or that social interest in
order to acknowledge the importance of identifying the particular
constellation of problems that history has presented to them, or to
recognize that the 'dialogue' in which they are engaged is not simply
a timeless debate with rootless philosophers but an engagement with
living historical actors, both those who dominate and those who resist.

To say this is not to claim that political theorists from another time
and place have nothing to say to our own. There is no inverse relation
between historical contextualization and 'relevance'. On the contrary,
historical contextualization is an essential condition for learning from
the 'classics', not simply because it allows a better understanding of
a thinker's meaning and intention, but also because it is in the context
of history that theory emerges from the realm of pure abstraction and
enters the world of human practice and social interaction.

There are, of course, commonalities of experience we share with our
predecessors just by virtue of being human, and there are innumerable
practices learned by humanity over the centuries in which we engage as
our ancestors did. These common experiences mean that much of what
great thinkers of the past have to say is readily accessible to us. But if
the classics of political theory are to yield fruitful lessons, it is not enough
to acknowledge these commonalities of human and historical experience
or to mine the classics for certain abstract universal principles. To
historicize is to humanize, and to detach ideas from their own material
and practical setting is to lose our points of human contact with them.

There is a way, all too common, of studying the history of political
theory which detaches it from the urgent human issues to which it is
addressed. To think about the *politics* in political theory is, at the very
least, to consider and make judgments about what it would mean to
translate particular principles into actual social relationships and
political arrangements. If one of the functions of political theory is
to sharpen our perceptions and conceptual instruments for thinking
about politics in our own time and place, that purpose is defeated by
emptying historical political theories of their own political meaning.

Some years ago, for instance, I encountered an argument about Aristotle's theory of natural slavery, which seemed to me to illustrate the shortcomings of an ahistorical approach.[14] We should not, the argument went, treat the theory of natural slavery as a comment on a historically actual social condition, the relation between slaves and masters as it existed in the ancient world, because to do so is to deprive it of any significance beyond the socio-economic circumstances of its own time and place. Instead, we should recognize it as a philosophical metaphor for the universal human condition in the abstract. Yet to deny that Aristotle was defending a real social practice, the enslavement of real human beings, or to suggest that we have more to learn about the human condition by refusing to confront his theory of slavery in its concrete historical meaning, seems a peculiar way of sensitizing us to the realities of social life and politics, or indeed the human condition, in our own time or any other.

There is also another way in which the contextual analysis of political

---

14 Arlene Saxonhouse, in a review of M.I. Finley's *Ancient Slavery and Modern Ideology*, writes dismissively of his approach as a 'social historian', which, apparently, can tell us a few unsurprising things about the predispositions of writers on slavery but cannot illuminate the deeper meaning of philosophical reflections such as those of Aristotle. 'Aristotle's reflections on the nature of slavery,' she writes, 'move us beyond a particular slave and a particular master. Instead, the slave's subordination to the master reflects our own subordination to nature. Slavery is not only the degraded position of one without control over his or her labour. It is the condition of all humans vis-à-vis nature. The master and the slave is not a relationship limited to the slave societies of the ancient and modern world to which Finley refers. The master and slave are perennial states which Aristotle exhorts us to understand so that we may understand our own place within society and within nature. Finley, the social historian, turns our attention to the specifics of a time and a place, and that is why, though he notes the importance of the study of American slavery to American society today, he does not explain the relevance of ancient slavery. For that we must turn to the ancient philosopher' (*Political Theory*, Vol. 9, No. 4, November 1981, p. 579). It is undeniable that Aristotle situates slavery in his all-embracing philosophical reflections on nature in general; but it seems perverse to deny that he is, in the process, reflecting on the very specific condition of slavery as he knew it in the Greek world. It might perhaps be possible to deny that Aristotle intends to *justify* slavery by treating it as a manifestation of humanity's general subordination to nature (though we may be inclined, on the contrary, to think that this naturalization of slavery serves precisely as justification). But there is, in any case, something rather troubling about the view that a 'philosophical' interpretation of Aristotle, which detaches his discussion of slavery from the concrete realities of the master–slave relation in historical time and space, tells us more about 'the relevance of ancient slavery' (or, indeed, Aristotle's views about it) than does mere 'social history', which treats the philosopher's reflections as, precisely, reflections on ancient slavery, not as a metaphor but as an all-too-concrete historical reality.

theory can illuminate our own historical moment. If we abstract a political theory from its historical context, we in effect assimilate it to our own. Understanding a theory historically allows us to look at our own historical condition from a critical distance, from the vantage point of other times and other ideas. It also allows us to observe how certain assumptions, which we may now accept uncritically, came into being and how they were challenged in their formative years. Reading political theory in this way, we may be less tempted to take for granted the dominant ideas and assumptions of our own time and place.

This benefit may not be so readily available to contextual approaches in which historical processes are replaced by disconnected episodes and traditions of discourse. The Cambridge mode of contextualization encourages us to believe that the old political thinkers have little to say in our own time and place. It invites us to think that there is nothing to learn from them, because their historical experiences have no apparent connection to our own. To discover what there is to learn from the history of political theory requires us to place ourselves on the continuum of history, where we are joined to our predecessors not only by the continuities we share but by the processes of change that intervene between us, bringing us from there to here.

The intention of this study, then, is not only to illuminate some classic texts and the conditions in which they were created but also to explain by example a distinctive approach to contextual interpretation. Its subject matter will be not only texts, nor discursive paradigms, but the social relations that made them possible and posed the particular questions addressed by political theorists. This kind of contextual reading also requires us to do something more than follow the line of descent from one political thinker to the next. It invites us to explore how certain fundamental social relations set the parameters of human creativity, not only in political theory but in other modes of discourse that form part of the historical setting and the cultural climate within which political theories emerged – such as, say, Greek tragedy, the Roman law or Christian theology.

While I try to strike a balance between contextual analysis and interpretation of the major texts, some readers may think that this way of proceeding places too much emphasis on grand structural themes at the expense of a more exhaustive textual reading. But the approach being proposed in this book is best understood not as in any way excluding or slighting close textual analysis but, on the contrary, as a way of shedding light on texts, which others can put to the test by more minute and detailed reading.

The Origin of Political Theory

Scholars have offered various explanations for the emergence of political theory in ancient Greece. There will be more in the next chapter about the specific historical conditions that produced, especially in Athens, the kind of confidence in human agency that is a necessary condition of political theory. In this chapter, we shall confine ourselves to the general conditions that marked the Greeks out from other ancient civilizations and set the agenda for political theory.

The most vital factor undoubtedly was the development, perhaps by the late eighth century BC, of the unique Greek state, the polis, which sometimes evolved into self-governing democracies, as in Athens from the early fifth to the late fourth century. This type of state differed sharply from the large imperial states that characterized other 'high' civilizations, and from states that preceded the polis in Greece, the Minoan and Mycenean kingdoms. In place of an elaborate bureaucratic apparatus, the polis was characterized by a fairly simple state admin- istration (if we can even call it a 'state' at all) and a self-governing civic community, in which the principal political relations were not between rulers and subjects but among *citizens* – whether the citizen body was more inclusive, as in Athenian democracy, or less so, as in Sparta or the city-states of Crete. Politics, in the sense we have come to understand the word, implying contestation and debate among diverse interests, replaced rule or administration as the principal object of political discourse. These factors were, of course, more prominent in democracies, and Athens in particular, than in the oligarchic polis.

It is also significant that by the end of the fifth century, Greece was becoming a literate culture, in unprecedented ways and to an unprece- dented degree. Although we should not overestimate its extent, a kind of popular literacy, especially in the democracy, replaced what some scholars have called craft literacy, in which reading and writing were specialized skills practised only, or largely, by professionals or scribes. What happened in Greece, and especially in Athens, has been described as the democratization of writing.

Popular rule, which required widespread and searching discussion of pressing social and political issues, and which provided new oppor- tunities for political leadership and influence, when coupled with economic prosperity, brought an increasing demand for schooling and teaching. An economically vital, democratic and relatively free culture with a growing means of written expression and exact argumentation, and an increasing audience for such discourse, created an atmosphere favourable to the birth and early thriving of political theory, a powerful

and ingenious mode of self-examination and reflection that continues
to the present.

But we need to look more closely at the polis, and especially the
democracy, to understand why this new mode of political thinking
took the form that it did, and why it raised certain kinds of questions
that had not been raised before, which would thereafter set the agenda
for the long tradition of Western political theory. There will be more
in the next chapter about Athenian society and politics, as the specific
context in which the Greek classics were written. For our purposes
here, a few general points need to be highlighted about the conditions
in which political theory originated.

The polis represented not only a distinctive political form but a
unique organization of social relations. The state in other high
civilizations typically embodied a relation between rulers and subjects
that was at the same time a relation between appropriators and
producers. The Chinese philosopher, Mencius, once wrote that 'Those
who are ruled produce food; those who rule are fed. That this is right
is universally recognized everywhere under Heaven.' This principle
nicely sums up the essence of the relation between rulers and producers
which characterized the most advanced ancient civilizations.

In these ancient states, there was a sharp demarcation between
production and politics, in the sense that direct producers had no
political role, as rulers or even as citizens. The state was organized to
control subject labour, and it was above all through the state that some
people appropriated the labour of others or its products. Office in the
state was likely to be the primary means of acquiring great wealth.
Even where private property in land was fairly well developed, state
office was likely to be the source of large property, while small property
generally carried with it obligations to the state in the form of tax,
tribute or labour service. It remained true of China, for instance,
throughout its long imperial history that large property and great
wealth were associated with office, and the imperial state did everything
possible – if not always successfully – to maintain that connection and
to impede the autonomous development of powerful propertied classes.

The ancient 'bureaucratic' state, then, constituted a ruling body
superimposed upon and appropriating from subject communities of
direct producers, above all peasants. Although such a form had existed
in Greece, both there and in Rome a new form of political organization
emerged which combined landlords and peasants in one civic and
military community. While others, notably the Phoenicians and
Carthaginians, may have lived in city-states in some ways comparable
to the Greek polis or the Roman Republic, the very idea of a civic

community and citizenship, as distinct from the principles of rule by a superimposed state apparatus, derive from the Greeks and the Romans.

The idea of a *peasant*-citizen was even further removed from the experience of other ancient states. The role of slavery in Greece and Rome will be discussed in subsequent chapters; but, for the moment, it is important to acknowledge the distinctive political role of producing classes, peasants and craftsmen, and their unique relation to the state. In the Greek polis and the Roman Republic, appropriators and producers in the citizen body confronted one another directly as individuals and as classes, as landlords and peasants, not primarily as rulers and subjects. Private property developed more autonomously and completely, separating itself more thoroughly from the state. A new and distinctive dynamic of property and class relations was differentiated out from the traditional relations of (appropriating) state and (producing) subjects.

The special characteristics of these states are reflected in the classics of ancient political thought. When Plato, for example, attacked the democratic polis of Athens, he did so by opposing to it a state-form that departed radically from precisely those features most unique and specific to the Greek polis and which bore a striking resemblance in principle to certain non-Greek states. In the *Republic*, Plato proposes a community of rulers superimposed upon a ruled community of producers, primarily peasants, a state in which producers are individually 'free' and in possession of property, not dependent on wealthier private proprietors; but, although the rulers own no private property, producers are collectively subject to the ruling community and compelled to transfer surplus labour to their non-producing masters. Political and military functions belong exclusively to the ruling class, according to the traditional separation of military and farming classes, which Plato and Aristotle both admired. In other words, those who are ruled produce food, and those who rule are fed. Plato no doubt drew inspiration from the Greek states that most closely adhered to these principles – notably Sparta and the city-states of Crete; but it is likely that the model he had more specifically in mind was Egypt – or, at least, Egypt as the Greeks, sometimes inaccurately, understood it.

Other classical writers defended the supremacy of the dominant classes in less radical and more specifically Greco-Roman ways. In particular, the doctrine of the 'mixed constitution' – which appears in Plato's *Laws* and figures prominently in the writings of Aristotle, Polybius, and Cicero – reflects a uniquely Greek and Roman reality and the special problems faced by a dominant class of private proprietors in a state that incorporates rich and poor, appropriators and producers, landlords and peasants, into a single civic and military community. The idea of the mixed constitution proceeded from the Greco-Roman classification of constitutions – in particular, the distinction among government by the many, the few, or only one: democracy, oligarchy, monarchy. A constitution could be 'mixed' in the sense that it adopted certain elements of each. More particularly, rich and poor could be respectively represented by 'oligarchic' and 'democratic' elements; and the predominance of the rich could be achieved not by drawing a clear and rigid division between a ruling apparatus and subject producers, or between military and farming classes, but by tilting the constitutional balance towards oligarchic elements.

In both theory and practice, then, a specific dynamic of *property* and *class* relations, distinct from the relations between rulers and subjects, was woven directly into the fabric of Greek and Roman politics. These relations generated a distinctive array of practical problems and theoretical issues, especially in the democratic polis. There were, of course, distinctive problems of social order in a society, like Athens, that lacked an unequivocally dominant ruling stratum whose economic power and political supremacy were coextensive and inseparable, a society where economic and political hierarchies did not coincide and political relations were less between rulers and subjects than among citizens. These political relations were played out in assemblies and juries, in constant debate, which demanded new rhetorical skills and modes of argumentation. Nothing could be taken for granted; and, not surprisingly, this was a highly litigious society, in which political discourse derived much of its method and substance from legal disputation, with all its predilection for hairsplitting controversy.

Greek political theorists were self-conscious about the uniqueness of their specific form of state, and they inevitably explored the nature of the polis and what distinguished it from others. They raised questions about the origin and purpose of the state. Having effectively invented a new identity, the civic identity of citizenship, they posed questions about the meaning of citizenship, who should enjoy political rights and whether any division between rulers and ruled existed by nature. They confronted the tension between the levelling identity of citizenship and the hierarchical principles of noble birth or wealth. Questions about law and the rule of law; about the difference between political organization based on violence or coercion and a civic community based on deliberation or persuasion; about human nature and its suitability (or otherwise) for political life – all of these questions were thrown up by the everyday realities of life in the polis.

In the absence of a ruling class whose ethical standards were accepted by the whole community as its governing principles, it was no longer possible to assume the eternity and inviolability of traditional norms. They were inevitably subjected to theoretical scrutiny and challenge. Defenders of traditional hierarchies were obliged to respond not by repeating old proverbs or reciting epics of aristocratic hero-kings but by constructing theoretical arguments to meet theoretical challenges. Questions arose about the origin of moral and political principles and what makes them binding. From the same political realities emerged the humanistic principle that 'man is the measure of all things', with all the new questions that this principle entailed. So, for instance, the Sophists (Greek philosophers and teachers who will be discussed in the next chapter) asked whether moral and political principles exist by nature or merely by custom – a question that could be answered in various ways, some congenial to democracy, others in support of oligarchy; and when Plato expressed his opposition to democracy, he could not rely on invoking the gods or time-honoured custom but was obliged to make his case by means of philosophic reason, to construct a definition of justice and the good life that seemed to rule out democracy.

Political Theory in History: An Overview

Born in the polis, this new mode of political thought would survive the polis and continue to set the theoretical agenda in later centuries, when very different forms of state prevailed. This longevity has not been simply a matter of tenacious intellectual legacies. The Western tradition of political theory has developed on the foundations established in ancient Greece because certain issues have remained at the centre of European political life. In varying forms, the autonomy of private property, its relative independence from the state, and the tension between these foci of social power have continued to shape the political agenda. On the one hand, appropriating classes have needed the state to maintain order, conditions for appropriation and control over producing classes. On the other hand, they have found the state a burdensome nuisance and a competitor for surplus labour.

With a wary eye on the state, the dominant appropriating classes have always had to turn their attention to their relations with subordinate producing classes. Indeed, their need for the state has been largely determined by those difficult relations. In particular, throughout most of Western history, peasants fed, clothed, and housed the lordly minority by means of surplus labour extracted by payment of rents, fees, or tributes. Yet, though the aristocratic state depended on peasants and though lords were always alive to the threat of resistance, the politically voiceless classes play little overt role in the classics of Western political theory. Their silent presence tends to be visible only in the great theoretical efforts devoted to justifying social and political hier- archies.

The relation between appropriating and producing classes was to change fundamentally with the advent of capitalism, but the history of Western political theory continued to be in large part the history of tensions between property and state, appropriators and producers. In general, the Western tradition of political theory has been 'history from above', essentially reflection on the existing state and the need for its preservation or change written from the perspective of a member or client of the ruling classes. Yet it should be obvious that this 'history from above' cannot be understood without relating it to what can be learned about the 'history from below'. The complex three-way relation between the state, propertied classes and producers, perhaps more than anything else, sets the Western political tradition apart from others.

There is nothing unique to the West, of course, about societies in which dominant groups appropriate what others produce. But there is something distinctive about the ways in which the tensions between them have shaped political life and theory in the West. This may be precisely because the relations between appropriators and producers have never, since classical antiquity, been synonymous with the relation between rulers and subjects. To be sure, the peasant-citizen would not survive the Roman Empire, and many centuries would pass before anything comparable to the ancient Athenian idea of democratic citizenship would re-emerge in Europe. Feudal and early modern Europe would, in its own way, even approximate the old division between rulers and producers, as labouring classes were excluded from active political rights and the power to appropriate was typically associated with the possession of 'extra-economic' power, political, judicial or military. But even then, the relation between rulers and producers was never unambiguous, because appropriating classes confronted their labouring compatriots not, in the first instance, as a collective power organized in the state but in a more directly personal relation as individual proprietors, in rivalry with other proprietors and even with the state.

The autonomy of property and the contradictory relations between ruling class and state meant that propertied classes in the West always had to fight on two fronts. While they would have happily subscribed to Mencius's principle about those who rule and those who feed them, they could never take for granted such a neat division between rulers and producers, because there was a much clearer division than existed elsewhere between property and state.

Although the foundations of Western political theory established in ancient Greece proved to be remarkably resilient, there have, of course, been many changes and additions to its theoretical agenda, in keeping with changing historical conditions, which will be explored in the following chapters. The Romans, perhaps because their aristocratic republic did not confront challenges like those of the Athenian democracy, did not produce a tradition of political theory as fruitful as the Greek. But they did introduce other social and political innovations, especially the Roman law, which would have major implications for the development of political theory. The empire also gave rise to Christianity, which became the imperial religion, with all its cultural consequences.

It is particularly significant that the Romans began to delineate a sharp distinction between public and private, even, perhaps, between state and society. Above all, the opposition between property and state as two distinct foci of power, which has been a constant theme throughout the history of Western political theory, was for the first time formally acknowledged by the Romans in their distinction between *imperium* and *dominium*, power conceived as the right to command and power in the form of ownership. This did not preclude the view – expressed already by Cicero in *On Duties* (*De Officiis*) – that the purpose of the state was to protect private property or the conviction that the state came into being for that reason. On the contrary, the partnership of state and private property, which would continue to be a central theme of Western political theory, presupposes the separation, and the tensions, between them.

The tension between these two forms of power, which was intensified in theory and practice as republic gave way to empire, would, as we shall see, play a large part in the fall of the Roman Empire. With the rise of feudalism, that tension was resolved on the side of *dominium*, as the state was virtually dissolved into individual property. In contrast to the ancient division between rulers and producers, in which the state was the dominant instrument of appropriation, the feudal state scarcely had an autonomous existence apart from the hierarchical chain of individual, if conditional, property and personal lordship. Instead of a centralized public authority, the feudal state was a network of 'parcellized sovereignties', governed by a complex hierarchy of social relations and competing jurisdictions, in the hands not only of lords and kings, but also of various autonomous corporations, to say nothing of Holy Roman emperors and popes.[15] Feudal relations – between king and lords, between lords and vassals, between lords and peasants – were both a political/military relation and a form of property. Feudal lordship meant command of property, together with control of legally dependent labour; and, at the same time, it was a piece of the state, a fragment of political and military *imperium*.

The feudal resolution of the tension between property and state could not last forever. In their relations with the peasantry, lords would inevitably turn to the state for support; and parcellized sovereignty, in turn, gave way, yet again, to state centralization. The new form of state that would emerge in the late Middle Ages and develop in the early modern period would forever be marked by the underlying conflict between monarchy and lordship – until capitalism completely transformed the relation between politics and property.

At each stage in this history of political practice, there were corresponding changes in theory and variations on old themes to accommodate new social tensions and political arrangements. The contradictory relations between property and state acquired new complexities, giving rise to new ideas about relations between monarchs and lords, the origins and scope of monarchical power, constitutional limits on state power, the autonomous powers of various corporate entities, conceptions of sovereignty, the nature of obligation and the right to resist. Developments in Christianity and the rise of the Church as an independent power introduced yet more complications, raising new questions about relations between divine and civil law and about the challenge posed by the Church to secular authority. Finally, the advent of capitalism brought its own conceptual transformations, in new ideas of property and state, together with new conceptions of 'public' and 'private', political and economic, state and 'society', and a resurrection of 'democracy', not in its ancient Greek form but in a new and distinctively capitalist meaning, which no longer represented a fundamental challenge to dominant classes.

Throughout this 'Western' history, there were also, as we shall see,

---

15 On the concept of 'parcellized sovereignty', see Perry Anderson, *Passages from Antiquity to Feudalism* (London: Verso, 1974), pp. 148ff. English feudalism, as we shall see, represented a partial exception. All property was legally defined as 'feudal' and conditional; but the Anglo-Saxon state was already relatively unified, and the Normans would consolidate that unity, so that 'parcellized sovereignty' never existed in England to the extent that it did on the Continent. The distinctive development of English capitalism was not unrelated to this distinctive 'feudalism'. But more on this later.

significant theoretical variations among diverse European states, not just because of linguistic and cultural differences but because social and political relations varied too. Not only were there several European feudalisms, but the dissolution of feudalism gave rise to several different transformations, producing forms as diverse as the city-states of Italy, the principalities of Germany, the absolutist state of France, and the commercial republics of the Netherlands, while the so-called 'transition from feudalism to capitalism' occurred only in England. For all the commonalities of European culture, and all the shared social issues that continued to make the Western tradition of political theory a fruitful common legacy, each of these transformations produced its own characteristic 'traditions of discourse'.

One further point is worth making. The ambiguous relation between ruling class and state gave Western political theory certain unique characteristics. Even while propertied classes could never ignore the threat from below, and even while they depended on the state to sustain their property and economic power, the tensions in their relations with the state placed a special premium on their own autonomous powers, their rights against the state, and also on conceptions of liberty – which were often indistinguishable from notions of aristocratic privilege asserted against the state. So challenges to authority could come from two directions: from resistance by subordinate classes to oppression by their overlords, and from the overlords themselves as they faced intrusions by the state. This helped to keep alive the habit of interrogating the most basic principles of authority, legitimacy and the obligation to obey, even at moments when social and political hierarchies were at their most rigid.

The Canon

A final introductory word needs to be said about why we should concern ourselves with the classics of Western political theory at all. Why select a few 'classic' works or 'great books', written by 'Dead White Males', largely confined to Western Europe and its cultural offshoots? Is it not true that, with very few exceptions, the 'canon' neglects the life experience of most of the world's population, the male domination of women, the oppression of racial and national minorities, the endemic violence in social relations, the whole history of colonialism and imperialism – when it does not actively support such domination and oppression?

For that matter, is it even meaningful to talk about the 'Western' tradition at all? The days are long gone when courses on 'Western

Civilization' were taken for granted, particularly in US universities, as a necessary introduction to higher education. Even the division between 'East' and 'West' is now recognized as problematic. What, for instance, does it mean to identify ancient Greek culture as belonging to the 'Western' tradition? 'East' versus 'West' is an artificial historical construct, and even 'Europe' is a concept that emerged fairly late. It is even more artificial to detach ancient Greece from, say, Egypt or Persia, as if the Greeks were always 'European', living a separate history, and not part of a larger Mediterranean and 'Eastern' world. Besides, the 'East' is even more diverse than Europe or the 'West', so there is no justification for treating it as some kind of residual category, encompassing everything not 'Western' or 'European'. And even if we accept the 'West' as a kind of shorthand, without lumping together the rest of the world as an undifferentiated 'other', which Western tradition are we talking about? Are there not, for instance, working class traditions as well as ruling class ideologies?

Let me offer at least a partial reply to these important doubts. First, for the purposes of this study, the main justification for using the shorthand 'Western' political theory has to do with the particularities of political life, since classical antiquity, within the geographic area we now call Europe. For all its internal diversity – which should be evident throughout this work – this 'Western' world has been marked by certain social and political peculiarities, which have been briefly outlined in this chapter and which have produced certain distinctive patterns of political thinking. The justification for treating ancient Greece and Rome as part of this 'tradition' is simply that we can trace the 'West's' political divergence back to Greco-Roman antiquity, and with it the development of political theory.[16]

The classic texts of political theory considered in this book, then, focus upon the Western state. Generally conceived by powerful minds and often written by first-rate literary stylists, they give us unparalleled access to the West's political history; and whether we like it or not, these works have indelibly stamped our modern culture and the world today. They have, in general, been the ruling ideas of ruling classes; and this also means, of course, that the imperial powers which have spread their tentacles throughout the world have taken these ideas with

---

16 See Paul Cartlege, *The Greeks* (Oxford: Oxford University Press, 2nd edn, 2002) for a masterful illustration of how our own political and cultural self-understanding can benefit from recognizing both the historical specificity of the Greeks and the continuities between them and us, both their 'otherness' and what we owe to them.

them. The spread of the West's ruling ideas, it must be said, has had its benefits, but they have also been invoked to justify colonial oppression. For better or worse, they have, in various ways, governed the world.

It is also true that, since classical antiquity, the Western state has been marked by a systemic inequality and domination of the many by a few. This reality, too, is reflected in the canon, since the voices we hear tend to be those of the ruling classes, propertied men (it is indeed men) and those who speak for them. Although we occasionally hear dissent from below, the peasants who have made up the majority of the population throughout most of the relevant history are largely silent. Yet this silence is not a reason for neglecting the voices of the masters. On the contrary, they are often our best access to the voiceless majority, to their grievances and the challenges they posed to those who dominated and exploited them. We are able, of course, to learn a great deal more when we can also listen directly to the words of those who opposed and resisted; but even when those words are unavailable, a careful and contextual reading of the canonical texts will tell us much about what dominant classes expected from their subordinates as well as what they feared from them.

This study works from the premise that it is wrong to treat the canon uncritically and to take its dominance for granted. It is equally wrong to write out of history identities and cultures not represented in canonical texts. But it is also a mistake to pretend that nothing like the canon exists or that the dominance of ruling ideas is not a major fact of history. The important thing is to recognize that this fact does indeed have a history. This means, among other things, trying to understand the conditions in which this canonical tradition emerged and developed, the social relations and struggles that shaped it. Without that kind of historical understanding, we cannot learn whatever universal lessons the classics may still have for us, but nor are we in any position to dismiss them as having nothing to teach us at all.

2

THE ANCIENT GREEK POLIS

The Invention of Politics

In his play, *The Suppliant Women*, Euripides interrupts the action with a short political debate between a herald from despotic Thebes and the legendary Athenian hero, Theseus. The Theban boasts that his city is ruled by only one man, not by a fickle mob, the mass of poor and common people who are unable to make sound political judgments because they cannot turn their minds away from labour. Theseus replies by singing the praises of democracy. In a truly free city, he insists, the laws are common to all, equal justice is available to rich and poor alike, anyone who has something useful to say has the right to speak before the public, and the labours of a free citizen are not wasted 'merely to add to the tyrant's substance by one's toil'.

This brief dramatic interlude may do little to advance the action of the play, but it nicely sums up the issues at stake in Athenian political theory. It also tells us much about the polis and the social conditions that gave rise to political theory. Contained in the conception of freedom exalted by Theseus are certain basic principles that the Athenians, and other Greeks, regarded as uniquely theirs, defining the essence of their distinctive state. The Greek word for freedom, *eleutheria*, and, for that matter, even the more restricted and elitist Latin *libertas* – in reference to both individuals and states – have no precise equivalent in any ancient language of the Near East or Asia, for instance in Babylonian or classical Chinese; nor can the Greek and Roman notions of a 'free man' be translated into those languages.[1] In Greek, these concepts appear again and again, in everything from historical writing to drama, as the defining characteristics of Athens.

---

1 See M.I. Finley, *The Ancient Economy* (Berkeley and Los Angeles: University of California Press, 1973), p. 28.

So, for instance, when the historian Herodotus offers his explanation for the Athenian defeat of Persia, he attributes their strength to the fact that they had shaken off the yoke of tyranny. When they were living under tyrannical oppression, 'they let themselves be beaten, since they worked for a master . . .' [2] Now that they were free, they had become 'the first of all'. Similarly, the tragedian, Aeschylus, in *The Persians*, tells us that – in contrast to subjects of the Persian king, Xerxes – to be an Athenian citizen is to be masterless, a servant to no mortal man.

It would, of course, be possible to attribute the Greeks' clear delineation of 'freedom' to the prevalence of chattel slavery, which entailed an unusually sharp conceptual and legal distinction between freedom and bondage. The growth of slavery certainly did clarify and sharpen the distinction. But the distinctive Greek conception of autonomy and self-sufficiency owes its origin to something else, and the uncompromising definition of servitude is a consequence of that conception more than its cause.

The distinguished medieval historian, Rodney Hilton, once remarked that 'the concept of the freeman, owing no obligation, not even deference, to an overlord is one of the most important if intangible legacies of medieval peasants to the modern world.' [3] If Hilton was right to trace this concept to the peasantry, he was surely wrong not to give the credit for it to the ancient Greeks. It was the liberation of Greek peasants from any form of servitude or tribute to lord or state, unlike their counterparts elsewhere, that produced a new conception of freedom and the free man. This conception was increasingly associated with democracy – so much so that an anti-democrat like Plato (who, as we shall see, thought that anyone engaged in necessary labour should be legally or politically dependent) sought to subvert the concept of *eleutheria* by equating it with licence. At the same time, the liberation of the peasantry wiped out a whole spectrum of dependence and left behind the stark dichotomy of freedom and slavery, the one an attribute of citizens, the other a condition to which no citizen could be reduced.

Although a leisurely life was no doubt a cultural ideal, the Greek conception of *eleutheria* has at its heart a freedom from the necessity to work for another – not freedom *from* labour but the freedom *of* labour. This applies not only to the masterless individual but also to

2 V. Herodotus, *The Persian Wars*, transl. George Rawlinson (New York: Modern Library [Random House], 1947), V.78.

3 Rodney Hilton, *Bond Men Made Free: Medieval Peasant Movements and the English Rising of 1381* (London: Temple Smith, 1973), p. 235.

the polis governed by a citizen body and one that owes no tribute to another state. In its emphasis on autonomous labour and self-sufficiency, this concept of freedom reflects the unique reality of a state in which producers were citizens, a state in which a civic community that combined appropriating and producing classes ruled out relations of lordship and dependence between them, whether as masters and servants or as rulers and subjects. That civic community, which was most highly developed in democratic Athens, was the decisive condition for the emergence of Greek political theory.

In the previous chapter, we outlined some of the ways in which the polis, and especially the democracy, generated a new mode of thinking, a systematic application of critical reason to interrogate the very foundations of political right. This mode of thinking was, it was suggested, rooted in a new kind of practice, which had less to do with relations between rulers and subjects than with transactions and conflicts among citizens, united in their civic identity yet still divided by class. The self-governing civic community and the practice of politics – action in the public sphere of the polis, a community of citizens – reached its apogee in democratic Athens, which was also home to the classic tradition of Greek political theory.

The Rise of the Democracy

The evolution of the democracy can be traced by following the development of the civic or political principle, the notion of citizenship and the gradual elevation of the polis, civic law and civic identity at the expense of traditional principles of kinship, household, birth and blood. To put it another way, the processes of politicization and democratization went hand in hand, and the most democratic polis was the one in which the political principle was most completely developed. The historic events commonly identified as the milestones in Athenian political development can all be understood in these terms. In each case, the strengthening of the political principle at the same time represented an advance in popular power and a reconfiguration of relations between classes.

Archaeology and the decipherment of Linear B, the script that preceded the Greek alphabet, have revealed much about the states that existed in Greece before the emergence of the polis. They were, as has already been suggested, analogous to other ancient states, albeit on a smaller scale, in which a bureaucratic power at the centre controlled land and labour, appropriating tax or tribute from subordinate peasant communities. Little is known about how this state-form disappeared or what intervened between its demise and the rise of the polis. Much of what is known about Greek society on the eve of the polis depends on the Homeric epics, which certainly do not describe the Mycenean civilization that is supposed to be their theme. Invoking myths and legends from an earlier time, they depict a social structure and social values of a later age. The Homeric poems may not exactly describe any society that ever existed in Greece; but, in general outline, they remain our best source of information about the aristocratic society that preceded the polis, a society already coming to an end when the poet(s) memorialized it. The epics at least allow us some access to the social and political arrangements that gave way to the polis.

The principal social and economic unit of 'Homeric' society is the *oikos*, the household, and especially the aristocratic household, dominated by a lord who is surrounded by his kin and retainers and supported by the labour of dependents. There is scarcely any 'public' sphere: duties and rights are primarily to household, kin and friends; and various social functions, such as the disposal of property and the punishment of crime, are dictated by the customary rules of kinship, while jurisdiction, such as it is, belongs exclusively to lords.

Yet when the epics were written, household and kinship ties were already being displaced by different principles. There were ties of territoriality, around an urban centre, while the bonds and conflicts of class were at work in relations between master and servant, or lord and peasant, and in the class alliances of lordship. 'Homeric' lords had become an aristocracy of property, bound together by common interests as appropriators, though often in vicious rivalry with one another, and increasingly isolated from their producing compatriots.

The aristocracy used its non-economic powers, especially its judicial functions, to appropriate the labour of subordinate producers. In that respect, it still had something in common with the ancient bureaucratic state, in which the state and state office were the principal means of appropriation. The status of lords may even have been a remnant of the old bureaucratic state and its system of state-controlled appropriation. But the critical difference is that there was, in post-Mycenean Greece, effectively no state, no powerful apparatus of rule to sustain the power of appropriators over producers. Property was held by individuals and households, and the aristocracy of property had to face its subordinates not as a well organized ruling force but as a fairly loose collection of such individuals and households, often engaged in fierce conflict with each other, and distinguished from their non-aristocratic compatriots less by superior power than by superior property and noble birth. Their relations with peasant producers were further complicated by the community's growing military reliance on the peasantry.

By the time we reach the first relatively well-documented moment in the evolution of Athenian democracy, the reforms of Solon, the conflict between lords and peasants had decisively come to the fore. Although Aristotle, in his account of the Solonian reforms, is no doubt exaggerating when he says that, at the time, all the poor were serfs to the wealthy few, there can be little doubt that dependence of one kind or another was very common. There was widespread unrest, which the aristocracy was in no position to quell by sheer force. Instead, there was an effort to settle the conflict between peasants and lords by means of a new political dispensation.

Whatever Solon's motivations may have been, the significant point for us here is *how* he sought to placate the unruly peasantry. He eliminated various forms of dependence which allowed Attic peasants to be exploited by their aristocratic compatriots. He abolished debt-bondage and prohibited loans on the security of the person, which could issue in slavery in case of default; and, by instituting his famous *seisachtheia*, the 'shaking off of burdens', he abolished the status of the *hektemoroi*, peasants whose land, and some portion of their labour, was held in bondage to landlords.[4] In other words, he eliminated various forms of 'extra-economic' appropriation through the medium of political power or personal dependence.

The effects of these reforms, liberating the peasantry from dependence and extra-economic exploitation, were enhanced by strengthening the civic community, extending political rights and elevating the individual citizen at the expense of traditional principles of kinship, birth and blood. Although citizens would still be classified into stratified categories, the old division among artisans, farmers and the aristocracy of well-born clans would no longer be politically significant and would be replaced by more quantitative criteria of wealth, based on an already existing system of military classification. While the former governing council, the Areopagus, was still confined to the two richest classes, the third class was given access to a new Council of 400, to act as a counterweight. The poorest military category, the *thetes*, was apparently admitted for the first time to the assembly, which became increasingly important as the power of the aristocratic council declined.

---

4 Hektemorage used to be understood as a consequence of default on a mortgage or loan, but it is now more commonly thought to be an old-established dependent condition in which, whether as serfs or clients, peasants were bound to a lord.

Solon also reformed the judicial system, creating a new people's court, to which all citizens had access. Any citizen could have his case transferred to this court, taking it out of the reach of aristocratic judgment and weakening the aristocracy's monopoly of jurisdiction. Traditionally, kinship groups had always had the initiative in avenging crimes against their members, according to age-old customs of blood vengeance. Now, any citizen could bring charges against anyone else on behalf of any member of the community. Crime was now defined as a wrong committed against a member of the civic community, not necessarily a kinsman; and the individual Athenian had the initiative as *citizen*, while the civic community, in the form of citizens' courts, had jurisdiction.

In various ways, then, Solon weakened the political role of noble birth and blood, kinship and clan, while strengthening the community of citizens. It is too much to say that his reforms were democratic; but they did have the effect of weakening the aristocracy, which was increasingly incorporated into the civic community and subject to the jurisdiction of the polis. Impersonal principles of law and citizenship were taking precedence over the personal rule of kings or lords. The new civic relationship between aristocracy and peasants, together with other labouring citizens, meant that the Athenians had moved decisively away from the old division between rulers and producers. The state, in the form of the polis, was becoming not a primary means of appropriation from direct producers but, on the contrary, a means of protecting citizen producers from appropriating classes.

The polis also created a new arena for aristocratic rivalries. Solon's reforms certainly did not end the influence of noble families, nor did they diminish the ferocity of intra-class rivalry. Athens would long continue to be plagued by aristocratic infighting, even to the point of virtual civil war, sometimes with help from Sparta for one or another of the contenders. But it was becoming harder for landlords to contend for power just among themselves. They now had to conduct their competition within the community of citizens, and this meant that they could advance their positions by gaining support from the common people, the *demos*. The paradoxical effect was that the civic community and the political principle were further strengthened by aristocratic rivalry. Although there has been much dispute about the 'tyrants' who followed Solon, who they were and what they represented, the most likely explanation is that they were a product of just such competition among Athenian aristocrats;[5] and the general

---

5 The Greek word, *tyrannos*, referred not necessarily to an evil or autocratic ruler but simply to a leader and sole ruler who had not been lawfully established.

tendency of their regime was, again, to strengthen the polis against traditional principles – for instance, building on what might be called 'national'
as against local loyalties, by such means as a national coinage, festivals
and cults, including the cult of the goddess Athena, patron of the polis.

After the expulsion of the last tyrant by Sparta, there followed, in
510–508 BC, a period of particularly violent struggle, in which the
principal contenders were Isagoras and Cleisthenes, both representing
noble families. When Cleisthenes prevailed, at least temporarily, he
instituted reforms that would later be regarded as the true foundation
of democracy. In a sense, he was simply following the logic established
by Solon and the tyrants. His reforms, in 508(?) BC, further weakened
the traditional authority of the aristocracy, their power over their own
neighbourhoods and over smaller farmers in their area. Like his predecessors, he accomplished this by elevating the polis and the whole
community of citizens over old forms of authority and old loyalties,
submitting local and regional power to the all-embracing authority of
the polis.

But what was most distinctive about this moment in the history of
Athens was that the demos had become a truly central factor in the
political struggle. By now, the people were a conscious and vocal political force. Cleisthenes did not create this force, but he had the strategic
sense to mobilize it in his favour. Whether he was himself a true democrat or simply another scion of a noble clan seeking to enhance the
position of his own aristocratic family, his appeal to the demos was
direct and unambiguous. Herodotus writes that, when Cleisthenes
found himself weaker than Isagoras, he made the demos his *hetairoi*
– a word difficult to translate but suggesting comrades or partners. It
also suggests the associations, friendship groups or clubs, the *hetaireiai*,
which formed the power base of the aristocrat in Athens.[6] The demos,
in other words, had replaced friends and kin of aristocrats as the

---

6 Paul Cartledge, who prefers to translate this passage from Herodotus to read that
Cleisthenes 'hetairized [the demos] to himself', has argued that this is a tendentious
formulation on the part of the historian ('Democracy, Origins of: Contribution to a
Debate', in Kurt Raaflaub et al., *Origins of Democracy in Ancient Greece*, Berkeley and
Los Angeles: University of California Press, 2007, pp. 155–69). Cleisthenes could not, of
course, have literally included the demos collectively in his *hetaireia* (if, indeed, he had
one). The effect of Herodotus's formulation, which makes the demos little more than a
pawn of its aristocratic leader, is to deny its revolutionary force; and the passage,
Cartledge suggests, represents the historian (or his aristocratic source) using traditional
aristocratic (and hence antidemocratic) language to describe, and traduce, a revolutionary
transformation of consciousness that had led to political revolution in practice.

source of political power. When Cleisthenes's enemy, Isagoras, drove him out, with the help of Sparta under its leader, Cleomenes, the demos rose in revolt, erupting into the political arena in an unprecedented way, as a conscious political force acting in its own right and in defence of its own interests.

Whatever his intentions, the result of Cleisthenes's reforms was the establishment of an institutional framework that was to govern Athenian democracy from then on, with only a few modifications. He changed the whole organization of the polis by removing the political functions of the four tribes, dominated by the aristocracy, which had been the traditional basis of political organization – for instance, in the conduct of elections – and replaced them with ten new tribes based on complex and artificial geographic criteria. More significantly, he subdivided the tribes into *demes*, generally (but perhaps not always) based on existing villages, and made them the foundation of the democracy, its fundamental constituent unit and the locale of citizenship. The new divisions cut across tribal and class ties and elevated locality over kinship, establishing and strengthening new bonds, new loyalties specific to the polis, the community of citizens.

Cleisthenes also effected other major reforms, introducing measures designed to create some kind of counterbalance to institutions still dominated by the aristocracy, such as the Areopagus, which continued to have a monopoly of jurisdiction in crimes against the state and in controlling magistrates. In particular, he gave the Assembly a new legislative role. But it was the institution of the demes perhaps more than any other institutional reform that vested power in the demos. It was in the deme that the peasant-citizen was truly born. Democratic politics began in the deme, where ordinary citizens dealt with the immediate and local matters that most directly affected their daily lives, and the democratic polis at the centre was constructed on this foundation. It was here that the traditional barrier between producing peasant village and appropriating central state was most completely broken down; and the new relation between producing classes and the state extended to other labouring citizens too.

Nothing symbolizes more neatly the effect of Cleisthenes's reforms than the fact that Athenian citizens were thereafter to be identified not by their patronymic or clan name but by their *demotikon*, the name of the deme in which their citizenship was rooted – an identification not surprisingly resisted by the aristocracy, which clung to the old identity of blood and noble birth. To be sure, the aristocracy continued to hold positions of power and influence, and Cleisthenes may or may not have intended to establish true popular sovereignty.

But his reforms did advance the power of the people. Cleisthenes himself seems to have described the new political order as *isonomia*, literally equality of law, which had to do not simply with equal rights of citizenship but with a more even balance among the various organs of government, giving the popular assembly a more active legislative role than ever before. Although the demos, who elected magistrates, would not achieve full sovereign control as long as the Areopagus retained its dominant role in enforcing state decisions and holding magistrates to account, the new legislative role that Cleisthenes gave to the Assembly was a major enhancement of popular power.

There were also other more intangible effects of Cleisthenes's reforms. We shall have more to say later about developments in the concepts of law, justice and equality; but it is worth mentioning here that Cleisthenes has been credited with a significant change in Greek political vocabulary, the application of the word *nomos*, instead of the traditional *thesmos*, to designate statutory law.[7] What is significant about this change is that, while *thesmos* implies the imposition of law from above and has a distinctly religious flavour, *nomos* – a word that suggests something held in common, whether pasture or custom – implies a law to which there is common agreement, something that people who are subject to it themselves regard as a binding norm. The application of *nomos* to statute became common usage in Athens, which had thereby adopted 'the most democratic word for "law" in any language.'[8]

Was the Democracy Democratic?

After Cleisthenes, popular power continued to evolve, with the Areopagus losing its exclusive jurisdiction in political cases, with popular juries playing an ever greater role (pay for attendance was introduced in the 450s under Pericles), and the Assembly gaining strength (though pay for attendance was introduced only in the late 390s). Since much of what we might regard as political business was dealt with in Athens by means of judicial proceedings, the power of popular juries was particularly important, and Aristotle – or whoever wrote the *Constitution of Athens* commonly attributed to him – would later describe it as one of the three most democratic features of the Athenian polis.

---

7 Martin Ostwald, *Nomos and the Beginnings of Athenian Democracy* (Oxford: Clarendon Press, 1969), p. 55.
    8 *Ibid.*, p. 160.

Athens's victory over Persia in the Battle of Marathon in 490 BC or, more especially, the naval victory at Salamis in 480 ushered in the golden age of the democracy, a new age of democratic self-confidence. When the historian Thucydides a few decades later depicted the most famous democratic leader, Pericles, he was able to put into his mouth a glowing account of democracy in his famous Funeral Oration. For all its rose-tinted prose, this speech tells us much about the realities, and even more about the aspirations, of Athenian political life.

Pericles, himself an aristocrat, tells us that Athens is called a democracy

> because its administration is in the hands, not of the few, but of the many; yet while as regards the law all men are on an equality for the settlement of their private disputes, yet . . . it is as each man is in any way distinguished that he is preferred to public honours, not because he belongs to a particular class, but because of personal merits; nor, again, on the ground of poverty is a man barred from a public career by obscurity of rank if he but has it in him to do the state a service . . . and we Athenians decide public questions for ourselves or at least endeavour to arrive at a sound understanding of them, in the belief that it is not debate that is a hindrance to action, but rather not to be instructed by debate before the time comes for action.[9]

And indeed the Assembly, which all citizens were entitled to attend, deliberated and decided on every kind of public question, while legal cases were commonly tried in popular courts. The council which set the agenda for the Assembly was now chosen by lot annually from among all citizens. Although election was regarded as an oligarchic practice, it was used for some positions, typically military and financial, which required a specialized skill. But in general public offices, which tended to be ad hoc, were not treated as specialized professional employments; and many officials were chosen by lot. In principle, then, and to a great extent in practice, all citizens could be involved in all government functions – executive, legislative and judicial. To be sure, aristocrats like Pericles (who reached his influential position in the democracy as a military leader chosen by the people) still enjoyed great influence, while wealthy and well-born citizens probably still had disproportionate weight in the assembly. Yet (as anti-democrats like

---

9 Thucydides, *The Peloponnesian War*, II.XXXVII.1 and XL.2–3, Loeb Classical Library translation.

Plato make very clear) we should not underestimate the day-to-day role of popular power in juries and assemblies, nor the significance of democratic practices like sortition (selection by lot) for various public positions.

Nevertheless, even taking into account the historically unprecedented, and in many ways still unequalled, power of the Athenian people, we must pause here to ask whether, or in what sense, it is appropriate to call the Athenian polis a democracy. After all, this was a society in which slavery played a major role, and in which women had no political rights. In fact, the evolution of democracy increased the role of slavery and in some ways diminished the status of women, especially in respect to the disposition of property. It can hardly be denied that the imperatives of preserving property had a great deal to do with restrictions on the freedom of women, and it is difficult to avoid the conclusion that the position of smallholders, the peasant-citizens of Athens, generated particularly strong pressures for the conservation of family property. It is even more obvious that the liberation of the peasantry and its unavailability as dependent labour created new incentives for enslavement of non-Greeks. So, while slavery was relatively unimportant in the days of Solon, in the golden age of the democracy, according to some estimates, there may have been as many as 110,000 slaves out of a total Attic population of 310,000, of which 172,000 were free citizens and their families (the number of citizens with full political rights would then have been somewhere in the region of 30,000), with another 28,500 metics or resident aliens, free but without political rights.[10]

Athens was a democracy in the sense – and only in the sense – that the Greeks understood the term, which they themselves invented. It had to do with the power of the demos, not only as a political category but as a social one: the poor and common people. Aristotle defined

---

10 These estimates come from an article on 'Population (Greek)' by A.W. Gomme and R.J. Hopper in the *Oxford Classical Dictionary* (1970). I am not offering this estimate as in any way decisive. There are other, different estimates, some of which suggest a far smaller slave population. The point for our purposes here is that the argument about Athenian democracy can be persuasive only if it can confront even large numbers of slaves. The role of slaves in the Athenian economy is just as controversial. This is not the place to deal with this matter, which is discussed in detail in Ellen Meiksins Wood, *Peasant-Citizen and Slave: The Foundations of Athenian Democracy* (London: Verso, 1988), especially Ch. 2 and Appendix 1. The essential point is that slavery did not free Athenians from labour and that the majority of the citizen body worked for a livelihood.

democracy as a constitution in which 'the free-born and poor control the government – being at the same time a majority', and distinguished it from oligarchy, in which 'the rich and better-born control the government – being at the same time a minority'. The social criteria – poverty in one case, wealth and high birth in the other – play a central role in these definitions and even in the end outweigh the numerical criterion. This notion of democracy as a form of class rule – rule by the poor – certainly reflected the views of those who opposed it, who may even have invented the word as a term of abuse; but supporters of the democracy, even moderates like Pericles, regarded the political position of the poor as essential to the definition of democracy.

The enemies of the democracy hated it above all because it gave political power to working people and the poor. It can even be said that the main issue dividing democrats from anti-democrats – as it divided Theseus and the Theban herald in *The Suppliant Women* – was whether the labouring multitude, the *banausic* or menial classes, should have political rights, whether such people are able to make political judgments. This is a recurring theme not only in ancient Greece, where it emerges very clearly in Plato's philosophy, but in debates about democracy throughout most of Western history.

The question raised by critics of democracy is not only whether people who have to work for a living have time for political reflection, but also whether those who are bound to the necessity of working in order to survive can be free enough in mind and spirit to make political judgments. For Athenian democrats, the answer is, of course, in the affirmative. For them, one of the main principles of democracy, as we saw in Theseus's speech, was the capacity and the right of such people to make political judgments and speak about them in public assemblies. The Athenians even had a word for it, *isegoria*, which means not just freedom of speech in the sense we understand it in modern democracies but rather *equality* of public speech. This may, in fact, be the most distinctive idea to come out of the democracy, and it has no parallel in our own political vocabulary. Freedom of speech as we know it has to do with the absence of interference with our right to speak. Equality of speech as the Athenians understood it had to do with the ideal of active political participation by poor and working people.

We can judge the significance of the Athenian definition only by comparing it to democracy as we understand it today. While we have to recognize the severe limitations of Athenian democracy, there are also ways in which it far exceeds our own. This is true of procedures such as sortition or direct democracy, with ordinary citizens, and not just representatives, making decisions in assemblies and juries. But even more important is the effect of democracy on relations between classes. It is true that modern democracy, like the ancient, is a system in which people are citizens regardless of status or class. But if class makes no (legal) difference to citizenship in either case, in modern democracy the reverse is also true: citizenship makes little difference to class. This was not and could not be so in ancient Greece, where political rights had far-reaching effects on the relations between rich and poor.

We have already encountered the peasant-citizen, whose political rights had wider implications. Peasants have been the predominant producing classes throughout much of history, and an essential feature of their condition has been the obligation to forfeit part of their labour to someone who wields superior force. Peasants have been in possession of land, either as owners or as tenants; but they have had to transfer surplus labour to landlords and states, in the form of labour services, rents or taxes. The appropriating classes which have made these claims on them have been able to do so because they have possessed not only land but privileged access to coercive military, political and judicial power. They have possessed what has been called 'politically constituted property'.[11] The military and political powers of lordship in feudal Europe, for instance, were at the same time the power to extract surpluses from peasants. If feudal lords and serfs had been politically and juridically equal, they would not, by definition, have been lords and serfs, and there would have been no feudalism.

This type of relationship, and even patronage (such as would exist in Rome), was absent in democratic Athens. Its absence certainly had the effect of encouraging the enslavement of non-Greeks. But it is, again, important to keep in mind that the majority of Athenian citizens worked for a living, mainly as farmers or craftsmen, and that citizenship in Athens precluded a whole range of legally and politically dependent conditions which throughout history have compelled direct producers to forfeit surplus labour to their masters and rulers. This is not to say that the rich in Athens had no advantages over the poor – though the gap between rich and poor was very much narrower in Athens than in ancient Rome. The point is rather that the possession of political

---

11 The phrase 'politically constituted forms of property' was originally proposed by Robert Brenner, who used it for the first time (probably) in the Postscript to his book, *Merchants and Revolution: Commercial Change, Political Conflict, and London's Overseas Traders, 1550–1653* (Princeton: Princeton University Press, 1993), p. 652.

rights made an enormous difference, because it affected how, and even whether, the rich could exploit the poor.

Here lies the great difference between ancient and modern democracy. Today, there is a system of appropriation that does not depend on legal inequalities or the inequality of political rights. It is the system we call capitalism, a system in which appropriating and producing classes can be free and equal under the law, where the relation between them is supposed to be a contractual agreement between free and equal individuals, and where even universal suffrage is possible without fundamentally affecting the economic powers of capital. The power of exploitation in capitalism can coexist with liberal democracy, which would have been impossible in any system where exploitation depended on a monopoly of political rights. The reason this is possible is that capitalism has created new, purely *economic* compulsions: the propertylessness of workers – or, more precisely, their lack of property in the means of production, the means of labour itself – which compels them to sell their labour power in exchange for a wage simply in order to gain access to the means of labour and to obtain the means of subsistence; and also the compulsions of the market, which regulate the economy and enforce certain imperatives of competition and profit-maximization.

So, both capital and labour can have democratic rights in the political sphere without completely transforming the relation between them in a separate economic sphere. In fact, it is only in capitalism that there *is* a separate economic sphere, with its own imperatives, and so it is only in capitalism that democracy *can* be confined to a separate political domain. It is also only in capitalism that so much of human life has been put outside the reach of democratic accountability, regulated instead by market imperatives and the requirements of profit, the commodification that affects all aspects of life, not just in the workplace but everywhere. Citizenship today, in the conditions of capitalism, may be more inclusive, but it simply cannot mean as much to ordinary citizens as it meant to Athenian peasants and craftsmen – even in the more benign forms of capitalism which have moderated the effects of market imperatives. Athenian democracy had many great shortcomings, but in this respect, it went beyond our own.

In one other respect, Athenian democracy was no less imperfect than is today's most powerful democracy. The commitment to civic freedom and equality among citizens at home did not extend to relations with other states. Athens increasingly exploited its growing power to impose imperial hegemony on allied city-states, largely for the purpose of extracting tribute from them. The Athenian empire was, to be sure, shaped and limited by the democracy at home. Imperial expansion was not driven by the interests of a landed aristocracy, and the Athenians often displaced local oligarchies in dependent city-states, establishing democracies friendly to Athens. Nor, while commercial interests were certainly at work, was the Athenian empire a mercantile project. The imperial mission was, in the first instance, to compensate for domestic agricultural deficiencies in order to ensure the food supply by controlling sea routes for the import of grain. This project was certainly a costly one, requiring ever-increasing revenues from tribute to maintain the Athenian navy; but the social property relations under-lying the democracy ensured that Athens never established a territorial empire, as the Romans would do. While Roman peasant soldiers, as we shall see, would be subject to years of service far away from home, leaving their properties vulnerable to expropriation by aristocratic landowners, Athenian military ventures were strictly limited by agri-cultural cycles and the needs of free peasant soldiers returning home to work their farms. Yet however limited their imperial objectives may have been, the Athenians could be spectacularly brutal in pursuit of their aims; and nothing in their democratic culture precluded such brutality.

The two faces of Athenian democracy would be eloquently captured by the historian, Thucydides, in two of the most famous passages in his *History of the Peloponnesian War*. In Pericles's Funeral Oration, the historian puts in the mouth of the great democratic leader a speech extolling, among other things, the virtues of civic equality. In Athens, Pericles suggests, inequalities between rich and poor, the strong and the weak, are tempered by law and democratic citizenship. In the Melian Dialogue, the Athenians, in debate with a recalcitrant city-state that refuses the status of tributary ally, are made to express with unadorned ruthlessness the imperial principle that 'right, as the world goes, is only in question between equals in power, while the strong do what they can and the weak suffer what they must.'

The Evolution of Political Theory

Political theory has been defined here as the systematic application of critical reason to interrogate political principles, raising questions not only about good and bad forms of government but even about the grounds on which we make such judgments. It asks the most funda-mental questions about the source and justification of moral and polit-ical standards. Do standards of justice, for instance, exist by nature, or are they simply human conventions? In either case, what, if anything, makes them binding? Are the differences between rulers and subjects, masters and slaves, based on natural inequalities, or have human beings who are naturally equal become unequal as a result of human practices and customs? These moral and political questions have inevitably raised even more fundamental issues. In fact, the tradition of Western philosophy emerged in ancient Greece in large part out of debates that were in the first instance political. In Athens, political debate opened up a whole range of philosophical questions discussed ever since by Western philosophers: not only ethical questions about the standards of good and bad but questions about the nature and foundations of knowledge, about the relation between knowledge and morality, about human nature, and the relation between human beings and the natural order or the divine.

It is easy to take these forms of thought for granted as emerging more or less naturally out of the human condition and the perennial problems humanity faces in its efforts to cope with its social and natural universe. We seldom stop to consider the very specific historical preconditions, intellectual and social, that made it possible to think in these critical terms. But it is worth asking what kinds of intellectual assumptions we must make in order systematically to raise questions about the foundations of good government, standards of justice, or the obligation to obey authority; and it is also worth asking what social conditions have given rise to such assumptions.

In order to question existing arrangements, there must, at the minimum, be some belief in humanity's ability to control its own circumstances, some sense of the separation of human beings from an unchangeable natural order, and of the social from the natural realm. There must be, to put it another way, a conception of *human* history instead of simply natural history or supernatural myth, an idea that history involves conscious human effort to solve human problems, that there is a possibility of deliberate change in accordance with conscious human goals, and that human reason is a formative, creative principle, to some extent capable of transcending the predetermined and inexorable cycle of natural necessity or divinely ordained destiny. Such a view of humanity's place in the world tends to be associated with some direct experience of social change and mobility, some practical distance from the inexorable cycles of nature, which is most likely to come with urban civilization, a well-developed realm of human experience outside the cycles and necessities of nature.

These conditions were present in all the 'high' civilizations of the ancient world and gave rise to rich and varied cultural legacies. But nowhere else had the emphasis on human agency taken centre stage in intellectual life, as it would do in Greece. The two most characteristic products of that distinctive legacy are history as practised by the Greek historians, notably Herodotus and Thucydides, and political theory, in the sense intended here. What distinguished Greece, and especially democratic Athens, from other complex civilizations was the degree to which the prevailing order, especially traditional hierarchies, had been challenged in practice; and conflict or debate about social arrangements was a normal, even institutionalized, part of everyday life. It was in this context that Athenians were faced, in new and unprecedented ways, with moral and political responsibility for shaping their own circumstances. Debate was the operative principle of the Athenian state, and the citizen majority had a deep-seated interest in preserving it. This was so because, and to the extent that, politics in Athens was not about sustaining the rule of a dominant power but about managing the relation between 'mass' and 'elite', with the public institutions of the state acting less as an instrument of rule for the propertied elite than as a counterweight against it, and with the common people in the role of political actors, not simply the object of rule. Reflection on the state was from the start shaped by that relation and by the tensions it inevitably generated.

To get a sense of how Greek political theory came into being, it is useful, again, to consider it against the background of the Homeric epics, the last major expression of ostensibly unchallenged aristocratic rule, at the very moment of its passing. When the epics were written down, whether by Homer himself or by someone else recording an oral tradition, traditional modes of transmitting cultural knowledge and values were no longer adequate, and conditions were emerging that required other forms of discourse, placing new demands on writing. In that respect, Homer was a transitional figure, both in the development of Greek literacy, as a poet still obviously steeped in the oral tradition but whose work was set down in writing, and as the poet of a dying aristocracy, no longer safe in its dominance, no longer able to take obedience for granted, and increasingly beleaguered by a challenge from below. Perhaps the very act of writing down the epics acknowledges the passing of the social order they describe (or the passing of a social order something like the one they have invented) and the need to preserve its principles in a form less ephemeral than oral recitation; but there is no evidence in the substance of the epics, in which the lower classes are scarcely visible, that aristocratic values now require a more robust and systematic defence than songs in praise of hero-nobles.

What happens to the concept of *dikē*, the Greek word for justice, is a telling illustration. In Homer, there is no real conception of justice as an ethical norm. The word *dikē* appears in *The Odyssey* several times but largely as a morally neutral term, describing a characteristic behaviour or disposition, or something like 'the way of things'. So, for example, the *dikē* of bodies in death is that flesh and bone no longer hold together, or the *dikē* of a dog is that it fawns on its master, or a serf does best when his *dikē* is to fear his lord. There are one or two usages that have a somewhat more normative connotation. On his return to Ithaca from the Trojan War, a still unrecognized Odysseus comes upon his father, Laertes, digging in the vineyard like a peasant or slave. Odysseus tells him that he looks more like a man of royal blood, the kind whose *dikē* is to sleep on a soft bed after he has bathed and dined. This could simply refer to the typical lordly way of life, but *dikē* here may also have about it the sense of a due right. Perhaps the closest Homer comes to a moral norm of justice appears in a passage suggesting that the gods do not like foul play but respect *dikē* and upright deeds, the *right* way. Yet even here, *dikē* does not refer to an ethical standard of justice so much as correct and proper behaviour, especially the behaviour of true nobles, in contrast to the intrusive rudeness of Penelope's suitors who, in their confidence that her husband, Odysseus, will never return to punish them, are breaking all the rules of decency.

Homeric usage, then, idealizes a society in which the way of things has not been subjected to serious challenge. *Dikē* does not appear as a standard of justice against which the prevailing order can and should be judged. But a very different meaning of *dikē* already appears in the work of Homer's near, if not exact, contemporary, Hesiod; and it is surely significant that the poet in this case is speaking not for nobles but for peasants. Himself a 'middling' farmer in Boeotia, Hesiod is no radical; yet his poem, *Works and Days,* is not only a compendium of farming information and moral advice but also a long poetic grumble about the lot of hard-working farmers and the injustices perpetrated against them by greedy lords. In this context, *dikē* appears in the figure of a goddess who sits at the right hand of Zeus. Hesiod tells us that she watches and judges 'gift-eating' or 'bribe-swallowing' lords who use their judicial prerogatives to exploit the peasantry by means of 'crooked' judgments. *Dikē*, Hesiod warns, will make sure that the crooked lords get their come-uppance. The poet, to be sure, is not calling for a peasant revolt, but he is certainly doing something of great conceptual significance. He is proposing a concept of justice that stands apart from the jurisdiction of the lords, a standard against which they and their judgments can and must themselves be judged.

It could hardly be more different from Homer's customary and unchallenged aristocratic way of things.

The difference between Homer and Hesiod is social no less than conceptual, the one idealizing an unchallenged dominant class whose values and judgments pass for universal norms, the other speaking for a divided community in which social norms, and the authority of dominant classes, are acknowledged objects of conflict. The issues raised here by poetry would become the subject of complex and abstract debates, for which writing would increasingly become the favoured medium, reaching fruition in the philosophical discourse of the fifth and fourth centuries BC, especially in democratic Athens. The kind of systematic enquiry that the Greeks had already applied to the natural order would be extended to moral rules and political arrangements. Dikē would pass from the poetry of Homer and Hesiod to the elaborate philosophical speculations of Plato on justice or dikaiosune in The Republic, as opponents of the democracy (of which Plato was the most notable example) could no longer rely on tradition and were obliged to construct their defence of social hierarchy on a wholly new foundation.

The Culture of Democracy

To get a sense of how much the issues of political theory permeated the whole of Athenian culture, it is worth considering how moral and political questions arose not only in formal philosophy but also in other, more popular cultural forms, notably in drama. The plays of Aeschylus, Sophocles and Euripides tell us a great deal about the atmosphere in which political philosophy emerged. We have already seen how political debate intruded into Euripides's Suppliant Women. In Aeschylus, the first of the major tragedians, the questions of political theory are introduced with greater subtlety but are also more integral to the dramatic action. Aeschylus was particularly well placed to judge the importance of the changes that Athens had undergone. He grew up in an age of tyranny and war. Having fought at Marathon, he saw the democracy come into its own. With experience of the past and steeped in its traditions, he was nevertheless very much a part of the new climate, in which citizens were forced to confront new questions about the moral and political responsibility of ordinary humans who no longer looked upon themselves as simply playthings of the gods or obedient subjects of lords and kings.

His classic trilogy, The Oresteia, appeared in 458 not long after the murder of the democratic leader Ephialtes, who had deprived the

Areopagus of its traditional functions, apart from its role as a homicide court. It is likely that Aeschylus was, among other things, conveying the message that this old aristocratic institution, while it still had a role to play in the democracy, had been rightly displaced by more democratic institutions. The trilogy has as its central theme a confrontation between two conflicting conceptions of justice, in the form of a contest between the endless cycle of traditional blood vengeance and new principles of judgment by judicial procedure. The first represents Destiny, the fury of uncontrollable fate; the other, human responsibility – an opposition that may also represent the antithesis of old aristocratic principles of kinship and blood rivalry as against the judicial procedures of a democratic civic order.

The murder of Agamemnon, king of Argos, by his wife, Clytemnestra, sets in train what could be an endless cycle of blood, as Orestes obeys an apparently natural law and avenges his father's death by killing Clytemnestra and her lover, Aegisthus. The inexorable laws of revenge mean that Orestes, pursued by the Furies, must also become the victim of blood vengeance, and so the cycle will go on and on. There is also, in a confrontation between the Furies and the god Apollo, a clash between old principles of kinship – represented by the Furies – and Apollo's commitment to patriarchal-aristocratic right, according to which the murder of a king is a crime in a way that matricide is not. The resolution comes in the last of the three plays with the establishment, on the instructions of Athena, of a court to hear the case of Orestes and end the matter once and for all. The jury will be manned not by gods or lords but by citizen jurors. Aeschylus still gives the gods a role, and fear will still play a part in enforcing the law – as the Furies become the more benign Eumenides. Nor does the tragedian repudiate the customs and traditions of the old Athens. But he is unambiguous about the importance of replacing the force and violence of the old order with new principles of reason, the rule of law and 'Holy Persuasion', the kind of order established by the polis and its civic principles – in particular, the democratic polis ruled by its citizens and not by kings or lords.

The attribution to Aeschylus of another play, *Prometheus Bound*, has been put in question, although his authorship was generally accepted in antiquity. Yet, whether or not it can be read as expressing his views, it tells us much about the culture of Athenian democracy, if we compare its telling of the Promethean myth to other versions of the story. The myth in what is probably its more conventional form appears in Hesiod. Prometheus steals fire from Zeus as a gift to humanity. In his anger, Zeus threatens to make humanity pay for this gift.

There follows the story of Pandora's 'box', a storage jar containing the threatened 'gift' from Zeus. Contrary to the advice of her brother-in-law Prometheus, she opens the jar and releases every evil, ending a golden age when the fruits of the earth were enjoyed without effort, and humanity was free of labour, sorrow and disease, although hope remains trapped inside. Hesiod combines this with another story about stages in the decline of humanity, which was once equal to the gods but is now a race that works and grieves unceasingly. For Hesiod, this is, in the main, a story about the pains of daily life and work. In Aeschylus's recounting of the Prometheus story, as in other variations on the same themes in Sophocles, and in the Sophist Protagoras, it becomes a hymn in praise of human arts and those who practise them.

In this first and only surviving play of a trilogy, (pseudo?) Aeschylus's Prometheus, being ruthlessly punished by Zeus for his pride, is presented as a benefactor to humanity. He has given them the various mental and manual skills that have made life possible and good, ending the condition of misery and confusion in which they had first been created. He also represents the love of freedom and justice, expressing contempt for Zeus's autocracy and the servile humility of the god's messenger, Hermes. As in *The Oresteia*, the tragedian is not here repudiating the gods or tradition, and there may be some right on both sides. But there is no mistaking the importance of the way he tells the Promethean story. Human arts, skills and crafts in his version betoken not the fall of humanity but, on the contrary, its greatest gift. The full political significance of this becomes evident not only when we contrast this view of the arts to the practices of Sparta, where the only 'craft' permitted to citizens was war, but also, as we shall see, if we compare it to Plato's retelling of the myth, where labour is again presented as a symbol of decline, in the context of an argument designed to exclude practitioners of these ordinary human arts, the labouring classes, from the specialized 'craft' of politics.

In Sophocles's *Antigone*, as in Aeschylus's plays, there are also two opposing moral principles in tragic confrontation, and again there is right on both sides. Eteocles and Polyneices, sons of the late ruler, Oedipus, and brothers of Antigone, have killed each other in battle. The new king of Thebes, Creon, has decreed that Eteocles, who fought on the side of his city, will be buried with full military honours, while Polyneices, who fought against the Thebans, will be left unburied. Antigone insists that she will bury her traitorous brother, in defiance of the ruler's decree and in obedience to immortal unwritten laws.

The play is sometimes represented as a clash between the individual conscience and the state, but it is more accurately described as an opposition between two conceptions of *nomos*, Antigone representing eternal unwritten laws, in the form of traditional, customary and religious obligations of kinship, and Creon speaking for the laws of a new political order. This is also a confrontation between two conflicting loyalties or forms of *philia*, a word inadequately conveyed by our notion of 'friendship' – a confrontation between, on the one hand, the ties of blood and personal friendship and, on the other, the public demands of the civic community, the polis, whose laws are supposed to be directed to the common good.

It cannot be said that Sophocles comes down decisively on one side or the other. It is true that we have great sympathy for Antigone, and increasingly less for the stubborn Creon; yet both the antagonists, Antigone and Creon, display excessive and uncompromising pride, for which they both will suffer. The tragedian here too clearly respects 'unwritten laws', but he also stresses the importance of human law and the civic order. Yet, for all of Sophocles's even-handedness, it becomes clear that Creon's chief offence is not that he insists on the supremacy of civic law but rather that he violates the very principles of civic order by treating his own autocratic decrees as if they were law.

In a dialogue with his son Haemon, Creon, having decreed Antigone's punishment, maintains that her act of disobedience was wrong in itself. Haemon believes it would be wrong only if the act itself were also dishonourable, and, he says, the Theban people do not regard it so. 'Since when,' Creon objects, 'do I take my orders from the people of Thebes?. . . I am king and responsible only to myself' – in a manner reminiscent of Xerxes in Aeschylus's *Persians*. 'A one-man state?' asks Haemon. 'What kind of state is that?' 'Why, does not every state belong to its ruler?' says the king, to which his son replies, 'You'd be an excellent king – on a desert island.'

In an ode that interrupts the action, the Chorus sings the praises of the human arts, and the rule of law which is the indispensable condition for their successful practice. We can deduce from this interlude that Sophocles regards the civic order and its laws as a great benefit to humankind, the source of its progress and strength. Yet he is also very alive to the dangers of allowing the polis to be the ultimate, absolute standard, discarding all tradition. Among the chief benefits of the civic order is the possibility of governing human interactions by moderation and persuasion. Perhaps the polis is, ideally, the place where different ethics can be reconciled. But one thing is clear: the possibility of resolution by discussion and persuasion, rather than by coercion, is greatest in a democracy, where one man's judgment cannot prevail simply by means of superior power.

There is also, in the ode, another indication of Sophocles's commitment to Athenian democracy. Of all the wonders of the world, he
writes, none is more wonderful than humankind. What distinguishes
humanity are the various human arts, from agriculture and navigation
to speech and statecraft. In this poetic interlude, as in Aeschylus's
Prometheus, human society is founded on the practical arts; and
Sophocles here sums up the central values of the democracy: not
only the centrality of human action and responsibility, but also the
importance of a lawful civic order and the value of the arts, from the
most elevated literary inventions to the most arduous manual labour.
In the interweaving of these themes – the centrality of human action,
the importance of the civic principle and the value of the arts – we
can find the essence of Greek political theory, the terrain of struggle
between democrats and those who seek to challenge them by over-
turning democratic principles.

Democracy and Philosophy: The Sophists

The plays of Aeschylus and Sophocles bespeak the rise of the civic
community, citizenship and the rule of law, as against traditional
principles of social organization. They reflect the evolution of the
democracy with its new conceptions of law, equality and justice, a
new confidence in human powers and creativity, and a celebration of
practical arts, techniques and crafts, including the political art. But
their tragedies also manifest the tensions of the democratic polis, the
questions it inevitably raises about the nature and origin of political
norms, moral values, and conceptions of good and evil.

The dramatists speak for a society which has certainly not rejected
the notion of unwritten and eternal laws, universal principles of behaviour, or obligations to family, friends and gods. But it is also a society
in which the very idea of universal and eternal values is open to
question and nothing can be taken for granted. The experience of the
democracy makes certain questions inescapable: what is the relation
between eternal laws and man-made laws, between natural and positive
law? It is all very well to connect the two by invoking some divinely
inspired lawgiver (as the Spartans did, while the Athenians did not);
but how do we account for the differences among various communities,
which all have their own specific laws? And what happens when democratic politics encourages the view that one person's opinion is as good
as another's? What happens then to universal and eternal laws or
conceptions of justice? Are these just man-made conventions, based
simply on expediency, human convenience, agreement among ordinary

mortals and the arts of persuasion? If so, why can we not change them at will, or, for that matter, disobey them?

From the middle of the fifth century BC, these questions were increasingly raised in more systematic form, first by the so-called sophists and then by the self-styled philosophers. There already existed a tradition of natural philosophy, systematic reflection on nature and the material world; and among the natural philosophers, some had begun to extend their reflections to humankind and society – such as the great atomist Democritus, who devoted his life to both science and moral reflection. But the sophists can claim credit for making human nature, society and political arrangements primary subjects of philosophical enquiry.

The sophists were paid teachers and writers who travelled from polis to polis to teach the youth of prosperous families. They flourished in Athens thanks to a keen and growing interest in education, especially in the skills required in the courts and assemblies of the democracy, the arts of rhetoric and oratory. Athens, with its cultural and political vitality, attracted distinguished teachers from other parts of Greece: Prodicus of Ceos, a student of language; Hippias of Elis, whose interests were encyclopedic; the brilliant rhetorician, Gorgias of Leontini, who came to Athens not as a professional teacher but a diplomat; and above all, the earliest and greatest of the sophists, Protagoras of Abdera, friend and adviser to Pericles, about whom more in a moment. Among the other sophists were Thrasymachus, whom we shall encounter in our consideration of Plato's *Republic*; and the second-generation sophists, such as Lycophron, who is credited with formulating an idea of the social contract; Critias, the uncle of Plato, who also appears in his nephew's dialogues; the possibly fictional Callicles, whom Plato uses to represent the radical sophists' idea that justice is the right of the strongest; the so-called 'Anonymous Iamblichi', who countered the radical sophists by arguing that the source of power is in community consensus; Antiphon, perhaps the first thinker to argue for the natural equality of all men, whether Greek or 'barbarian'; and, much later, Alcidamas, who insisted on the natural freedom of humanity.

We should not be misled by the unflattering portraits of these intellectuals painted in particular by Aristophanes and Plato, for whom they represented the decline and corruption of Athens. It is impossible to judge the portrayal of the sophists by these critics without knowing something about the historical moment in which they were writing. During this phase of the democracy, even democratic aristocrats like Pericles were being displaced by new men such as the wealthy but 'common' Cleon. In Plato's aristocratic circles, there was, not surprisingly, an atmosphere of disaffection and nostalgia for the good old days. Unfortunately, the aristocratic grumbles of a small minority have tended to colour views of Athenian democracy ever since, creating a myth of Athens in decline which has been very hard to shift.

Aristocratic disaffection did have more serious consequences, which left a deep mark on the democracy. There were two oligarchic revolutions: a brief episode in 411 but more particularly the coup in 404 which, with the help of Sparta, established the bloody rule of the Thirty (the Thirty Tyrants). With the support of a 700–man Spartan garrison on the Acropolis, the Thirty murdered and expelled large numbers of Athenians. Thousands fled the city, and only 3,000 Athenians – perhaps 10 per cent of the citizenry – retained full rights of citizenship. Yet, when the democracy was restored in the following year, it displayed remarkable restraint in dealing with the oligarchic opposition, instituting, at Sparta's behest, an amnesty which ruled out the political persecution of the oligarchs and their supporters; and despite the catastrophes that brought the golden age to a close, the fourth century was to be the most stable period of the democracy, which enjoyed widespread support among the poor and even the rich. This was also a period in which the culture of Athens flourished and when it truly became what Pericles had earlier called 'an education to Greece'. There was no further serious internal threat to the democratic regime, and it came to an end only when Athens effectively lost its independence altogether to the Macedonians in the last quarter of the century.

The notion that the late democracy was a period of moral decay is largely a product of class prejudice. To be sure, there were serious problems, especially economic ones; and the Athenians had paid a heavy price in the Peloponnesian War, to say nothing of the plague. But the myth of democratic decadence has more to do with the social changes that marked the decline of the old aristocracy, which were accompanied by political changes in both leadership and style, a new kind of popular politics that brought to maturity the strategy adopted by Cleisthenes at the beginning of the democracy, when he made the people his *hetairoi*. Critics described these changes as the triumph of vulgarity, materialism, amoral egoism, and 'demagogic' trickery designed to lead the ignorant demos astray. What is most striking about the attacks on a leader like Cleon – by figures as diverse as Thucydides, Aristophanes and Aristotle – is that they invariably suggest objections of style more than substance. Aristotle, for instance, can think of nothing worse to complain about than Cleon's vulgar manner, the way he shouted in the Assembly and spoke with his cloak not girt about him, when others conducted themselves with proper decorum.

For critics like Aristophanes and Plato, the sophists became the intellectual expression of this alleged moral decadence and were made to stand for the decline of traditional values. They were portrayed as representing a polis where even young aristocrats had given up the high moral standards of their ancestors, a polis in which all standards of right and wrong had been abandoned, and even those who knew the difference were likely to prefer wrong to right. The rhetorical strategies perfected by the sophists, and the lawyer's adversarial principle that there are two sides to every question, were interpreted by critics as simply a way of 'making the worse cause seem the better'. But, while some sophists may indeed have been unprincipled opportunists, among them were thinkers who made substantial and innovative contributions to Greek culture and the traditions emanating from it. Even while their ideas have come down to us only in fragments or in second-hand accounts, especially in the dialogues of a generally hostile Plato, enough remains to justify the claim that the sophists, and Protagoras in particular, effectively invented political theory and set the agenda of Western philosophy in general.

The sophists varied in their philosophical ideas no less than in their politics. What they generally had in common was a preoccupation with the distinction between *physis* (nature) and *nomos* (law, custom or convention). In a climate in which laws, customs, ethical principles, and social and political arrangements were no longer taken for granted as part of some unchangeable natural order, and the relation between written and unwritten law was a very live practical issue, the antithesis between *nomos* and *physis* became the central intellectual problem. The very immediate political force of this issue is dramatically illustrated by the fact that, with the restoration of the democracy, magistrates were prohibited from invoking 'unwritten law', an idea that now had powerfully antidemocratic associations.

The sophists in general agreed that there is an essential difference between things that exist by nature and things that exist by custom, convention or law. But there were disagreements among them about which is better, the way of nature or the way of *nomos*, and, indeed, about what the way of nature is. In either case, their arguments could be mobilized in defence of democracy or against it. Some, in support of oligarchy, might argue that there is a natural division between rulers and ruled and that natural hierarchy should be reflected in political arrangements. Others, in defence of democracy, might argue that no such clear division exists by nature, that men are naturally equal, and that it is wrong to create an artificial hierarchy, a hierarchy by *nomos* as against *physis*. But other permutations were possible too: a democrat could argue that a political equality created by *nomos* has the advantage of moderating natural inequalities and permitting men to live in harmony. Or it could be argued that, however similar men may be by nature, life in society requires differentiation, a division of labour, and hence some kind of inequality by *nomos*.

If sophists could be either oligarchs or democrats, it was democracy itself that had brought such issues into sharp relief. In the context of civic equality, the seemingly self-evident observation that, as Thucydides put it in the Melian Dialogue, 'the strong do what they can and the weak suffer what they must' could no longer simply be taken for granted and was up for discussion in unprecedented ways. There were now indeed two sides (at least) to the question. The juxtaposition in practice of civic equality and 'natural' inequality, the inequality of strength and weakness, produced particularly fruitful tensions in theory, which found expression both in Thucydides's history and in philosophy.

It is not as easy as Plato would have us believe to distinguish between the intellectual activities of the sophists and true 'philosophy', or love of wisdom, as practised by Plato himself and the man more commonly credited with its invention, Socrates. To be sure, Socrates was not a paid teacher, though he could always rely on the largesse of his almost uniformly wealthy and well-born friends and acolytes – such as his great-est pupil, the aristocratic Plato. But both Socrates and Plato conducted their philosophic enterprise on the same terrain as the sophists. Not only were the 'philosphers' also concerned primarily with human nature, society, knowledge and morality, but they also proceeded in their own ways from the distinction between *nomos* and *physis,* between things that exist by law or convention and those that exist by nature. They certainly transformed this distinction, in a way that no sophist did, into a philosophical exploration of true knowledge. Unlike the sophists, who tended towards moral relativism or pluralism and never strayed far outside the sphere of empirical reality, Socrates and Plato were concerned with a different kind of 'nature', a deeper or higher reality which was the object of true knowledge. The empirical world was for them, and more particularly for Plato, a world of mere appearances, the object of imperfect conventional wisdom, at best (more or less) right *opinion* but not real knowledge. The philosophers drew a distinction between learn-ing and persuasion, suggesting that the sophists, like lawyers, were not really interested in learning the truth but only in making a case and persuading others of it. Yet even if, for instance, Plato's conception of the division between rulers and ruled is grounded in this hierarchy of knowledge and not on a simple test of brute strength or noble birth, we can still see the connections between the philosopher and those sophists who opposed the democracy on the grounds that it created an

artificial equality in defiance of natural hierarchy. More particularly, we
can see that the sophists, especially the democratic ones and Protagoras
in particular, set the questions the philosophers felt obliged to answer.

Socrates and Protagoras

Socrates, probably the ancient Athenian most revered in later centuries,
is also in many ways the most mysterious. He left none of his ideas
in writing, and we have to rely on his pupils, especially Plato but also
Xenophon, for accounts of his views. Although the differences between
Plato's and Xenophon's Socrates have often been vastly exaggerated,
it is certainly true that each of these two very different witnesses, the
philosopher and the rather more down-to-earth and unphilosophical
general, brings something of his own disposition to the portrait of his
teacher. There has been heated debate about the 'real', 'historical'
Socrates; about the degree to which Plato's philosophy represents an
extension of Socratic teachings or a clear departure of his own; and,
not least, about Socrates's attitude to the democracy.

The trial and death of Socrates have presented enormous problems
of their own. While commentators seem, on the whole, to agree that
the death sentence was a grave injustice, they differ on what it tells us
about the democracy. On the one hand, there are those who see only
an injustice perpetrated by a repressive democracy against a man of
conscience, the model of the courageous intellectual who follows his
reason wherever it takes him in defiance of all opposition and threats.
On the other hand, some commentators see not only an injustice but
also a beleaguered democracy, which had just come through a period
of oligarchic terror and mass murder after a coup against the democratic regime; and they see in Socrates not only a philosopher of courage
and principle but also a man whose friends, associates and pupils were
among the leading oligarchs – a man who, as democrats fled the city,
remained safely in Athens among his oligarchic friends, with every
indication that they were confident of his support.

This is not the place to rehearse all these debates.[12] We can confine
ourselves to a few less controversial facts about Socrates, his life and

---

12 For detailed discussion of these disagreements, see Ellen Meiksins Wood and
Neal Wood, *Class Ideology and Ancient Political Theory: Socrates, Plato, and Aristotle
in Social Context* (Los Angeles and Berkeley: University of California Press, 1978), Ch. 3;
and Wood and Wood, 'Socrates and Democracy: A Reply to Gregory Vlastos', *Political
Theory*, Vol. 14, No. 1, February 1986, pp. 55–82.

work, and then proceed to an analysis of those ideas that had the greatest consequences for the development of political theory. All we can confidently say about his life is that he was an Athenian citizen of the deme of Alopeke, born around 470 BC, son of Sophroniscus and Phaenarete; that he participated in some military campaigns, most likely as a hoplite (which required enough wealth to arm oneself and support a retainer) during the Peloponnesian War; that he took part as a member of the Council in the trial of the generals of 406 BC; and that he was tried and condemned to death in 399. There is little evidence to support the tradition that his father was a sculptor or stonemason (he may have owned slaves employed as craftsmen, as did the fathers of Isocrates and Cleon) and his mother a midwife, and even less that Socrates followed in his father's footsteps. There is some evidence that he was a man of comfortable means, though certainly not among the very wealthiest. His friends and associates, however, were almost uniformly wealthy and well born; and the picture of Socrates regularly holding philosophical discussions with artisans around the streets and markets of Athens should be taken with a grain of salt.

During the oligarchic coup and the regime of the Thirty, Socrates stayed safely in Athens, as one of the privileged 3,000 citizens. Some time after the democracy was restored, a charge was brought against him for not duly recognizing the gods of Athens, introducing new gods and corrupting the youth. It seems likely that these accusations were, at least in part, a substitute for more overtly political charges ruled out by the amnesty; but, in any case, there can be no doubt that Athenians looked upon the philosopher with suspicion because of his association with the enemies of the democracy. This does not detract from his dignity and courage; and the main reason given for his refusal to escape with the help of his friends – that he must honour the laws of his polis – testifies to his principled commitment to the rule of law. In this respect, he was quite different from many of his oligarchic friends. But nor do his courage, dignity and loyalty to principle make him a supporter of the democracy.

The question then is whether the suspicions aroused by his associations are supported by what we know of his ideas. Here, again, we have little to go on. What we know with some degree of certainty is that he adopted a particular method of inquiry: engaging in dialogue with one or more interlocutors, he begins with a very general question about the nature of knowledge or the meaning of a concept such as virtue or justice, proceeding by a painstaking series of questions and answers to enumerate the manifold particular instances of 'virtuous'

or 'just' actions; and, with his characteristic irony, he searches out the
inconsistencies and contradictions in his interlocutor's definitions.
Although he typically professes ignorance and an inability to teach, it
becomes clear that, by seeking the common qualities of all the specific
instances of 'virtuous' or 'just' actions, he attempts to find a 'real'
definition of virtue or justice – not a rule-of-thumb characterization
of specific acts in the empirical world but a definition that expresses
an underlying, universal and absolute principle of virtue or justice.
The object of the philosophic exercise is to elevate the soul, or *psyche*,
the immortal and divine element in human nature to which the flesh
should be subordinate. Applied to politics, the object of philosophy
is to fulfill the higher moral purpose of the polis.

In itself, neither the Socratic method nor even the conception of
absolute knowledge associated with it has any necessary political
implications. But Socrates's most famous paradox, that virtue is knowledge, is altogether more problematic. On the face of it, this principle
simply implies that people act immorally out of ignorance and never
voluntarily; and, whatever we may think of this as a description of
reality, it seems at least benevolent in its intent, displaying a tolerance
and humanity towards those who do wrong which appears to rule out
retribution. Nor is there anything political in the admirable first
principle of Socrates's moral teaching: that it is better to suffer wrong
than to inflict it. But there is more to the identification of virtue with
knowledge, which has far-reaching consequences, not least political
and antidemocratic implications. The combined effect of this identification and the moral purpose he attributes to the state is, for all
practical purposes, to rule out democracy and even to make 'democratic
knowledge' an oxymoron.

The implications of Socrates's formulation become most visible in
the confrontation with the sophist Protagoras, depicted in Plato's
dialogue, *Protagoras*. If we can rely on Plato's reconstruction of the
sophist's argument, he seems to have laid out a systematic case for
democracy; and it is based on conceptions of knowledge, virtue and
the purpose of the polis opposed to those of Socrates. What we know
from Plato's portrayal and from the very few genuine surviving
fragments of the sophist's writings is that Protagoras was an agnostic,
who argued that we cannot really know whether the gods exist; that
we can rely only on human judgment; and that, since there is no certain
arbiter of truth beyond human judgment, we cannot assume the existence of any absolute standards of truth and falsehood or of right
and wrong. Human beings, indeed every individual, must be the final
judges – an idea famously summed up in his best-known aphorism,

'Man is the measure of all things, of things that are that they are and of things that are not that they are not.'

Such ideas were significant enough. But in Plato's *Protagoras*, there is a discussion between Socrates and Protagoras which effectively sets the agenda for the whole of Plato's mature philosophical work and the intellectual tradition that follows from it. Although this dialogue is no longer commonly regarded as among the earliest of Plato's works, it has been described as the last of his 'Socratic' dialogues, after which he strikes out on his own, developing his ideas more elaborately and independently of his teacher. *Protagoras* opens up the questions to which the philosopher will devote the rest of his working life and which will, through him, shape the whole of Western philosophy.

What is most immediately striking about the dialogue is that the pivotal question is a political one. Socrates presents Protagoras with a conundrum: like others of his kind, the sophist purports to teach the art of politics, promising to make men good citizens. This surely implies, argues Socrates, that virtue, the qualities of a good citizen, can be taught. Yet political practice in Athens suggests otherwise. When Athenians meet in the Assembly to decide on matters such as construction or shipbuilding projects, they call for architects or naval designers, experts in specialized crafts, and dismiss the views of non-specialists, however wealthy or well born. This is how people normally behave in matters regarded as technical, involving the kind of craft or skill that can and must be taught by an expert. But when the Assembly is discussing something to do with the government of the polis, Athenians behave very differently:

> . . . the man who gets up to advise them may be a builder or equally well a blacksmith or a shoemaker, merchant or shipowner, rich or poor, of good family or none. No one brings it up against any of these, as against those I have just mentioned, that he is a man who without any technical qualifications, unable to point to anybody as his teacher, is yet trying to give advice. The reason must be that they do not think this is a subject that can be taught.[13]

Protagoras gives a subtle and fascinating answer, introduced by yet another story about Prometheus. He sets out to show that Athenians 'act reasonably in accepting the advice of smith and shoemaker on

---

13 *Protagoras* 319c–d, transl. W.K.C. Guthrie.

political matters'.[14] There is no inconsistency, he says, between the claim that virtue can be taught and the assumption that civic virtue, or the capacity to make political judgments, is a universal quality, belonging to all adult citizens regardless of status or wealth. His argument turns out to be less a case for his claims as a teacher of the political art than a defence of Athenian democratic practice, insisting on the capacity of ordinary, labouring citizens to make political judgments.

Although there is a brief defence of democracy in Herodotus (III.80), Protagoras's speech is the only substantive and systematic argument for the democracy to survive from ancient Greece. It is true that we have to rely on Plato to convey the sophist's views, and we have no way of knowing how much of it Protagoras actually said. But, in contrast to Plato's attacks on other sophists, Protagoras emerges as a fairly sympathetic and deeply intelligent figure, and Socrates somewhat less so than is usual in Plato's dialogues. In any case, whether or not these are the authentic ideas of Protagoras, they certainly express a coherent democratic view; and Plato spends the rest of his career trying to counter it. Much of his philosophy thereafter, including his epistemology, seeks to demonstrate that virtue is a rare and lofty quality and the political art a specialized craft that can be practised only by a very select few, because it requires a special and elevated kind of philosophic knowledge.

It is not always clear that Plato regards natural inequalities among human beings as great enough in themselves to justify the division between rulers and ruled. But there is no ambiguity in his belief that there is an absolute and universal hierarchy of knowledge, which must be reflected in the organization of the polis. Whatever the innate qualities of human beings and their natural capacities to acquire knowledge, it is impossible, in the real world, for the majority to achieve the kind of philosophic knowledge required to make sound political judgments. In particular, the practioners of ordinary and necessary crafts – Protagoras's shoemakers and smiths – are politically incapacitated not only by their lack of time and leisure to acquire philosophic knowledge, but even more by their bondage to labour and material need, their life 'among the multiplicity of things'. True knowledge requires liberation from the world of appearance and necessity.

Protagoras's argument proceeds, first, by way of an allegory. Human beings, he recounts, at first had no means of providing for themselves as other animals did. Prometheus found them 'naked,

---

14 *Ibid.* 324d.

unshod, unbedded, and unarmed.'[15] So he gave them the gifts of fire and skill in the arts. But, while they now had the resources to keep themselves alive, they were unable to benefit from the arts they had acquired, because they lacked political wisdom. They had speech and the means to make houses, clothes, shoes, and bedding, and to get food from the earth; but, unable to live together and cooperate for their mutual benefit, they scattered and were devoured by wild beasts. Zeus instructed his messenger, Hermes, to give humanity the qualities of respect for others (*aidos*) and a sense of justice (*dikē*), to create a bond of friendship and union among them, so they could live together in civilized communities. Hermes asked Zeus whether these qualities should be distributed just to a few, on the grounds that only one trained specialist is enough for many laymen – as one doctor is enough to care for many untrained people – or should they be given to all alike. Zeus replied that all should have their share, because there could never be cities or civilized life if only a few had these virtues.

Protagoras's allegory from the outset entails a conception of the state's purpose quite different from that of Socrates. The polis exists not to achieve some higher moral purpose but to serve ordinary human interests by providing conditions in which human beings can live reasonably peaceful and comfortable lives. The allegory is intended to demonstrate that political society, without which humanity cannot benefit from the arts and skills that are its only distinctive gift, cannot survive unless the civic virtue that qualifies people for citizenship is a universal (male?) quality. He then goes on to show how virtue can be a universal quality that nonetheless must and can be taught – and here the argument moves from allegory to what might be called anthropology.

The necessary qualities are not, he argues, the kinds of characteristics that are given by nature or chance. They require instruction and learning. Yet the required instruction is available to all. Everyone who lives in a civilized community, especially a polis, is from birth exposed to the learning process that imparts civic virtue, in the home, in school, through admonition and punishment, and above all through the city's customs and laws, its *nomoi*. In a remarkable passage, Protagoras illustrates his point by insisting that no rational man would inflict punishment for a crime simply to avenge the offence, which in any case cannot be undone. Because we believe that civic virtue can be taught, punishment looks not to the past but to the future, either to prevent the same person from repeating the offence or to teach by example to others.

---

15 *Ibid.* 321d.

No man, argues Protagoras, can be a layman in civic virtue if the state is to exist at all, and any civilized community has the means to ensure that all its members can obtain the necessary virtue. Life in a civilized and humane community, which has courts of justice and the rule of law, as well as education, is the school of civic virtue; and the community's customs and laws are the most effective teachers. Civic virtue is both learned and universal in much the same way as one's mother tongue, which is taught and learned in the normal transactions of everyday life. The sophist who, like Protagoras himself, claims to teach virtue can only perfect this continuous and universal process, and a man can possess the qualities of good citizenship without the benefit of the sophist's expert instruction. Again, the object here is not to defend the claims of expert teachers but, above all, to give credit for virtue and civilized life to the *nomoi* generated especially by a democratic community.

Protagoras's emphasis on the universality of virtue is, of course, critical to his defence of democracy. But equally important is his conception of the process by which moral and political knowledge is transmitted. Virtue is certainly taught, but the model of learning is not so much scholarship as apprenticeship. Apprenticeship, in so-called 'traditional' societies, is more than a means of learning technical skills. It is also the means by which the values of the community are passed from one generation to another. There is no better way of characterizing the learning process described by Protagoras, the mechanism by which the community of citizens passes on its collective wisdom, its customary practices, values and expectations.

It is not quite so easy to interpret the argument of Socrates. He begins the discussion apparently suggesting that virtue cannot be taught and mischievously concludes at the end of the dialogue that he and Protagoras seem to have changed sides on the question. But he is being somewhat disingenuous. It is, after all, not Socrates himself who begins with the view that virtue is not teachable and that it is effectively a universal quality. He is, with a fair degree of irony, suggesting that the Athenians themselves behave as if this were so. The essence of his argument is not that virtue is unteachable, or requires no teaching, but rather that it is inconsistent to argue both that virtue is teachable and that it is a universal quality.

The point, of course, is that Socrates and Protagoras, from the beginning, have different conceptions of knowledge. Although Socrates does not here lay out a systematic argument, he is certainly moving in the direction of identifying virtue – the condition for enjoying political rights – with philosophic wisdom, the knowledge of a universal and absolute good. Protagoras, as we saw, is talking about a different and more mundane kind of knowledge, as the condition of a more mundane kind of political virtue and to serve the mundane purposes of the polis. His position on virtue and how it is acquired never changes throughout the discussion. What Socrates mischievously presents as a contradiction in Protagoras's argument is simply his refusal to accept the identification of virtue with philosophic wisdom. Socrates, too, remains consistent; and, while he never quite answers the question about political virtue himself, he already hints at an answer, to be developed by Plato, which effectively repudiates Athenian democratic practice: virtue can and must be taught (though Plato makes it clear that the final perception of the Good, after painstaking guidance by the teacher, is not something that is directly taught but occurs as an almost mystical illumination); but if virtue is taught and learned, it is as a rare and highly specialized knowledge, a knowledge that only a few can acquire. The dialogue ends with a tantalizing suggestion that the discussion of virtue will be left for another occasion. In fact, Plato will devote much of his life to it.

The principle invoked by Socrates against Protagoras – at this stage, still rather tentatively and unsystematically – is the principle that virtue is knowledge; that is, philosophic knowledge, the knowledge of one single good that underlies the appearances of many particular goods. This is the kind of knowledge that allows its practitioner not only to display this or that specific ordinary virtue but to grasp the fundamental and all-encompassing principle of virtue as a single entity, which underlies all the qualities we associate with various multiple virtues. The principle that virtue is knowledge was to become the basis of Plato's attack on democracy, especially in *The Statesman* and *The Republic*. In Plato's hands, it represents the replacement of Protagoras's moral and political apprenticeship in the community's values and norms with a more exalted conception of virtue as philosophic knowledge – not the conventional assimilation of the community's customs and values but a privileged access to higher universal and absolute truths, which are unavailable to the majority who remain tied to the world of appearance and material necessity.

So the political question posed by Socrates opens up much larger questions about the nature of knowledge and morality. Epistemological and moral relativism, as Protagoras formulates it, has, and is intended to have, democratic implications. Plato responds to this political challenge by opposing Protagoras's relativism with a new kind of universalism. In the democracy, in the atmosphere of public deliberation and debate, there could be no ruling ideas, no individual or social group whose unchallenged dominance allowed it to claim universality for its own values and impose them on others. The only effective way of challenging the conventional wisdom of shoemakers and black-smiths, and their ability to participate in public speech and deliberation, was to trump conventional wisdom altogether with some higher form of knowledge, a knowledge not of mundane empirical realities but of absolute and universal truths.

Platonic universalism is of a very special kind, and it is perhaps only in relation to this philosophical universalism that Protagoras's ideas can be called morally relativist at all. He certainly did reject the notion that there are higher moral truths accessible only to philosophic knowledge, but he put in its place what might be called a practical universalism, rooted in a conception of human nature and the conditions of human well-being. His argument presupposes a conviction not only that men are in general capable of making political judgments, and that their well-being depends on participation in a civic order, but also that they are *entitled* to the benefits of civic life. It is true that, in his view, the specific requirements of well-being will vary in the infinite diversity of the human condition in different places and times, and social values will vary accordingly. But the underlying human substratum remains the same, and the well-being of humanity does provide a kind of universal moral standard by which to judge social and political arrangements or to assess the relative value of opposing opinions, not on the grounds that some are *truer* than others but that they are *better*, as Protagoras is made to formulate it in Plato's dialogue, *Theaetetus*.

In these respects, Protagoras and Plato are poles apart both politically and philosophically, and the differences between them are traceable to their very different attitudes towards democracy. Nevertheless, there is one respect in which they proceed from a common starting point, and both of them are equally rooted in the democracy. Plato too draws on the common experience of democratic Athens, appealing to the familiar experience and values of the labouring citizen by invoking the ethic of craftsmanship, *technē*, and seeking to meet the democratic argument on its own terrain by constructing his definition of political virtue and justice on the analogy of the practical arts. Only this time, the emphasis is not on universality or the organic transmission of conventional knowledge from one generation to another, but on specialization, expertise and exclusiveness. Just as the best shoes are made by the trained and expert shoemaker, so the art of politics should be practised only by those who specialize in it. No more shoemakers and smiths in the Assembly. The essence of justice in the state is the principle that the cobbler should stick to his last.

Only the few who are not obliged to work for a living, whether in farming, craftsmanship or trade, can have the qualities required to rule.

Both Protagoras and Plato, then, place the cultural values of *technē*, the practical arts of the labouring citizen, at the heart of their political arguments, though to antithetical purposes. Much of what follows in the whole tradition of Western philosophy proceeds from this starting point. It is not only Western *political* philosophy that owes its origins to this conflict over the political role of shoemakers and smiths. For Plato the division between those who rule and those who labour, between those who work with their minds and those who work with their bodies, between those who rule and are fed and those who produce food and are ruled, is not simply the basic principle of politics. The division of labour between rulers and producers, which is the essence of justice in the *Republic*, is also the essence of Plato's theory of knowledge. The radical and hierarchical opposition between the sensible and the intelligible worlds, and between their corresponding forms of cognition, is grounded by Plato in an analogy with the social division of labour which excludes the producer from politics.[16]

Plato: The *Republic*

After the *Protagoras*, Plato would never again directly confront a democratic argument. He certainly continued his debate with the sophists; and every attack on them was in a sense an attack on democracy, since, even when they were antidemocratic, he often treated them as products or expressions of democracy (which, of course, in a sense they were) on the grounds that they reflected and encouraged the moral and intellectual decadence of a polis in which one man's opinion was as good as another's. In the *Gorgias*, for instance, we are given to understand

---

16 It has been suggested that this opposition is the most distinctive characteristic of Greek thought, which has set the agenda for Western philosophy ever since. See, for instance, Jacques Gernet in 'Social History and the Evolution of Ideas in China and Greece from the Sixth to the Second Century BC', in Jean-Pierre Vernant, *Myth and Society in Ancient Greece*, transl. Janet Lloyd (Sussex: Harvester Press, 1980). The suggestion that the opposition between sensible and intelligible worlds is uniquely Western may be misleading; but there is a uniquely antagonistic conception of the relation between them in the Western philosophical tradition since Plato; and this owes much to the antidemocratic convictions on which his argument is based. The connection drawn by Plato between this epistemological division and the division between rulers and ruled is critical here; and a philosopher who could take for granted the division between rulers and producers (as Mencius did, for instance) might not have felt the same compulsion to emphasize the antithesis between these two worlds, with their corresponding forms of cognition.

that the amoral, unprincipled Callicles, with his contention that justice is the right of the strongest, is the logical outcome of the democratic attitude, even when the idea that might makes right is invoked in support of oligarchy. Yet, while Plato conducted his case against democracy without ever directly engaging a serious argument in its favour, Protagoras remained his primary, if nameless, adversary.

Protagoras, as we have seen, presented the practical arts as the foundation of society. The 'argument from the arts', which lies at the heart of Plato's political theory, is intended to turn Protagoras's principle against itself. It uses the ethic of craftsmanship, which was so much a part of Athens's democratic culture, to argue against the democracy. We can understand the full significance of this argument for Plato only if we consider its relation to the culture of the Athenian aristocracy and its disposition at that historical moment.

Plato, born in 427, belonged on both his parents' sides to the most distinguished of Athenian families, perhaps not among the very wealthiest – though his wealth was not inconsiderable – but certainly among the most noble in pedigree. There can be little doubt about the generally antidemocratic feeling among his associates, and his close relatives were leaders of the oligarchic coup that established the reign of the Thirty Tyrants. Plato himself, if we are to believe the *Seventh Epistle*, had political ambitions in his youth and had great hopes for the regeneration of Athens by the oligarchic revolution.[17] But he was, to his credit, unable to accept the excesses of the regime established by his friends and relations, refusing to join them as he was expected to do. When the Thirty were overthrown, his political ambitions were briefly renewed, only to subside again with the restoration of the democracy. Plato praised the moderation of the returning democrats, who generally treated their enemies with great restraint, especially in contrast to the bloody excesses of the oligarchs; and this remained his judgment despite the trial and death of Socrates. Yet the restored democracy seemed to him to signal the moral corruption of Athens, which 'was no longer ruled by the manners and institutions of our forefathers', and where 'the whole fabric of law and custom was going from bad to worse at an alarming rate'.[18]

After the death of Socrates, Plato embarked on an extended journey, not only to expand his own education but offering his wisdom to the

---

17 The authenticity of the *Epistles* is controversial, although the *Seventh Epistle* is more generally accepted as Plato's own work.
18 *Seventh Epistle*, 325d–e.

royal court of Syracuse in Sicily. He visited Syracuse both under Dionysius I and his successor, Dionysius II, with whom the philosopher fell out. In about 385 BC Plato founded the Academy, about a mile outside the city walls, to teach subjects such as mathematics, astronomy, harmonics, and philosophy, both natural and political. His own political ambitions were never again revived and, given his associations, were in any case unlikely ever to succeed. But the political purposes of the Academy are unmistakable. Its students – the sons of wealthy Athenians and foreign families – were educated in Platonic politics and sent forth as consultants to rulers and cities throughout the Mediterranean world.

At home in Athens, disaffected aristocrats were withdrawing from politics, and Plato's philosophical enterprise developed in this climate of disaffection and withdrawal. There would still be aristocratic leaders even in the late third century, notably Lycurgus; but politics was no longer the favoured career it had once been. The historical moment of popular politics and aristocratic estrangement, when well-born and educated men turned their backs on the polis, posed itself for Plato as a philosophical problem: the separation of thought and action. He set himself the task of reuniting them. Wisdom as he conceives it is in its very essence related to practice and especially to politics. We cannot hope to understand how he envisaged his philosophical task if we abstract it from the political problem as he perceived it. His philosophical project was never divorced from Athenian political realities, and his search for absolute and universal truths was never dissociated from the mission to regenerate Athens. Plato cannot be dismissed as simply an ideologue of the aristocratic-oligarchic faction in Athenian politics, nor is his conception of philosophic virtue reducible to the values of aristocratic culture. But his political philosophy leaves little doubt that his hopes of moral and political regeneration required the reconciliation of aristocracy and politics. Nor is this a simple matter of replacing one political form with another. The separation of thought and action has very specific social conditions, and to reunite them will require a social transformation.

The democracy, as we saw, had evolved in tandem with the civic principle; and the estrangement of the aristocracy from politics was the culmination of that historical process. The establishment of the Athenian polis as the dominant principle of association, the civic community with its laws and the new identity of citizenship, had at the same time been a consolidation of popular power, in opposition to aristocratic dominance. Civic identity, the jurisdiction of the polis and the rule of *nomos* in Athens all tended towards a kind of equality, set against aristocratic principles of rule and hierarchy. Plato's task was to reclaim the polis for the aristocracy. This required breaking the bond between politics and democracy and making hierarchy, not equality, the essence of the polis. The polis, in other words, had to replace the hierarchical *oikos*, the lordly household of the Homeric epics, as the natural terrain of aristocracy. So Plato had to devise a conception of the polis in which the essential political relation would no longer be interaction among citizens but, again, the division between rulers and subjects, even rulers and producers. He also needed to elaborate a conception of justice that would reverse the increasingly close association, in the democracy, between the concept of *dikē* and the notion of *isonomia*. In his great classic, the *Republic*, Plato constructed a conception of *dikaiosune* which identified it with inequality and the social division of labour between rulers and producers.

The dialogue begins with an exchange between Socrates and his interlocutors concerning three conventional conceptions of justice: first, the simple morality of the honest businessman whose basic rules of right conduct are that one should always tell the truth, never cheat anyone, and pay one's debts; second, the traditional maxim of helping one's friends and harming one's enemies; and finally, the observation that justice is defined by the interest of the strongest. Plato, in the person of Socrates, quickly dismisses the first, on the grounds that specific actions, such as returning something borrowed, may be good and just in some circumstances but not in others. Polemarchus tries to deal with this by proposing, first, that justice is giving every man his due. But that, of course, raises questions about what is due to whom, and here Plato already introduces the analogy of the arts which will be the core of his whole argument: to judge what is due to someone is akin to the expert judgment made by the practitioner of a specialized art, *technē*, about what good practice is in any particular circumstances; and this requires knowledge about the purpose of the art involved, the ends it is meant to achieve. Just as doctors, builders or shoemakers must have specific knowledge about the ends and means appropriate to their arts, so a man can live a good and just life only if he knows the true purpose of life and how to achieve it. Polemarchus then specifies that justice means doing good to friends and harm to enemies. This, too, is found wanting, since it cannot be just, for instance, to do harm to enemies who are themselves good. Polemarchus is forced to concede that what he means is that we should do good to friends who are good and harm to enemies who are bad. But this simply opens him to the objection that it surely cannot be just to harm others, especially since the only real harm we can do them is to make them worse than they are. How can it be just to make someone less good? So we must still seek out the underlying principle of justice that stands apart from any specific example and allows us to judge any particular action by a universal standard that applies to all cases.

The argument with Thrasymachus and his definition of justice as the interest of the stronger is the most revealing and significant. He begins with a descriptive observation that, in any given situation, the interest of the stronger or ruling elements will be defined as just. This is not, at first, intended as a moral judgment. At this stage, Thrasymachus is expressing the kind of anthropological insight we might expect from a serious sophist, with which even Protagoras could agree. It is a simple proposition about the conventional foundations of morality, with the added observation that the ideas of ruling groups, for better or worse, have tended to be the ruling ideas of their societies. But Plato creates a trap for the sophist, which allows the philosopher not only to mobilize and elaborate the arts analogy but also to transform a reasonable sophistic insight into an objectionable amorality.

Socrates responds to Thrasymachus's original observation with the objection that rulers can be wrong about their interests and leads the sophist to the conclusion that a ruler is only a ruler insofar as he makes no mistakes – a conclusion that leads easily to the proposition that ruling is a specialized art. Thrasymachus shifts his position, moving away from his purely empirical observation and boldly asserting the moral principle that 'might makes right'. As is typical of Plato's dialogues, Socrates's interlocutor has conveniently been pushed to a conclusion that need not follow from his first premise. There is no logical reason why Thrasymachus's anthropological insight is more consistent with the moral judgment that might makes right than with Protagoras's principle that justice is something like the greatest good of the greatest number. But Plato's strategy, as a prelude to his own exploration of justice, is not to grapple with the useful insights of the sophists so much as to undermine even the reasoned arguments of Protagoras through a kind of guilt by association, while also establishing the principle that government is a specialized art. He goes on to suggest that justice is the specific virtue of the soul which allows the soul to perform its special function most effectively. That function is to live well, and Plato here also establishes a principle that will prove crucial to his argument: that among the basic functions of the soul essential to the truly good life, functions that only the soul can perform, are actions such as 'deliberating or taking charge and exercising control'. We begin to understand that justice has something to do with a proper balance among various functions, with reason in control.

It is striking that, in seeking a definition of justice, Plato never engages a conception that expresses the principles of the democracy. He never, for instance, directly confronts an argument that justice has something to do with equality, that *dikaiosune* has something to do with *isonomia*. If anything, apart from the first definition canvassed in the *Republic*, which he lightly dismisses, he conducts a debate with conventional principles that were fundamental to the old aristocratic ethic. Here, the division between friends and enemies, as well as between rulers and subjects, had a special meaning, deriving from a society in which aristocratic power was rooted in a network of friendship groups, the *hetaireiai*, and the values of a ruling class were meant to be a universal standard. Plato challenges these principles not on behalf of democratic values but rather in the conviction that conventional aristocratic principles are far too vulnerable in the democracy. In democratic Athens, the main political arena is not *hetaireia* but polis; and the demos, not the aristocracy, can be regarded as the strongest or the ruling element. What is needed is a new aristocratic ethic, which is less dependent on convention and tradition, far more universalist and absolute, and yet rooted in the polis.

Plato then sets out to replace the conventional wisdom of the oligarchic faction with a *philosophical* defence of inequality. One distinguished classicist has even suggested that Plato's doctrine of Ideas is 'directly descended' from the old aristocratic ethic of hero-models, as in Homer. But now the *paradeigma* or example for imitation, which was so central to the old aristocratic code, is translated into, as Plato himself defines the Ideas, 'patterns established in the realm of Being'.[19] His argument depends on situating justice within the realm of absolute Ideas, the ultimate reality to which only philosophical reason has access, beyond the sphere of everyday life, the world of appearances and 'the multiplicity of things'.

The stated objective of the dialogue is to find a conception of justice that is not merely conventional, nor merely concerned with appearances, rewards and punishments. The task is to discover an absolute and universal idea of justice as something that is good in itself. Socrates suggests that, although he hopes to identify the qualities of the just man, it is easier first to seek out justice in the larger model of the state. Some commentators have taken this to mean that the *Republic* is not essentially a political work and that Plato's fictional state appears in it simply as a means of defining justice in the soul by analogy. But

---

19 Werner Jaeger, *Paideia: The Ideals of Greek Culture* (New York: Oxford University Press, 2nd edn, 1945), Vol. I, p. 34. The definition of Ideas appears in *Theatetus*, 176–e.

as the argument proceeds, it becomes increasingly clear that the philosopher is laying out some essential principles of politics, which are never
secondary to, and are always served by, the analogy of the soul.

Socrates proposes to follow a state in imagination as it comes into
being and develops from a simple form to a more prosperous society
of luxury, so that we can observe the point at which justice enters the
picture. The very first essential principle laid down in this imaginary
reconstruction is that the state is based on a division of labour. This
means that the state is not simply a conventional creation but is based
on the natural principle of human interdependence, the inability of
any single human being to perform all the functions necessary for
survival, and the variety of innate abilities which fit different people
for different occupations. As Socrates builds his imaginary state, it
begins to emerge that justice will have something to do with this
division of labour, the proper balance among the constituent elements.

We should here take note of the fact that there is nothing in the
social division of labour as such that makes it intrinsically hierarchical.
Yet Plato requires a hierarchical division of labour in which some
elements control or rule over others, and establishing this hierarchical
principle may be the most important step in his argument. It is at this
point that we can appreciate the function of the analogy between
individual soul and the state.

We might expect the typical Athenian citizen to dispute the notion
that there is a natural division between those who rule and those who
must be ruled. He would, at any rate, object to the application of this
notion to himself and other Athenians. But he might more readily
accept the principle that a healthy soul, the one more conducive to a
morally good life, is one in which reason commands the 'lower'
appetites. We need not assume that the notion of a two-part soul was
conventional wisdom in Athens; but at least such a principle would
not violate the fundamental values of the democratic culture, and the
citizen would probably have little difficulty in appreciating the distinction between reason and the appetites. Now, analogy can be a persuasive
tool of argumentation only if there is some basic agreement about
one of its terms, which can then be extended – by analogy – to support
a more contentious proposition. To an Athenian audience, the political
principle in Plato's argument is undoubtedly the controversial one, and
it would be pointless to invoke it in support of some other allegedly
analogous proposition. Despite what the philosopher tells us about
his primary intention to elucidate the nature of the soul and the just
individual, his strategy makes far more sense if we understand that
the object of his argument is to defend a deeply controversial political

principle, by drawing on a less contentious notion of the soul. In any case, in spite of what Socrates tells us about the order of argumentation, he has already introduced the notion of a balance between the controlling, rational element of the soul and the lower appetites before he embarks on his reconstruction of the state, and he freely draws on the analogy as he proceeds.

It is worth noting, too, that to make the critical move in his argument, establishing the natural division between ruler and ruled, Plato invokes only two parts of the soul, 'better' and 'worse', or reason and the appetites, although he will go on to propose a tripartite soul. The tripartite soul, which appears only sporadically in Plato's work, has its own, more specific political purpose in devising a kind of tripartite state – or rather, a bipartite state with a ruling class exercising two distinct functions. But the more fundamental division between rulers and ruled is supported by a two-part soul. In his other major political work, the *Laws*, he again requires only a division between reason, the 'natural sovereign', and the passions, appetites or lower functions of the soul; and even in the *Republic* the essential division is between the sovereign reason and the baser elements, just as the primary division in the state is between rulers and producers. The tripartite soul, in which a 'spirited' element ideally assists deliberative reason, simply allows him to delineate the two distinct functions of a ruling class, deliberative and military, as against the 'lower' functions of the farming classes and the practitioners of other practical arts. At every stage of his argument, in every aspect of the analogy between the soul and the state, it is difficult to mistake the direction of argumentation: the doctrine of the soul serves the theory of the state.

As Plato spells out the qualities of the good soul, he is also elaborating the qualities appropriate to a ruling class and those characteristics that must consign men to political subjection. What is particularly striking about his delineation of the 'philosophic nature', the qualities of the soul appropriate to rule, is the extent to which the philosophic virtues correspond to more conventional aristocratic traits. It is impossible to detach moral qualities from social status in Plato's doctrine, in much the same way that the English concept of 'nobility' implies both a moral attribute and a social position; and like other aristocratic critics of democracy, the philosopher attaches great importance to style and deportment as reflections of some deeper moral virtue. More particularly, the realization of the philosophic nature depends on the life conditions of a leisured aristocracy, able to appropriate the labour of others and free from the need to engage in productive work.

Plato's argument here is significant for several reasons. It means that social conditions are more decisive than innate differences in determining the qualities of soul that divide human beings into rulers and ruled. To be sure, people are born with varying abilities – which is, again, why the division of labour is a natural principle. Yet the differences among them are not enough to account for the vast and permanent division between rulers and ruled. Even the differences between 'gold' or 'silver' souls, on the one hand, and 'iron' or 'brass', on the other, turn out, in the main, to be socially determined. The unbridgeable gulf between the few who are by nature qualified to rule and those who must be ruled is grounded in more profound differences in the conditions of life which divide the privileged classes from the labourers, craftsmen, merchants and farmers tied to the world of material necessity. Each condition of life has its own specific virtue, the qualities best fitted to fulfil its proper role. But the majority engaged in base and menial occupations can never rise above the relative virtues of their station, and it soon emerges that the highest virtue of these classes is voluntary submission to their betters. True virtue requires liberation from the 'multiplicity of things'. The conditions for the realization of true virtue, however, are not simply the social circumstances of the individual. A polis governed by the lower appetites – that is, a polis in which 'banausic' classes dominate – will inevitably corrupt the most admirable soul. The life of the virtuous soul can be achieved only in a polis that allows the necessary social conditions to flourish and is governed by rulers who personify the soul's higher elements. At the very least, it requires a philosopher king who embodies the necessary virtues and rules the polis absolutely according to his philosophic wisdom, unfettered by law.

When Plato goes on to trace the stages in the decline of the polis, he confirms the dependence of virtue on social conditions. The watershed in the decline is the fall of the second-best form, timocracy, a warrior state like Sparta, which is motivated by the love of honour, and its replacement by oligarchy, which is driven by the love of money. Oligarchy is rule not just by the wealthy but specifically by those in possession of alienable property, not a landed aristocracy but moneyed men; and the transition from timocracy to oligarchy marks the beginning of rule by the lower parts of the soul, as the 'spirited' element gives way to baser appetites. Nothing could be clearer than the close association in Plato's moral doctrine between qualities of soul and social conditions. Even the prevailing form of property is decisive in shaping the moral disposition of the polis. A change from aristocratic and hereditary property to moneyed wealth crosses the critical dividing line between, on the one hand, a society in which the ruling class –

in timocracy, the fighting class – 'will abstain from any form of business, farming, or handicrafts', and on the other hand, a society in which the leading elements are men who have scraped together a fortune by earning their living.

The fact that the ruling class in the ideal polis of the *Republic* has no property at all, while subordinate classes apparently do, should not mislead us about the aristocratic values that permeate the dialogue. References to Plato's 'communism' – in relation to the communal property, and the community of wives and children associated with it – are particularly misguided. What is important for Plato in his conception of property is that the rulers belong to a group that can live on the labour of others and are free of material necessity, the most fundamental distraction from pure intellection. In the real world, the closest approximation to his ideal – a ruling class that can 'abstain from any form of business, farming, or handicrafts' – is a hereditary landed class, secure in its possession of largely immobile and inalienable property, commanding the labour of others and never reduced to sordid commercial dealings. In the *Laws*, Plato will make explicit this connection between the ideal and the 'second-best' polis.

It is significant, too, that when Plato blames 'bad upbringing' for the corruption of promising individuals, what he has in mind is not the ill-effect of the wrong kind of family life or a poor education but rather, above all, the corrupting influence of the mob. Here, Plato again turns Protagoras against himself. He adopts the sophist's view that the community, and not any individual instructor, is the most effective teacher, best able to transmit its values and promote the character traits it most prizes. But while Protagoras regarded the democratic polis, with its customs and laws, as the surest source of virtue, for Plato it is the breeding ground of vice. The demos is capable only of a relative virtue specific to its lowly station, but its corruption is more absolute. The vice of the banausic multitude is not only its specific class attribute but the source of the corruption infecting other classes too – as it infected, Plato tells us in the *Gorgias*, even its greatest leader, Pericles.

The possession of true virtue and the 'philosophic nature', then, depends both on the individual's social position and on the quality of the polis as a whole, in particular the social character of the people who dominate it. The importance Plato assigns to the social conditions of virtue must inevitably affect how we understand his theory of knowledge and the practice of philosophy. It is clear that for Plato true knowledge, which Socrates has identified with virtue, requires not only epistemological liberation from the material world of appearances but also social liberation from material necessity in everyday life. We already know that freedom from material necessity is a requirement for those who practise the 'Royal Art' of politics or statesmanship; and, as Plato explains the process of acquiring true knowledge, he makes it clear that the essential qualification for the Royal Art is knowledge of the 'Human Good', the true purpose or *telos* of humanity, which is not mere pleasure, power, or material wealth but the fulfilment of the human essence as a rational being. The social condition Plato requires of his ruling class, in other words, is also the minimal condition of true knowledge.

As Plato lays out the programme of the philosophic education, freedom from material necessity begins to appear not simply as a precondition but an integral step in the process of acquiring knowledge of the Good. The object of Plato's education is to lead the student to a knowledge of goodness in itself, the ultimate Idea or Form of the Good as a single, unchanging essence beyond all specific instances of goodness. This, in his view, requires understanding of a greater cosmic order, the expression of a higher Reason. Plato never offers us a definition of the Good, because its apprehension is a kind of revelation, even a mystical experience. But the process that leads the student to the point of revelation is spelled out in great detail, as Plato enumerates the various forms of cognition, together with their proper objects, in ascending order. The essential dividing line is between the world of appearances and the intelligible world, and each of these is subdivided into lower and higher forms: the form of cognition most tied to appearances is imagining, the object of which is images, and above that is belief or opinion, which concerns visible things. We cross the line to the intelligible world in the process of *thinking* about mathematical objects, and from there we rise to intelligence or knowledge of the Forms. This takes us finally to the threshold of the Good.

The process of education is a gradual progression in detaching the soul from 'the multiplicity of things' and mere appearances; and the freedom of body and soul from material necessity is no less a part of that progression than is the hierarchy of cognition. The practical liberation from everyday material necessity is the first and essential moment of the soul's epistemological liberation from the world of appearances.

The *Statesman* and the *Laws*

We shall return to Plato's theory of knowledge as laid out in the *Republic* to consider how, or even whether, our judgment of his whole philosophical system – not only his political philosophy but also his epistemology – should be affected by its material presuppositions and ideological implications. For the moment, a brief consideration of his two other important political works, the *Statesman* and the *Laws*, will help to clarify the political assumptions that permeate his philosophic project.

It can be misleading to look upon the progression from *Republic* to *Statesman* to *Laws* as simply a two-stage descent from the ideal. It is certainly true that the *Laws* is explicitly presented as a 'second-best' polis, and it is also true that the *Statesman* provides a conceptual transition to the later work. But it is important to acknowledge that all three dialogues express the same fundamental principles, which Plato elaborates from different vantage points. The *Republic* undoubtedly displays a greater allegiance to philosophic principles than to aristocratic politics, and it certainly reflects his disillusionment with the attempt to establish an Athenian oligarchy. In the *Laws*, Plato will spell out in great detail a constitution that does not depend so much on rule by philosophic wisdom as on carefully crafted institutions and laws designed to imitate as much as possible the effects of philosophic rule. Although this polis is at best an imitation of the ideal, adapted to the harsh realities of material and social life, there is a sense in which it is even more revolutionary than the *Republic*. If the *Republic* represents a kind of thought experiment, not intended as a model for the ideal polis but rather as statement, in poetic or metaphorical style, of certain fundamental principles – the *Laws*, however utopian it may be, converts those principles into an institutional blueprint. It proposes a complete transformation of political and social relations as they are in the Athens of Plato's day, a radical departure from everything essential in Athenian political practice and its social underpinnings, down to the most basic conditions of property and labour. The polis of the *Laws* makes Plato's political commitments even clearer than the ideal state in the *Republic*. The *Statesman*, while it presents no blueprint for an ideal or even second-best constitution, elaborates political principles introduced in the *Republic* and develops them to lay a foundation for the revolution of the *Laws*.

The *Statesman* is above all an elaboration of the argument from the arts, which already played a major role in the *Republic*; and it redefines the rule of law, which will be given concrete form in the *Laws*. In effect, it creates a bridge between the rule of philosophy and a philosophic rule of law. The first premise, again, is that politics is a specialized art, requiring refined expertise – though here, more than in the *Republic*, Plato stresses the differences between statesmanship and more conventional arts, in order to emphasize the incompatibility between the art of politics and ordinary occupations. The emphasis, as ever, is on expertise and the exclusiveness of specialized arts, and perhaps the most critical point is that the true expert must have free rein in the practice of his art. This principle, which absolves the states- man from obedience to law, will set the stage for redefining the rule of law.

But first, Plato seeks the best analogy for the art of statesmanship. He begins by suggesting that the art of politics is essentially one with the arts of household management. We should hardly need reminding how significant it would have been in Plato's Athens to treat the polis as an *oikos* writ large, with everything this implies about its hierarchical structure; and Plato is especially provocative in identifying the states- man with the household lord, even the slave-master, the *despotes*. Yet this is not enough to characterize the political art, so Plato ventures further afield. Here, he introduces the myth of the cosmic cycle, which we encountered in our discussion of the Promethean story. Human beings in the philosopher's own time are living in the Age of Zeus, the bottom of the cosmic cycle, with all its pains and labours and bereft of divine guidance or assistance, in sharp contrast to the Age of Kronos, when the herd of humanity was governed and physically nurtured by the divine shepherd. This suggests the possibility of an analogy between statesman and shepherd; but, although Plato acknowl- edges certain affinities, he cannot unequivocally accept this analogy. To be sure, it has the advantage of emphasizing that the art of politics is about rule and not citizenship; but, for reasons that will soon become apparent, he is unwilling to accept that the political art, like the art of tending sheep, entails the physical nurture of its subjects.

The art that most resembles statesmanship, Plato finds, is weaving. The art of weaving selects appropriate materials, rejects others, and joins a multiplicity of different strands into a variegated but unified fabric. The art of politics is similar to weaving because its object is to create a social fabric out of various human types. The statesman supervises the selection and rejection of materials and creates the web of state out of the warp and woof of humanity. He must weave together the strands that truly belong to the web of state, while 'enfolding' in it other elements, not integral parts of the state but necessary for its maintenance. Plato distinguishes between the art of weaving itself and other, ancillary arts: those that are 'subordinate' to weaving but part of the process, such as carding and spinning, and those that are merely 'contributory', in the sense that they do not belong to the process of weaving but simply produce the necessary tools, such as shuttles. Analo- gously, there are subordinate and contributory arts in the realm of politics. In particular, those who practise the contributory arts can have no share in the royal art of politics – and these politically excluded arts turn out to embrace everything that produces the community's physical requirements: its food, tools, clothing, shelter, conveyances, and other materials used to maintain existence and health, provide amusement, or give protection. Aristotle, who joined the Academy in 367 when Plato's *Statesman* was taking shape, would later make a distinction with similar political effect, between the 'parts' and the 'conditions' of the polis: those that have a share in politics and those who simply create the conditions that make it possible.

Having established the nature and purpose of the royal art, Plato is able to redefine the rule of law accordingly. His first premise is that law, at least as it is commonly understood in democratic Athens, is incompatible with art. *Nomos* and *technē* are antithetical, because the rule of law restricts the free play of the craftsman's art and because non-experts are effectively dictating to experts. Doctors, for instance, cannot be told what to do by those who are ignorant of medical arts. They must be free to respond creatively to each situation as their knowledge and skill best instruct them. The rule of law as understood by the Athenians violates that principle of art and ties the hands of those who govern them. *Nomos* acts as a check on leaders no less than on those who are led; and (as we saw earlier in considering the contrast between *nomos* and *thesmos* as two very different conceptions of law) it is an expression of the people's role – the role of non-experts – in determining their common life.

Yet Plato finds a way of reappropriating the law by redefining its function. The rule of law, in his new definition, should imitate, not thwart, the political art. Its object should be to create and maintain a certain kind of social fabric, not to introduce an element of civil equality into the polis but, on the contrary, to embody inequality, in particular to fix in place the hierarchical relation between those who practise the political art and those who simply 'contribute' by serving the needs of the polis.

Plato goes on to classify the types of constitution, adopting the traditional distinctions among rule by one man, rule by the few and rule by the many, but dividing each into law-abiding and lawless forms. Just as one-man rule can be a lawful monarchy or a lawless tyranny, rule by the few can take the form of aristocracy or oligarchy, which are distinguished not on the grounds that one is rule by the 'best' and the other simply rule by the rich but rather on the basis that one form of rule by the rich abides by the law and the other does not. Here, Plato makes a grudging concession to democracy, suggesting that, among the evil constitutions, the lawless form of democracy is easiest to bear – not because it is more virtuous than others but simply because it is weaker and can do less harm. Yet the most revealing point is his suggestion that among the law-abiding constitutions, democracy is the worst, the most distant from the art of politics and its objectives.

Plato puts these principles into practice in the *Laws*, which delineates in great detail a polis governed by a system of laws designed to imitate the art of politics. As the *Statesman* has led us to expect, the rule of law is here conceived as a way of rigidly structuring social behaviour by means of a legally fixed separation of human types. Its principal objective is to divide the inhabitants of the polis permanently into predetermined social positions or classes, even castes, to prohibit any confusion among them, and especially to separate those who are suited to citizenship from those engaged in occupations that corrupt the soul and disqualify their practitioners from political participation. This will be accomplished by establishing a sharp and legally defined distinction between landowners, who are free of necessary labour, and non-landowning labourers, who will perform all necessary labour. Land will be carefully allotted to prospective citizens and made entirely inalienable. The landed class produced by this means will have access to the labour of others and will hence be qualified for citizenship. Although the citizen class contains people of modest means (in movable property), as well as those of more substantial wealth, Plato has effectively restored the rule of a hereditary agrarian aristocracy, except that now the polis, not the *oikos*, is its principal platform. The remaining landless inhabitants, ranging from slaves and farm labourers to craftsmen and merchants, will have no political rights. Indeed, anyone performing necessary labour will be scarcely distinguishable from slaves in dependence and servility.

It soon becomes clear that Plato has very consciously set out to subvert the Athenian constitution, deliberately replacing its democratic principles with antithetical aristocratic standards. He even signals his intention by ostensibly adopting certain Athenian institutions – like the Solonian division into classes of wealth and Cleisthenes's division of the population into tribes – and adapting them to his antidemocratic purposes. The classes of Solon, for instance, become not a means of conferring a political identity even on the poorest classes but rather a reinforcement of their exclusion. The new classification simply subdivides the ruling class itself into four sections based on the amount of their movable wealth, and the rest of the population are defined by their complete omission.

This legally fixed class structure is designed to make the polis less dependent on the judgment of wise rulers. In separating good from bad, as little as possible will be left to chance, to guard against the danger that virtue will be contaminated by a confusion of noble and banausic. Yet if much of philosophy's work will be done in advance by a rigid system of law, philosophy will still play a major role in the daily life of the polis. Nowhere, in fact, are the political intentions of Plato's philosophy more evident than in his account of the Nocturnal Council, which will oversee the laws. With a striking resemblance to Plato's Academy, engaging in philosophical studies with an emphasis on mathematics, astronomy and theology, the Council is nonetheless an overtly political institution, with a central role in governance, like the unreformed Areopagus in Athens. It will act as a supreme court to interpret the laws, a continuous constitutional convention to revise them when necessary, a school for public officials and a moral censor; and as guardian of the law, its principal function will be to protect the rigid class system which for Plato is the essence of lawfulness. In the *Laws*, it is even harder than in the *Republic* to avoid the political implications of his philosophic system.

Philosophy and Ideology

Let us, then, return to the *Republic* and the question of how we should judge the philosophy of Plato if we accept that knowledge and virtue as he conceives them have a clear and forceful ideological meaning. Considering this question in relation to Plato, at this founding moment in the development of Western philosophy, may also shed light on our whole historical enterprise and the implications of a 'social history' for our appreciation of political theory.

Even if we interpret the *Republic* as above all a discussion of the individual soul, a dialogue on the attainment of knowledge rather than an essentially political work, there is no escaping the social conditions of true knowledge as Plato conceives it. Even if the polis appears only for the purpose of analogy, it remains significant that he defines knowledge in these terms. Plato's philosophical idealism turns out to be remarkably materialist: true knowledge, the knowledge of Ideas or Forms, has very concrete material conditions. Again, the material freedom of the person is an irreducible condition of true knowledge not only in the sense that the long and arduous process of education leading to knowledge of the ultimate Good requires leisure time but, more particularly, because a life of necessary labour damages the soul and makes it unfit for philosophy. Philosophy is inevitably dishonoured when it is illegitimately pursued by those 'whose souls a life of drudgery has warped and maimed no less surely than their sedentary crafts have disfigured their bodies.'[20]

What does all this mean for our appreciation of Plato's philosophical project? If we acknowledge its social and political meaning, even its ideological motivations, are we obliged to disparage his philosophy? Is it still possible, for instance, to derive profound epistemological or moral insights from the *Republic* even while we recognize its anti-democratic purpose? These are the kinds of questions we inevitably confront with every great thinker who is also politically engaged – as all the political theorists of the Western canon were, in one way or another.

The simple answer is that no amount of disagreement with their ideological propensities obliges or permits us to dismiss the theoretical merits of their ideas or to suspend our intellectual judgment. The historicity of an idea or even its partisanship does not preclude significance and fruitfulness beyond its time and place or outside the politics of its originator. The object of a contextual reading, in the sense intended here, is not to discredit or to validate ideas by their ideological origins or purposes but rather to understand them better by identifying the salient issues that confronted the theorist and the terms in which those issues were being contested. This kind of reading has the added advantage of enabling a critical distance from our own unexamined assumptions. Our assessment of ideas cannot end with recognition of their historicity, but that is certainly a useful place to start. To appreciate the philosophers' answers, we need to understand the questions they are addressing, and those questions are historically constituted, however much the theorist may be looking for a universal answer.

The notion of universality itself has a history of changing meanings rooted in specific social conditions and steeped in ideology. Plato's idea of universal truths, for example, is something very different from the universalism of the Enlightenment; and the differences in philosophical substance are grounded not only in different historical conditions but also in divergent social and political motivations. The characteristically Greek identification of universal truth and philosophic reason grew out of a distinctive social and political experience. While Plato was addressing questions already raised by thinkers before him about the existence of universals and whether, or how, it is possible to know them, these questions posed themselves to him not only as philosophical but also as practical, political problems. We need not insist that Plato's

---

20 495d–e.

motivation was solely political in order to acknowledge the ways in which his conception of reason and universal truth grew out of an engagement with the politics of the democracy. He was nothing if not clear about the practical intentions of his philosophy and about the central role of politics in achieving the good life, which was the object of the philosophic quest. So the problem of reason and truth was for him immediately and essentially political.

The nature of truth and human access to it had a particular meaning in the democratic culture, which ascribed to human reason an unprecedented role in determining the fate of humanity and in judging, indeed creating, authority. Plato's philosophical mission was driven not only by his engagement with thinkers like Pythagoras or Parmenides but by a confrontation with the politics of the democracy, its conception of authority and its apparently indiscriminate attention to all kinds of opinion, whatever their source. His solution, while directed against the democratic conception of reason and truth, was still characteristically Greek. He did not deny the power of reason. If anything, reason, as the guide to higher universal truths, became still more powerful. But he redefined its appropriate object, and in so doing placed true rationality for all practical purposes outside the reach of ordinary people. Yet, for all his antidemocratic motivations, who can deny that his struggle with the culture of democracy was exceptionally fruitful, or that debate on the nature of knowledge was immeasurably advanced by his attempt to find a truth beyond the transience and mutability of empirical reality?

We cannot go far wrong if we begin by acknowledging that passionate engagement, while it can often overwhelm the critical faculties, can also be the surest source of human creativity. It is, indeed, difficult to think of any lasting contribution to the culture of humanity, from the arts to science and philosophy, that has not been driven by some kind of passion. In the case of political theory, it seems reasonable to suppose that the relevant engagement is political; perhaps a passion for social justice, however defined, or even something less exalted, like a fear of losing power or a drive to guard the interests of one's class. We shall hardly do justice to the philosophers if we simply point out the political commitments secreted even in their most ostensibly abstract, disinterested and universalistic ideas. But neither will we give them their due if we evade the issue altogether by assuming that any idea that claims to be disinterested or universalistic cannot also serve partisan interests.

At the same time, we should also acknowledge the complexities of the relation between ideas and contexts. Even if we were inclined to judge Plato's philosophy on primarily political criteria, we would have to recognize its inextricable connection with Athenian democracy. Although – or, more precisely, because – his elaboration of Greek rationalism and his particular brand of universalism were in deliberate opposition to the prevailing democratic culture, his philosophical approach was determined as much by the democracy as by his own aristocratic inclinations.

Aristotle

It has been said – most notably by Samuel Taylor Coleridge – that 'one is born either a Platonist or an Aristotelian'. This observation may have more to do with temperament than philosophy, but there are also differences in philosophic style. In some respects, indeed, the two philosophers do seem to represent polar opposites: Plato's abstract idealism against Aristotle's materialism, or at least his abiding interest in the material world; Plato's Socratic 'dialogical' method against Aristotle's 'technical' approach; Plato's eyes fixed on the heavens and pure, disembodied Forms, seeking the kind of knowledge captured by astronomy and mathematics, against Aristotle's grounding in the physical world of animate and inanimate bodies, the world of physics and biology; Plato's insistence on the primacy of absolute, eternal and universal truths, against Aristotle's preoccupation with motion and change, his sympathy for conventional opinion and his pragmatism; Plato's insistence that virtue is knowledge, against Aristotle's less demanding acceptance of ordinary, unphilosophical virtues, gentlemanly behaviour and the golden mean. Seen from a slightly different angle, the more down-to-earth Aristotle seems the more disinterested scholar, a cool logician and a man of scientific temperament, as against Plato, whose literary style suggests an artist's disposition, while his political passions are present at every level of philosophy, beginning with epistemology.

However we look at them, these two philosophers present a host of striking contrasts. We shall consider some of these at least briefly in what follows, but it may be necessary to acknowledge at the outset the challenge they may seem to pose to the social history of political theory advocated in this book. It will be argued here that whatever else may divide these two philosophical giants, their social values and political commitments are, for all intents and purposes, the same. They are both opposed to the Athenian democracy, from the standpoint of aristocratic values. Might it not be possible, then, to object that, if the connection between politics and philosophy is as close as we say it is for these great political thinkers, the same political commitments and social ideologies should produce essentially the same philosophies? Or, at the very least, are we not entitled to question the usefulness of this social-historical approach if the connections between politics or social attitudes and philosophy is so variable, so lacking in what might be called predictive value?

Nothing argued here so far would justify a simplistic reading of what is entailed or promised by a contextual analysis of political theory, even one that attaches great importance to the political and social dispositions of the theorist. But it may be worth emphasizing a few points. While it should be fairly obvious that any ideology can be sustained by a wide variety of theoretical strategies, even this is not the crucial issue. The point is rather that, for the truly great and creative theorists, historical contexts and political commitments present themselves not as ready-made answers but as complex questions. A historical and political reading of the classics can never predict the thinker's theoretical solutions. It can only illuminate them after the fact – and this is surely no small benefit – by shedding light on the questions to which the theorist was seeking an answer, questions that were posed and contested in historically specific forms.

At the same time, it should also be obvious that no two contexts are ever the same, however close in time and space they are, to say nothing of differences in temperament and personal experience, family background, and education. Plato was an Athenian citizen, Aristotle a metic in Athens, a resident alien from Stagira in Macedonia. For that matter, Plato's philosophy already belonged to the historical context in which Aristotle conceived his ideas. There is also a critical difference between the political moment in which Plato was writing, after the golden age of Periclean democracy but at a moment of declining aristocracy, and, by contrast, the period of Macedonian hegemony, which was Aristotle's context and very present in his mind as he thought about the polis. The Macedonian conquest of Greece effectively marked the end of the polis as an independent political form, but Aristotle saw new possibilities for it within the imperial embrace. While Plato's aristocratic authoritarianism was fairly hopeless and nostalgic, at a time when a rampant democracy seemed to have triumphed, only a few years later Aristotle could imagine a political dispensation more congenial than Athenian democracy, watched over and enforced by a Macedonian garrison.

Aristotle was born in 384 BC, the son of a distinguished family. His father was physician to Amyntas III, King of Macedonia, and the philosopher was probably brought up in the royal household, beginning his lifelong friendship with the king's son, two years his junior, who would become Philip II, conqueror of Greece. The political environment in which Aristotle grew up – both the oligarchy of Stagira and the tribal kingdom of Macedonia – was very different from democratic Athens; and Aristotle's first exposure to Athenian democracy came through the antidemocratic medium of Plato's Academy, where he came to study in 367, escaping the bloody dynastic struggle following the death of Amyntas. He remained as a teacher apparently until 348, the year before Plato's death, perhaps compelled to flee by the growing anti-Macedonian sentiment in Athens. Although evidence is scanty, according to tradition he served from 343 or 342 to 340 as tutor to Philip's son, the future Alexander the Great. It is likely that he also undertook other missions for Philip, such as negotiations with various *poleis* before the final conquest of Greece in 338.

The philosopher returned to Athens in 335, after Philip's assassination and Alexander's suppression of various revolts, including one in Athens. This time, Aristotle came as a member of the Macedonian establishment, with the support of local aristocratic-oligarchic factions; and he lived under the protection of his close friend and patron, Antipater, Alexander's autocratic viceroy in Greece. The philosopher would live and teach in Athens for another dozen years; and, although the famous Lyceum was technically founded by his friend and student, Theophrastus, it was essentially Aristotle's intellectual creation, as the Academy was Plato's. On Alexander's death, Aristotle was forced yet again to leave Athens. When, the following year, he died in Chalcis, a wealthy man with an estate far larger than Plato's, the executor of his last will and testament was Antipater. A few years later, the new ruler of Athens, Demetrios of Phaleron – an Athenian of the pro-Macedonian aristocratic-oligarchic faction, student of Theophrastus and possibly of Aristotle, and something like a philosopher king who apparently lectured at the Lyceum himself – introduced political reforms in the spirit of Aristotle and his philosophic predecessors.

Aristotle, then, was probably more directly engaged in the politics of his day than Plato had been. Although he never directly took part in everyday politics, he was certainly closer to power. But his engagement expressed itself in his philosophy in rather different ways. We have seen how Plato attacked the very foundations of the democratic culture; how, with his epistemology and the principle that virtue is knowledge, he set out to uproot the conceptions of knowledge and virtue that justified democracy. His higher reality of absolute and universal Forms, accessible only to philosophic wisdom, was intended to displace the world of change and flux that was the object of conventional opinion, a world in which there was no higher good than the ordinary virtues of the common citizen. Aristotle challenged Plato's conception of truth and the process of knowing, rejecting the notion of Forms as a separate reality, while placing high value on conventional morality and practical wisdom, accessible without some special philosophic vision. In this, he seems closer to Protagoras. To be sure, he concurred with Plato in rejecting epistemological and moral relativism, of the kind proposed by sophists; but he was very critical of Plato's failure to confront the realities of change and motion, regarding the Platonic theory of Forms as particularly unhelpful. Although the natural state of things was rest, according to Aristotle, and everything tended towards a motionless state, the world was constantly in motion. There was, in his view, a critical need for a form of knowledge capable of dealing with the problem of motion and change; and Plato's theory of immutable Forms, which seem to have an independent existence separate from the changing world of particulars and sensible experience, could contribute little to that kind of knowledge.

For Aristotle, every substance is a complex of matter and form, which are conceptually distinguishable but always exist, and must be studied, together. He agrees with Plato that form, which persists through change, is the proper object of knowledge, and that we can distinguish universal forms from concrete particulars; but for Aristotle this means that the primary objective of knowledge is not to abandon the natural world for a higher, immutable reality but rather to discover the *order* of nature, that which is permanent and unchanging in a world of change. Instead of escaping the world of particulars to contemplate the Universal Forms, we acquire knowledge by proceeding from particular to general, investigating generality by studying particulars, the mutable world we inhabit, which is best known to us. This conception of knowledge attaches importance not only to observed facts but also to commonly held opinions, and in that respect could hardly be more different from Plato's counterposition of empirical fact and opinion, on the one hand, to knowledge and truth, on the other. Since that counterposition lies at the very heart of Plato's moral and political philosophy, in particular his challenge to democracy, we might expect to see a commensurate difference in ethics and political theory.

Aristotle, like Plato, denies that standards of right and wrong are mere conventions; but, he argues, we have no way of discovering rigorous absolute rules. There is no single Form of the Good, no single definition that applies to all cases; and even if there were, the kind of knowledge that could apprehend it would be of little use in understanding particular goods as they apply to us in our everyday lives.

That kind of knowledge could not make someone a better craftsman
or doctor; nor could it ensure a morally good life. Morality is more
a matter of habituation than of philosophic learning. Aristotle certainly
distinguishes between intellectual and ethical virtues or virtues of character; and, having also distinguished between two intellectual virtues,
theoretical and practical wisdom, he identifies contemplation or *theoria*
as the highest virtue. But ethics, like medicine, is a practical, not a
theoretical discipline, whose aim is action, not just understanding. In
determining the good, we can only proceed from what is given in experience, with all its confusions and uncertainties, and try to reach some
kind of reasoned universal judgment. This means that we must consider
conventional opinion and adopt as much as possible of popular morality.
To be sure, the practical intelligence that guides us to the good life is
an intellectual as well as a practical quality; and the best and most
complete life, the fulfilment of humanity's true nature, includes not only
bodily goods but goods of the soul, the contemplative life, the life of
reason. But moral virtue is not knowledge, in the Platonic sense. It is
something closer to what Plato might call right opinion.

The most general and universal feature that defines Aristotle's virtues
is adherence to the mean in every quality. Every practice, every temperament, has its excess as well as its inadequacy; and the morally good
person is the one who consistently displays a disposition to that golden
mean – as (there is here a certain circularity in Aristotle's argument)
the man of practical intelligence would define it. His moral principles
are more like universal rules of thumb than abstract absolutes. Yet he
tells us enough about the qualities of the virtuous man to make it
clear how closely tied the virtues are to aristocracy. The four most
important ethical virtues – generosity; magnificence; the nameless
mean between ambition and its absence; and, 'the crown of the virtues',
great-souledness or high-mindedness (*megalopsychia*) – are qualities
available only to the wellborn and wealthy. The great-souled man in
particular is by definition an aristocrat, whose qualities include a (justified) feeling of superiority, pride, self-confidence and even haughtiness.
He can concern himself with 'great and lofty matters' because he (like
Plato's philosophic nature) is free of the petty and vulgar preoccupations that come with having to work for a living. 'A high-minded
person', the philosopher writes in a passage that could have come from
a handbook of aristocratic manners,

> is justified in looking down upon others for he has the right opinion
> of them, but the common run of people do so without rhyme or
> reason. . . . He will show his stature with men of eminence and

fortune, but will be unassuming toward those of moderate means. For to be superior to the former is difficult and dignified, but superiority over the latter is easy. Furthermore, there is nothing ignoble in asserting one's dignity among the great, but to do so among the lower classes is just as crude as to assert one's strength against an invalid. He will not go in for pursuits that the common people value. . . . He cannot adjust his life to another, except a friend, for to do so is slavish. That is why . . . all flatterers are servile and people from the lower classes are flatterers. . . . He is a person who will rather possess beautiful and priceless objects than objects which are profitable and useful, for they mark him more as self-sufficient.[21]

The philosopher then goes on to list the elements of style – the slow gait, low voice and deliberate manner of speaking, the absence of hurry and excitement that mark the great-souled man. Readers may remember that Aristotle (if he was indeed the author), in *The Constitution of Athens*, singles out the lack of just such gentlemanly style as the principal defect of the democratic leader, Cleon. Vulgarity, it seems, is a serious breach of morality.

Aristotle's *Politics*

The moral conventions that Aristotle respects clearly have more to do with aristocratic codes than with popular morality. And yet, the fact remains that, far more than Plato, he is prepared to give consideration to conventional opinion, not only in the aristocracy but even among the 'middling' sort. This is reflected in his politics not in the sense that his attitude to democracy and his preference for aristocratic oligarchy are any less pronounced than Plato's, but rather in the sense that he raises questions which Plato never bothers to confront – at least in part, perhaps, because the younger philosopher has more hope of seeing his principles put into practice. Just as in his approach to the sciences and metaphysics Aristotle grapples with the material world of change and motion, instead of turning his gaze immediately to a world beyond mundane reality, in his political theory he looks not only for the ideal state but for the sources of motion and unrest in the polis as it is, with a view to correcting them.

Aristotle enumerates several different forms of polis, based on the

---

21 *Nichomachean Ethics*, transl. Martin Ostwald, 1124b5–1125a16.

numbers who rule – monarchy, aristocracy, polity, and their perversions, tyranny, oligarchy and democracy. This classification is accompanied by another, which plays a smaller part in his own political theory but which would, as we shall see in subsequent chapters, figure more prominently in medieval philosophy: the distinction among different forms of authority – despotic, economic, regal and political. But in his attempts to identify the principal causes of civil strife, he is mainly concerned with the two principal types of the Greek state, democracy and oligarchy, not only to judge them against some abstract ideal but to investigate what kinds of safeguards are needed to preserve each actually existing form by reducing the strains that engender conflict and civic disorder, or *stasis*.

To understand the vantage point from which Aristotle constructs his theory of politics, we can consider it in light of what has been said here, earlier in this chapter and in Chapter One, about the distinctive development of the polis, especially in Athens, and the very particular problems it posed for the maintenance of social order in general and the position of propertied classes in particular. Here is a particularly striking illustration of how historically specific questions, posed by specific social conditions, have set the agenda for philosophy and shaped the template on which a system of ideas has been constructed.

Two essential and related features of the polis stand out: the absence of a clear demarcation between rulers and producers, in a civic community combining landlords and peasants, together with other producing classes; and the lack of a powerful state apparatus to act on behalf of propertied classes in maintaining order and their dominance over producers. In other precapitalist societies, appropriators have been directly organized in the state, as in the ancient bureaucratic kingdoms, or have been able to rely on state power to maintain their positions of dominance and to suppress unrest among subordinate producers. There have been some cases, notably in the feudal West, in which dominant classes have, for a time, managed without a strong central state; but even a strongly militarized dominant class could not stave off the threat of disorder forever. Feudal lords were under great pressure to create a unified power to defend them, to counter the centrifugal forces generated by their intraclass conflicts; and the 'parcellized sovereignty' of feudalism gave way to a process of state centralization. While the modern European state was certainly marked by tensions between monarchs and propertied classes, it was the best available protection of property and class domination and was accepted as such, with varying degrees of reluctance, by Europe's ruling classes.

In ancient Greece, as we have seen, a loosely organized propertied class never had such a state at its disposal. The polis presents a rare, even unique, case in precapitalist history in which a propertied class for various historic reasons had neither the military nor the political predominance required to sustain its property and powers of appropriation. Instead, post-Homeric landlords were compelled to rely on various political accommodations to maintain social order and protect their property. The reforms of Solon and Cleisthenes illustrate how the distinctive class relations of ancient Attica were managed in the absence of a clear class dominance, in a civic order where appropriators and producers confronted one another directly as individuals and as classes, as landlords and peasants, not primarily as rulers and subjects. Without assuming that these reformers were driven by democratic sympathies, we can recognize how the configuration of social power in the ancient polis obliged them to reach accommodations with the demos if civic order was to be maintained and, indeed, if the rich and well born were to protect their own positions.

Aristotle's political theory can be situated in this long political tradition. Just as early modern European political theory would be shaped by the three-way relationship among landlords, peasants and monarchical states, so Aristotle's theory responded to the specific questions thrown up by the polis and its own very particular disposition of social power. He made it very clear that his preference, like Plato's, would have been for a clear division between rulers and producers. But in the actually existing social order, with its distinctive class configuration, he felt obliged, like Athens's legendary reformers, to consider what kind of civic accommodation could save the polis from the social conflicts that threatened to destroy it. We can better understand him if we keep in mind that his conception of political order, as it is possible in the real world, is always informed by his conviction that ruling and production are best kept apart. In the states he clearly favours, such as Egypt or, in Greece, Crete, something like this division exists, for instance in the separation of military and farming classes; and in his outline of the ideal polis (to which we shall return), he proposes just such a division.[22] But in dealing with realities in which the ideal is impossible, he compromises this principle, while always keeping it in view.

Aristotle, then, argues that the general cause of *stasis* in both the two principal forms of polis, especially in recent times, is inequality,

---

22 *Politics*, 1328a–b.

specifically the conflict between the rich and well born on one side and the common people on the other. These social conflicts are expressed politically in different conceptions of justice, a democratic conception which demands equality and an oligarchic one which insists on inequality, or, to put it another way, two opposing conceptions of equality: 'numerical' and 'proportionate', or arithmetic and geometric. It is true, the philosopher argues, that there should be political equality among men who are equal, and also that unequal men should have unequal political rights. But both democratic and oligarchic conceptions are incomplete, because they ignore the proper criteria of equality and inequality, the qualities that properly dictate what is, in true justice, due to each man. The democrat assumes, in effect, that all free-born men are equal, while the oligarch treats wealth as the measure of inequality. But true justice requires that political rights and offices should vary according to the contribution men make to the fulfilment of the state's essential purpose. That purpose is not mere life, material prosperity or even safety and security. Although the state does serve all these ends, its essential purpose is the truly good life; so honours and offices should, in true justice, be distributed according to a principle of civic excellence apart from wealth or free birth. Nevertheless, if both oligarchic and democratic notions are imperfect, the oligarchic commitment to proportionate equality is the best of the incomplete conceptions of justice, the one that more closely approximates the perfect form, while the democratic idea of justice as numerical equality is certainly the worst.

Yet, since the rich and the poor will always exist, there will always be conflicting conceptions of justice in both democracy and oligarchy; and means must be found to contain the conflicts generated by this inescapable reality. In oligarchies there are also the problems posed by conflicts within the ruling oligarchic class itself. At the same time, the rich and well born are, as we know, uniquely equipped to pursue the good life in ways denied to those whose bodies and minds are bound to the necessities of work. This means that preserving, or even advancing, the well born and wealthy minority, with its natural superiority and its critical role in any kind of state, is for Aristotle an essential objective in both cases. The measures intended to eliminate *stasis* must never go beyond the minimum necessary to avoid instability. His general prescription is a judicious combination of oligarchic and democratic principles, in various forms depending on the circumstances; but while the avoidance of *stasis* may require concessions to democracy, the presumption is clearly in favour of oligarchy, because it is among the oligarchic aristocrats that at least a handful of virtuous men will be found.

The 'best practicable' polis, the 'polity' (an Anglicization of *politeia*, which Aristotle is using here in a narrower sense than the general term often translated as 'constitution'), would be just such a combination, in which, despite some democratic elements, the effective primacy of oligarchic principles is clearly visible. Property would be a qualification for active citizenship, even for membership in the Assembly; and, while independent farmers of moderate means would be included and might belong, as hoplites, to the fighting element that is the backbone of the polity, ordinary shopkeepers, artisans and wage-labourers would not qualify. When Aristotle describes the best forms of democracy and oligarchy, they turn out to be very like the polity; and even in democracy, the role of the solid citizen of moderate means, the middling independent farmer, would be limited, because such men, as Aristotle points out, 'not having any great amount of property, are busily occupied; and . . . have thus no time for attending the assembly'[23] – which is all to the good, as government will, for all practical purposes, be concentrated in the hands of the rich and well born.

The philosopher's political values are most clearly visible in the incomplete outline of the ideal polis in what are conventionally numbered Books VII and VIII of the *Politics*. There are significant similarities between this ideal polis and the polity, and indeed the best forms of oligarchy or democracy. But the fundamental principles are more explicitly stated. In particular, the proposal is based on one fundamental premise:

> In the state, as in other natural compounds, [there is a distinction to be drawn between 'conditions' and 'parts']: the conditions which are necessary for the existence of the whole are not organic parts of the whole system which they serve. The conclusion which clearly follows is that we cannot regard the elements which are necessary for the existence of the state, or of any other association forming a single whole, as being 'parts' of the state or of any such association.[24]

We encountered a similar principle in Plato's *Statesman*, in his distinction between the art of statesmanship and other, ancillary – 'subordinate' and 'contributory' – arts, which excluded from citizenship all those who worked to serve the daily needs of the polis. Aristotle's

---

23 *Pol.*, 1218b.
24 1328a.

ideal polis, too, relegates such people to the sphere of necessary 'conditions' and not integral 'parts' of the polis. 'The state', he declares, 'is an association of equals, and only of equals' – though now he makes it plain that the relevant criterion of equality is after all a social one, even in the ideal state: we must, he seems to suggest, always assume that those who do the necessary work cannot make a contribution to the essential, higher purpose of the polis. The presumption must always be in favour of those whose material conditions and social position suit them for the good life, whether or not they actually achieve or contribute to it; and they are the integral parts of the polis:

> Upon these principles it clearly follows that a state with an ideal constitution – a state which has for its members men who are absolutely just, and not men who are just in relation to some particular standard – cannot have its citizens living the life of mechanics or shopkeepers, which is ignoble and inimical to goodness. Nor can it have them engaged in farming: leisure is a necessity, both for growth in goodness and for the pursuit of political activities.[25]

There are, of course, necessary functions not subject to this political exclusion: the functions of governance themselves, military and deliberative. These functions are in some respects separate, if only because young men do the fighting and deliberation is best left to older, more experienced citizens. But together they constitute the practice of rule, and they must be performed by men of property, never by those engaged in other necessary arts. Nor should farmers, craftsmen and day-labourers be allowed to serve as priests. The state should be divided into classes, and, in particular, there should be a division between farming and fighting classes. Indeed, all cultivation should be done by slaves or serfs, preferably non-Greeks.

Although Aristotle criticizes Plato's political theory in various ways, the similarities between his own ideal state and Plato's 'second best' polis should already be clear. Nor is this likeness accidental. The affinities between them are indicated even in specific proposals, such as Aristotle's suggestion that every citizen should have two plots of land, one near the central city and one on the frontier, which, like other measures, he borrows directly from Plato's *Laws*. That this polis is for Aristotle a perhaps unrealizable ideal and for Plato only 'second best' tells us very little about any differences between them in their

---

25 1328b–1329a.

opposition to democracy or their commitment to aristocratic principles. It tells us more about the differences in the tasks each man set himself and the very specific historical moment in which he thought about the polis. Even Aristotle's criticisms of his predecessor are often motivated by the values they share, on the grounds that some of Plato's proposals, such as his views on property or the community of wives and children in the *Republic*, would endanger, not advance, the goals both philosophers would like to achieve. Such proposals are not only impracticable but tend to dilute the differentiation of men and the self-sufficiency which both agree is essential to the polis.

Politics and Nature

We must also consider how Aristotle's antidemocratic sentiments, while moderated for the real world, penetrated his most fundamental ideas and even his most analytic or descriptive 'science'. At the beginning of the *Politics*, he lays out his basic definitions and applies his 'analytic-genetic' method to politics as he does elsewhere to other natural phenomena. His political preferences are already visible here; and when we move from the *Politics* to the non-political works in which his philosophical and scientific methods are developed, it is hard to escape the political assumptions that imbue them.

Aristotle begins the *Politics* by defining the basic forms of human association, of which the polis is the highest. Each one has its own specific purpose or *telos*, corresponding to various aspects of human nature. The most basic form is the *oikos*, the household, which deals with biological necessity, the daily recurrent needs of life. Then comes the village, an association of households, which contributes to the satisfaction of material necessities but also deals with something more than daily recurrent needs and is, in a sense, a bridge to the highest form, the polis. The polis, though it also incorporates and adds to the functions of the other two, has as its distinctive purpose the realization of humanity's essential nature. It is natural in the sense that it develops from other natural associations; but, more particularly, it is natural in the sense that it is the perfect completion of human development. 'Man is by nature a polis-animal', a creature intended to live in a polis, because it is only in the polis that he can fulfil his own *telos* as a rational and moral being.

The nature of the polis is defined in relation, as well as in contrast, to the *oikos*. The household is characterized by three principal sets of relationships: master and slave, husband and wife, parents and children. It is in its very essence a hierarchical and patriarchal institution marked by fundamental inequalities. At the very outset, the philosopher lays out his theory of natural inequality, on the premise that there is a principle of rule and subordination operating throughout all nature, and that the soul rules the body. In this respect, he is in agreement with the fundamental dualism in Plato's theory of knowledge and the cosmos. Aristotle goes on to say that, while slaves, women and children do possess the different parts of the soul, they do so in different ways. Women possess the faculty of deliberation, but in an incomplete form; and in children it is immature. They are therefore naturally subordinate to the man of the house. But there are some men whose powers are basically those of the body, while their understanding is capable of no more than following the orders of someone else's reason. It follows that some men are naturally suited to rule and others to be ruled, some are by nature free and others are natural slaves. Since the master is the rational being, the subordinate condition of the slave is both just and beneficial to all concerned.

Aristotle goes beyond most Greeks, and indeed Romans, in justifying slavery on the grounds of natural inequality. While the ancients were prepared to justify slavery on other, often simply pragmatic, grounds, the idea of natural slavery, based on innate differences among individuals or races, seems never to have been widely accepted. The distinctiveness of the philosopher's justification is certainly significant, but it is also important to note that the natural division between rulers and ruled operates for him also in the absence of such innate inequalities. The principle of hierarchy remains natural, even if it corresponds to no naturally inborn inequalities among human beings. Indeed, his political theory requires a principle of natural hierarchy between rulers and ruled that applies not only to the relation between masters and slaves – or even between men and women, adults and children – but also to aristocracy and common people, the leisured few and the labouring many. To widen the scope of this hierarchical principle Aristotle, like Plato, relies not only on fundamental innate differences among men to justify rigid divisions between those who are suited to rule and those who should be ruled. Even without substantial innate inequalities, those whose lives of labour bind them to necessity – and such men must always exist – cannot possess the qualities of soul required to rule.

It is true that Aristotle explicitly distinguishes between the slave and the free artisan, on the grounds that their degrees of servitude are different, the artisan less bound to a master; nor is the artisan naturally what he is in the way that the slave is by nature a slave. Yet the conclusion the philosopher draws from this is simply that the master has an obligation to produce in the slave the limited moral goodness of which he is capable, while there is no such obligation to the free man. The differences between free artisan and slave turn out to be less important in establishing Aristotle's political principles than are the similarities in their respective conditions, in particular their function in supplying the basic necessities of life. The division between 'banausic' types and those whose life conditions fit them to rule is, in its way, no less grounded in nature than that between natural masters and natural slaves.

Those who labour for a livelihood, whether in farming, commerce or the crafts, lack the leisure and freedom of spirit to fulfil the essential nature of humanity. Their bondage to necessity places them on the wrong side of the divide between those who contribute to the fulfilment of the state's essential purpose, its natural *telos*, and those who merely serve its basic needs – even if Aristotle acknowledges that, in practice, political concessions must sometimes be made to 'banausic' men of free birth. The polis, in contrast to the *oikos*, is an association of equals and only of equals; yet the principle of hierarchy established in the *oikos* is critical to the definition of relations in the polis too. The criterion of equality and inequality that Aristotle regards as appropriate in the distribution of political rights derives from the distinction between the principles of necessity and freedom established in the household.

There is also another way in which the *oikos* sets the terms of political right. It is in his discussion of the *oikos* that Aristotle lays out his views on property and the art of acquiring it, and these are essential in defining the character of the proper ruling class. The art of household management (*oikonomia*) strictly speaking is concerned with the use, not the acquisition, of things necessary for life and comfort; but the art of household management must involve itself with acquisition, or, more precisely, with supervising the process of acquisition. We must, then, distinguish between 'natural' forms of acquisition, having to do with obtaining and securing things required by the household, and the unnatural mode of acquisition whose object is the making of money, retail trade for profit. There are certainly legitimate forms of exchange in which households acquire from others things they do not produce for themselves, and some gain may even be involved. But because monetary gain is not the object, these are in a sense extensions of *oikonomia*, or, in any case, they represent a more natural form of *chrematistic*, the art of acquisition. Unnatural *chrematistic*, exchange for the primary purpose of monetary gain, is concerned not with well-being or 'true wealth' but the acquisition of money, and this kind of exchange has become increasingly prevalent.

Aristotle here makes a distinction that was to become theoretically fruitful many centuries later and serves as a fine illustration of how an idea shaped by its specific historical context and even by particular social values can reach far beyond its time, place and ideology. 'All articles of property', he argues, 'have two possible uses . . . The one use is proper and peculiar to the article concerned; the other is not.'[26] A shoe, for example, can be worn or it can be used as an object of exchange for profit. More particularly, there is a distinction between production for use and production for profitable exchange. A shoe produced for one's own use, or even simply to exchange it for necessary money or food, is one thing, while a shoe produced for making profit is something else; and these forms of production are quite different in their consequences. One is associated with acquisition which is limited in its objectives, while the other is in principle unlimited. Karl Marx would develop the distinction to quite different ends, but for Aristotle it plays an essential role in establishing the aristocratic principles that inform his conception of the polis.

As the argument proceeds, it becomes increasingly clear that the philosopher's political preferences are embodied even in his most basic and ostensibly neutral definitions. Even as he develops his definitions of the various associations and applies his analytic-genetic method to them, we form a picture of the 'equals' who properly constitute the polis. They are, to begin with, heads of patriarchal households, engaged in supervision but not in labour, while slaves do the necessary work. Since the truly natural form of acquisition is from land and animals, the political class is properly a class of landowners; and, if the *telos* of the polis is truly to be realized, their property is substantial enough to free them from the need to work. Nor should their property be acquired by sordid commercial means. The hereditary property of the well born is certainly the cleanest kind of property. Those practising 'unnatural' *chrematistic*, retail trade or any other form of money-making such as usury, as well as those engaged in necessary labour, do not properly belong in the political realm, however important they may be to its maintenance. The fact that Aristotle is prepared to compromise on these principles in varying degrees in various circumstances does not make them any less significant in identifying his social values and political preferences, which play their part even in his most pragmatic proposals.

It is even difficult to detach his non-political theory from his politics.

---

26 1257a.

The argument of the *Politics*, as we have seen, deliberately proceeds from certain basic principles derived from his general theory of nature. Aristotle's objective in studying nature is to explain the anomaly of constant motion in a natural world where everything tends toward rest. He seeks to discover the principles of order that remain constant throughout the processes of change. Two themes are essential to his explanation: the first is the notion of purpose or the *telos* towards which every process tends, and the second is the intrinsic hierarchy of the natural order.

When we speak of the *telos* or 'final cause' of objects created by humans, we mean the conscious, deliberate purpose of the craftsman who creates them; but we can still speak of such 'final causes' even where, as in the natural world, there is no deliberate purpose, no divine mind controlling natural change from without (here Aristotle tends yet again to differ from Plato, who sometimes seems to be suggesting a divine intelligence). In nature, the *telos* is immanent in the object itself, the final state 'for the sake of which' the natural processes of growth and development take place – as the oak is the *telos* of the acorn; and every immature object or being, including the human child, is *potentially* what it will (or ought to) be when it matures. Moreover, these processes, while not consciously willed, are not random but orderly and regular. Different outcomes are possible, if things go wrong, but there is only one true *telos* for every thing and every being in nature. How Aristotle puts this principle to use in his political theory is clear enough, as he develops his conception of the human *telos* and the political conditions necessary for its realization. Even clearer is the political application of his second principle: that there is, everywhere in nature, a ruling element and a ruled. Aristotle insists that the natural order is universally hierarchical and that the condition of rest towards which all nature tends forms a Great Chain of Being, in which every natural being is situated, from the highest to the lowest. The polis must in its way reflect that natural hierarchy.

It may be difficult to determine what comes first, the natural 'science' or the politics, or, more precisely, which has the overriding force. No doubt this doctor's son was exposed very early to his lifelong scientific interests, particularly in biology, and no doubt these continued to shape his thinking in every domain. But it is also possible that Aristotle's conception of nature was affected by his predisposition to social and political hierarchies. The issue here, however, is not whether we can unravel the complex order of causality in Aristotle's thinking, or, indeed, in that of any other complicated human being. If, in his philosophy, aristocratic principles govern both the natural and political order, it is enough for us to recognize that the questions he was seeking to answer in both his scientific and political speculations were put to him by his social no less than his natural context.

3

FROM POLIS TO EMPIRE

From Aristotle to Alexander

Plutarch, in one of his accounts of Alexander the Great and his achievements, writes that Aristotle advised his pupil to distinguish between Greeks and barbarians and to deal with the former as a leader or *hegemon*, while behaving towards the latter as a master, a *despotes*. Alexander, says Plutarch, did just the opposite. Refusing to divide men between Greek friends and barbarian foes, he chose rather to distinguish simply between good men and bad, whatever their origin. Alexander, it has been said, was in effect inventing the notion of a *cosmopolis*, which received its theoretical expression in Stoic philosophy, replacing the polis with a universal human community and stressing the equality and fraternity of humankind as against the particularisms of the polis.

Whether or not the story of Aristotle's advice to Alexander is authentic, it does correspond to a distinction between different kinds of rule that the philosopher draws in the *Politics*:

> There is rule of the sort which is exercised by a master [over slaves] ... But [besides rule of the sort exercised by their ruler over persons in a servile position] there is also rule of the sort which is exercised over persons who are similar in birth to the ruler, and are similarly free. Rule of this sort is what we call political rule; and this is the sort of rule which [unlike rule of the first sort] the ruler must begin to learn by being ruled and by obeying – just as one learns to be a commander of cavalry by serving under another commander ... [1]

Aristotle later elaborates on this distinction by contrasting two modes of government: 'One way is to govern in the interest of the governors: the other, to govern in the interest of the governed. The former way is what we call "despotic" [i.e. a government over slaves]; the latter is

---

1 *Pol.*, 1277b.

what we call "the government of freemen."'[2] The rule of a master over
slaves, 'though there is really a common interest which unites the natural
master and the natural slave, is primarily exercised with a view to the
master's interest, and only incidentally with a view to that of the slave,
who must be preserved in existence if the rule itself is to remain.'[3]
Here, he introduces another category, household management (*oikonomia*), rule over wife, children and the household in general, which 'is
either exercised in the interest of the ruled or for the attainment of
some advantage common to both ruler and ruled.'[4]

The philosopher's distinctions did not preclude a despotic relation
between rulers and ruled in a polis; or a polis governed by a community
of citizens rather than a single ruler, in which the relation between citizens
and non-citizens might be comparable to that between a despotic ruler
and his subjects. Aristotle wanted to preserve the civic ideal of the polis,
its principles of freedom and equality, while giving new life to old
principles of rule, grounded in a natural division between ruler and ruled.
The political relation among citizens was a relationship among equals,
but there remained a fundamental inequality between the civic community
and those outside it. The notion of rule applied to the life of citizens
only in the sense that citizenship involved an alternation between governing
and being governed, and, ideally, a capacity in every citizen for both. But
a far more rigid and permanent division was preserved for relations
between the 'parts' and the 'conditions' of the polis, between true citizens
and all those subordinate human beings whose purpose was to serve their
rulers' interests, just as the purpose of slaves is to serve the *despotes*.

If Alexander really did refuse his teacher's advice, he surely cannot
have done so because he rejected the principles of rule, a deep and
abiding division between ruler and ruled or the duty of subjects to
serve their imperial master. Readers hardly need reminding that he
was a ruthless conqueror, an absolute ruler who built a vast empire
on the foundations laid by his father, Philip, and declared his own
divinity. His imperial ambitions and policies hardly bespeak a doctrine
of human equality and brotherhood. If the accounts of Alexander's
ostensibly humanitarian views are correct, it would be absurd to take
them at face value without considering their ideological or rhetorical
function in his imperial project. Perhaps he had in mind something
like what Aristotle himself hints at in the *Politics*:[5] that if only the
Greeks could achieve a single *politeia*, they would rule the world.

---

2 *Pol.*, 1333a.
3 1278b.
4 1278b.
5 1327.

To be as explicit as Aristotle was about the nature of despotic rule and its purpose of serving the interests of the ruler would not, to be sure, have been the most effective way of justifying it to its victims. But stressing the equality and brotherhood of all human beings is not, in general, the most obvious way to justify the subjection of some of them to others, whether in the form of monarchy or imperial hegemony. If Alexander did adopt this paradoxical strategy, he did so because in the Greek world it had a special propaganda value. It would have evoked the deeply rooted principles of Greek political life, their professions of freedom and equality. It is true that Alexander, and even more his successors in their struggles for power, invoked old principles of *eleutheria, autonomia* and even democracy in seeking the support of prospective subjects by promising them the right to live under their own laws and ancestral gods, free of tribute and imperial garrisons. But if this represented an appeal to the older particularistic values of the autonomous polis, Alexander's (putative) idea of the cosmopolis could have been intended to transfer those old political principles and loyalties from the polis to the all-embracing imperial state, while depriving citizenship of its political arena and replacing active citizenship with passive membership in a cosmic community. If Alexander really did think in cosmopolitan terms, his usage would have been largely ideological in its purpose, to describe and to justify empire and even its attempted, if not entirely successful, suppression of politics.

Whatever its ideological purpose, however, the cosmopolitan idea did express a historical reality. Not only was polis replaced by empire – if not, 'world order', certainly a unit much wider in geographic scope – but the empire established by Alexander was also composed of very diverse populations which were united under Macedonian rule. While Greek culture was already widespread in the Mediterranean world before the conquests of Alexander, he consciously utilized the strategy of Hellenizing subject peoples as an instrument of hegemony. The cosmopolitan principle found expression sometimes in the coercive suppression of difference but also in the encouragement of mixing and intermarriage among the various ethnicities, in the emergence of religious cults without frontiers instead of particularistic tribal and civic cults, and above all in the unifying dominance of Greek language and culture. Increasing commercial relations among the imperial cities were also a major factor in promoting the cosmopolitan idea. Transport and communication were enhanced by new roads, a more widely recognized currency was established, and Greek became the main commercial language from Massalia (modern Marseilles) to the borders of India.

In general, however, Hellenistic cosmopolitanism meant the Hel-
lenization of local elites. Macedonian and Greek populations, together
with Greek-speaking local elites, tended to remain apart from the
subjects whose labour supported them; and lower classes, if they spoke
Greek at all (or, at least, the simplified demotic form that would become
the language of the New Testament), would have had little access to
the glories of Greek culture. A similar mechanism would operate in
the Roman Empire, which already by 30 BC included half of what had
been the 'Hellenistic' world. Roman imperial rule too would rely on
the cultural transformation and allegiance of Romanized local
aristocracies. And just as Alexander had defined his imperial rule as
cosmopolitan, the idea of the cosmopolis would be translated into the
'universal' Roman Empire and, above all, into Christianity, the
'universal (literally *catholic*) Church'.

This mode of imperial rule through the medium of local aristocracies
allowed Alexander, like the Romans after him, to govern a far-flung
empire without a massive imperial state. In this respect, both Hellenistic
and Roman empires contrasted sharply with other great imperial
civilizations like the Chinese, whose imperial states were more directly
in command of their subjects, by means of much larger imperial
bureaucracies. This also meant that the 'cosmopolitan' empire did in
a sense preserve, or revive, at least the form of the Greek polis. Reliable
cities could be permitted a degree of local self-government; and
Alexander founded cities (often called Alexandria, like the most famous
centre in Egypt) in his various domains, which were allowed a certain
autonomy and laws of their own, although they were clearly subject
to his imperial rule.

After his death, as his empire fragmented into the Macedonian or
Antigonid, Seleucid and Egyptian kingdoms, the idea of a king governing through the medium of local municipal entities played a particularly
important role in the power struggle over the successor kingdoms.[6] At
least, the old liberties of the polis, their *eleutheria* and *autonomia*,
served a useful propaganda purpose – though there were cases in which,
with the help of one or another imperial rival, oligarchies established,
for instance, by Antipater, actually were overthrown in favour of
'democracy'. Reality may not have measured up to rhetoric; but the
old Greek culture of the polis, and even of democracy, was so deeply
ingrained that no imperial ideology was likely to succeed without

---

6 See Eric S. Gruen, *The Hellenistic World and the Coming of Rome* (Berkeley and
Los Angeles: University of California Press, 1984), Vol. 1, esp. Ch. 4.

invoking it. Thereafter, this strategy would survive, even if only in rhetorical form, as a means of maintaining friendly relations among monarchs and cities, as an excuse for war, or as a form of diplomatic language to describe the relations of domination by stronger over weaker powers.[7]

For all its 'cosmopolitanism', however, the 'Hellenistic' period, generally dated from Alexander's life to the late second century BC, was a period of political and social crisis. Alexander's conquests and the power struggles that followed his death aggravated existing social and political instabilities in the Greek world. The worsening conditions of the poor and the growing numbers of the landless led to demands for redistribution of land and the abolition of debts, giving rise to social conflicts, even a social revolution, which has been described as 'one of the great historic processes of Hellenistic Greece'.[8] Inevitably expressed in political upheavals, in conflicts between democrats and oligarchs, this social unrest intensified as the successor kingdoms vied for influence in Alexander's domains by mobilizing those ever-present social and political antagonisms and seeking to install or promote friendly governments. Sparta, paradoxically, which had remained a vigorous and independent polis, was also the site of a particularly notable revolution in the third century BC under kings Agis IV and Cleomenes III, instituting land reforms, cancellation of debts and an extension of citizenship based on fairly extreme conceptions of equality. The effect was to alarm the propertied classes throughout the Greek cities. Fearing social unrest and reform at home more than they did Macedonian dominance, they allied themselves with the Macedonians; and Sparta was finally defeated. The pervasive unrest, and the fear it inspired in propertied classes, form the background against which Hellenistic thinkers embarked on their philosophical projects.

Hellenistic Philosophy: Epicureans and Stoics

Hellenistic philosophy remained deeply indebted to its Hellenic past, but its ground had shifted in fundamental ways. Not only was Athens displaced as the cultural centre by Alexandria and Pergamum, with their great libraries, but philosophy was obliged to adapt itself to a

---

7 *Ibid.*, p. 156.

8 A. Fuks, 'Social Revolution in Greece in the Hellenistic Age', *La Parola del Passato* 111 (1966), p. 441, quoted in Andrew Erskine, *The Hellenistic Stoa: Political Thought and Action* (Ithaca: Cornell University Press, 1990), p. 36.

new imperial reality. If it is possible to speak of political theory in this period, its principal subject was no longer the polis of Plato and Aristotle.

The Hellenistic *cosmopolis*, to be sure, presupposed the *polis*. This is true not only in a purely etymological sense but also in the sense that the cosmopolitan idea absorbed and adapted the principal themes that had emerged from the life of the polis: themes such as *nomos*, *eleutheria*, *autonomia*, the principles of citizenship and the civic community, and even the democratic concept of *isonomia*. It is even possible to say that if Alexander, his successors or those who lived under their rule had any systematic notion of 'empire' at all, the idea of an imperial *state* played little part in it. The primary idea of the state that Hellenistic rulers had to work with was the old conception of the polis as a community of citizens. Imperial rhetoric, and even, up to a point, imperial reality, oscillated between, on the one hand, a conception of empire as a collection of poleis, each allowed at least nominal autonomy and governed by its own particular laws, and, on the other, the idea of the cosmopolis as one universal polis, with its *nomoi* writ large.

The Hellenistic period did produce theories of kingship, especially to legitimize the three kingdoms that succeeded Alexander; and the idea of monarchy was inevitably called upon to play a larger role than it had in the age of the free polis, if only to support the dynastic claims of particular rulers. The importance of monarchy in post-classical Greek political theory – such as it was – reflected the decline of the polis and the civic community. This gave rise to a literature on ideal kingship, which has no parallel in classical Greek culture and which draws on Persian, Egyptian and Mesopotamian ideas as well as Greek traditions going back as far as Homer, together with a tendency to deify kings.

Yet Hellenistic conceptions of kingship never completely detached themselves from the polis, at least in the sense that they were obliged to confront the cultural and ideological legacies of the polis and its civic principles. So, for instance, one of the most important ideas emanating from the Hellenistic theory of kingship is the notion of the king as 'living law' (*nomos empsychos*, in Latin *lex animata*), which would be transmitted to the medieval West via the Roman Empire in the Code of Justinian. The idea of the king as 'living law' has much in common with – and is related to the polis in much the same way as – Plato's redefinition of *nomos* in the *Statesman*. As we saw, he argues that *nomos* in its conventional Athenian sense is opposed to the art, the *technē*, of statesmanship; and he elaborates a new conception of the rule of law which would imitate, not thwart, the political art. Plato reappropriates *nomos* by detaching the rule of law from the community of citizens and personifying it in the monarchical statesman, who must be free to exercise his art on behalf of the community, unchecked by a self-governing community of non-expert citizens. Absolute rule replaces the civic traditions of the democratic polis by turning them against themselves.

There were other, more philosophically fruitful responses to the shift from polis to empire. As civic identity and agency gave way to different ways of being in the social world, philosophers such as the Epicureans and Stoics concerned themselves less with political order than with the individual's place in the cosmos. It is, indeed, sometimes said that a kind of individualism represents the greatest departure of Hellenistic philosophy from its Hellenic predecessors. While this judgment tends to neglect the role of human association in Hellenistic doctrines, it is certainly true that these philosophers were inward-looking in a way that their predecessors were not.

At the same time, even this inward-turning individual has roots in the polis. Stoic and Epicurean philosophy both, in their different ways, are responding to questions raised with particular force by the life of the polis. In the previous chapter, it was suggested that the conflict and debate that characterized the polis, the direct experience of shaping the conditions of everyday life and social arrangements, the constant challenge to prevailing political relations and values – meant a confrontation, in unprecedented ways and to unprecedented degrees, with the problems of human agency and responsibility. The civic consciousness was both confident in the possibilities of human agency and, at the same time, uneasy about the uncertainties, dangers and responsibilities associated with it. Stoic and Epicurean philosophies seem to derive their special character from a confrontation with the joys and fears of autonomy and self-determination, the consciousness of the citizen, but now in the absence of the polis. It may be too much to say that the individual of Hellenistic philosophy is, in one form or another, an introversion of the active citizen; but the dynamism of this introspective soul surely bears the mark of civic activism.

It remains true, nonetheless, that the period is marked by a conception of human agency and the possibilities of human action that no longer has the polis as its principal terrain. It is possible to read both Stoicism and Epicureanism as more or less apolitical responses to the decline of the polis or to the general uncertainty and turbulence of the times. It is certainly true that, as polis gave way to empire, the main arena of philosophical reflection shifted. The sphere of civic action and deliberation receded, bringing into focus the private individual at one extreme – most notably in Epicureanism – and the universal order of the cosmopolis at the other, especially as conceived by the Stoics. While there was certainly a place in Stoicism, especially in its later Roman form, for civic duty and political activism, both these major Hellenistic schools located human happiness not in the polis but in the individual's inner resources. In the case of Epicureanism, the shift away from politics is explicit and unambiguous. The case of the Stoics is rather more difficult, and we shall shortly explore its complexities (always keeping in mind that very little remains of their work, or, indeed, the work of any Hellenistic philosophers).

Epicurus was born in Samos in 341 BC, the son of Athenian parents. He would experience very directly the effects of the Macedonian conquests when, after the death of Alexander, the Athenian settlers were driven out of Samos by Perdiccas, the imperial regent. Epicurus eventually settled in Athens in 306, where he founded a school, from which derived a philosophical tradition that would retain its popularity and influence for something like six centuries. His work has survived only in fragmentary form or in the words of his followers. The most important extant Epicurean classic would be the epic poem by Lucretius (about whose life little is known), *De Rerum Natura* (*On the Nature of Things*), written much later, in the first century BC, in republican Rome.

For Epicurus and his followers, the highest good, even the purpose of life, is pleasure (though not in the amorally hedonistic sense commonly attributed to 'epicureans') and the avoidance of pain. Above all, happiness requires the peace that comes with the absence of fear, and this means in particular fear of death and the afterlife. If there is one single overriding purpose in Epicurean philosophy and its conception of nature, it is to banish such fears, which requires liberation from religion. This involves an explanation of natural processes without the intrusion of divine or supernatural forces, relying on a conception of material bodies composed of atoms, and an account of the human psyche in terms of materially generated sensations, which are, on the whole, accurate sources of knowledge. The consequence of this materialism is that death need not be feared, because it means complete annihilation. Nowhere, at any time in history, has this theme been more eloquently played out than in Lucretius's *De Rerum Natura*. But the materialist bent of Epicureanism and its unambiguous concentration on the goods (intellectual as well as, and more than, material) of this life were not expressed in a conception of human self-determination through the medium of the self-governing polis. Its central theme was not the life of the citizen but the experience and ethics of the individual person; and the highest relation among individuals was not the civic bond but personal friendship.

At the same time, while the shift from polis to empire created a powerful impetus to apolitical withdrawal, we need to remember that Hellenistic philosophers were writing against a background of war and social turmoil, particularly as, in various city-states, conflicts between classes or between democrats and oligarchs were drawn into imperial power struggles. Social upheaval and political instability certainly encouraged a search for comfort in the cultivation of one's own garden; but they also gave a new urgency to questions of order, hierarchy, domination and subordination. Stoic philosophers in particular responded in ways quite different from, and often consciously opposed to, their great predecessors, Plato and Aristotle.

The foundation of Stoicism is credited to Zeno of Citium (333–264 BC); but it would undergo various significant changes after its foundation and is generally divided into three periods, the Old, Middle and Later or Roman Stoa. Nothing but fragments remain from the earlier periods; and the only complete works belong to the later, Roman imperial phase, the works of Seneca (4 BC–AD 65), Epictetus (c.55–135) and the Emperor Marcus Aurelius (121–80), which are largely devoted to ethics. It is only from fragments or from reconstruction by later thinkers that we can piece together anything like a coherent picture of the epistemological and cosmological ideas of the earlier Stoics. What can be said with some degree of confidence is that significant shifts took place in Stoic philosophy as the Hellenistic age passed into imperial Rome and philosophers began to respond to the needs of Roman elites. An important shift undoubtedly took place some time between Zeno and the Middle Stoics, Panaetius (185/180–110/108) and Posidonius (135–51), who, though Greek in origin, spent time in Rome, were well connected with Rome's elite and supported Roman imperial rule.

Like Epicureanism, Stoicism is concerned above all with ethics and the well-being of the individual. The self-control, even self-abnegation, that we associate with 'stoicism', the aspiration to eliminate the passions that cause human misery and the emphasis on the internal goods of the soul, may seem to argue for a withdrawal from political life altogether. Although civic life did play an important part in the ethical philosophy of Stoicism, at least in some of its forms, Stoic cosmopolitanism, with its emphasis on the universal bonds of humanity against all social and political particularities, may seem to have an apolitical charge. There is, nonetheless, much to be said in favour of a more political reading of what the Stoics were about – although their doctrines are compatible with a fairly wide range of political attitudes.

The most important known political work of early Stoicism is Zeno's *Republic*, which can only be reconstructed on the basis of comments left by his critics and successors. Zeno was born in Citium in Cyprus, the son of a merchant, and seems to have been a merchant himself until, after studying with the Cynic philosopher, Crates, he founded his own school, the Stoa, named after the Stoa Poikile, the Painted Porch in Athens where he taught. His *Republic* portrayed an ideal polis lacking the familiar institutions of the real city-state, such as courts of justice, schools, temples, property and money, and relying for its cohesion entirely on harmonious relations among virtuous individuals. On the one hand, it has been described as a youthful aberration, depicting a completely imaginary, perhaps even playful, ideal which can hardly be taken seriously. On the other hand, it has been interpreted as a mature, radical critique of contemporary social and political realities, which eliminates from the ideal republic all the injustices and sources of conflict that plague existing states – not only confining its inhabitants to wise and virtuous men but removing all existing sources of inequality, domination and subordination, in direct opposition to Plato's *Republic*.

Whatever Zeno may have intended in this political dialogue, there are more fundamental questions to be asked about Stoic epistemology, psychology and cosmology; and, while their political implications are not self-evident, we can attempt to tease them out. At the heart of Stoic doctrine is the notion of *logos*, the universal reason of a divine cosmic order, the dynamic principle in material nature. The universe is completely unitary. In sharp contrast to the Platonic dualism of sensible and intelligible worlds, the rational and the non-rational, body and intellect, there is in Stoic philosophy – at least in its original form – no division between mind and matter. Mind permeates all material things, as the universe is united by the dynamic principle of cosmic reason, *logos*, which both activates the universe and holds it together. Human reason partakes of this universal *logos*. It is effectively one with the cosmic or divine *logos*. Epistemologically this means that human sensation and perception, which have direct access to reality, are reliable foundations of knowledge – not the imperfect sources, at best, of mere opinion, to be distinguished from the true knowledge that is accessible only to reason. It also means that, since there is no mind–body split in Stoic psychology, Stoic philosophy departs radically from the principles underlying the fundamental Platonic division between ruling element and ruled.

The ethical implications of this Stoic monism are even more significant, though not entirely unambiguous. Although all living beings and inanimate objects belong to the rational cosmic order, only human beings possess the rational capacity to understand it. At the same time, and for the same reason, Stoicism suggests that human beings are capable of acting in opposition to the *logos*, that is, in a less than rational manner. In that sense, they have the freedom to choose or repudiate virtue. If humans simply acted unconsciously or non-rationally in accordance with the laws of nature, as animals do, it would be impossible to speak of human virtue. But, by definition, the truly rational – hence virtuous – person is the one who can live only in accordance with the universal principle of nature, aligning the individual soul with the divine cosmic order.

The suggestion of a natural law which applies to all human beings, and the notion of a universal human community, can be understood in different ways and with different moral or political effects. The idea of a universal community, subject to a universal law, can be understood as a counsel of universal compassion; but it can also support a harsh moral rigidity. It can underwrite deeply egalitarian principles; but, as we have seen, it can also be used to justify empire. The idea of a transcendent natural equality, which attributes to all human beings a common *logos*, can be used to underwrite social and political equality, even the equality of women, and the repudiation of slavery. But it can also serve as a pretext for accepting inequality in the material world, while relegating equality to some higher realm which leaves existing social and political hierarchies intact. This, as we shall see, was certainly the effect of Stoic influences in Rome and, for instance, in the political theory of Cicero. It would also find its way into Christianity.

We can perhaps gain a deeper insight into the political implications of Stoic doctrine by considering the provenance of their philosophy, as they themselves perceived it. This will require us to go back further in the history of Greek philosophy, even beyond the classical age of Plato and Aristotle. In rejecting the dualism of Plato and Aristotle, the Stoics purport to be returning to the Presocratics, and to Heraclitus (535–475 BC) in particular. Heraclitus is the first thinker known to have given a metaphysical meaning to the word *logos*, a wide-ranging word commonly used to denote everything from the spoken or written word to thought or opinion, measure, proportion, the truth of the matter, an account of something, right reason, and so on. He has also been credited with the first known philosophical use of the word *cosmos* to denote the world order. The remaining fragments of his thought are still controversial, and commentators cannot agree on whether the universal *logos* that gave order to the cosmos had epistemological implications for him as it later would for the Stoics. It is presumably significant that he used the term commonly applied to human word, thought or reason to denote the universal principle of cosmic order; and it seems reasonable to suppose that, if the *logos* represented both the cosmic order and human intelligence, this had implications for the possibilities of human knowledge. Nevertheless, it is possible that the Stoics drew out these epistemological implications for their own purposes. Heraclitus, who more than once expressed his contempt for the ignorant many, would have been unlikely to accept the egalitarian consequences of Stoic psychology. His *logos* was certainly that which is common; but the trouble with most human beings, according to him, is that they live in ignorance of what is truly common, as if according to a private wisdom of their own. It is possible that, in their opposition to Platonic doctrines, the Stoics invoked the authority of Heraclitus not because they wished to reproduce his views faithfully but precisely because of Plato's objections to the great Presocratic philosopher.

What, then, can we learn from Plato's objections? In the first instance, they concern two related ideas that are central to Heraclitus's philosophy: that everything is in continuous motion, so that, while the cosmos is lawful, its operative principle is a law of change; and that the cosmic order is constituted by opposites in tension, a harmony of opposites, so that strife and war are the universal principle of nature. For Plato, Heraclitus's conception of the cosmos leaves no room for the dichotomy between the constant change of becoming and the permanence of being, or for the essential distinction between knowledge and opinion and the two distinct levels of reality that correspond to them. Nor would Plato have approved of Heraclitus's strictures against Pythagoras. For Heraclitus, Pythagoras represented precisely the idea of cosmic peace and harmony he was opposing; while for Plato, Pythagoras epitomized the orderly, motionless world of true being. Aristotle (who cannot abide what he takes to be Heraclitus's violation of the principle of non-contradiction: the unity of opposites suggested by Heraclitus's view that things, in the process of flux, are the same and not the same at once) even suggests that Plato devised his conception of absolute Forms in reaction to Heraclitus and the unknowable world which, as Plato saw it, followed from the Presocratic philosopher's ideas.

In short, Heraclitus failed to acknowledge the dualisms that would unite Plato's epistemology with his political theory. It does not, however, follow that Heraclitus himself drew the political conclusions from his own cosmology that Plato ascribed to philosophical monism. If anything, though little is known of Heraclitus's political preferences, the evidence suggests that he had aristocratic leanings. But it is likely that the differences between Heraclitus and Plato had less to do with the logic of philosophical argumentation than with the historical changes that had intervened between them.

Heraclitus, whose birthplace Ephesus was near the Ionian city of Miletus, where Greek philosophy was born, was writing probably in the late sixth century BC, before the golden age of Greek democracy. Plato, of course, lived through the democratic golden age in Athens, into what he regarded as its decadent phase, and was obsessed with its consequences for all he held dear. When Heraclitus conceived his ideas on cosmic strife, Ionia, and Miletus in particular, had just passed through 'some of the most extreme civil conflicts of the archaic period'.[9] There had been a struggle for control between the Wealthy (*Ploutis*) – possibly those who derived their wealth from trade, since they were also called Perpetual Sailors (*Aeinautai*) – and the Manual Workers (*Cheiromachai*); and, 'after a number of atrocities on both sides over two generations', the conflict was settled by arbitrators from another city who placed control in the hands of the landowners – or, as Herodotus puts it:

> they called the people together . . . and made proclamation that they gave the government into the hands of those persons whose lands they had found well farmed; for they thought it likely (they said) that the same persons who had managed their own affairs well would likewise conduct aright the business of the state. The other Milesians who in times past had been at variance they placed under the rule of these men.[10]

Is it fanciful to suppose that Heraclitus's conception of the cosmic order was shaped by these events? There is a striking correspondence, at any rate, between the recent social experience of Miletus and the philosopher's notion of strife as the operative cosmic principle, resolved not by complete suppression of one or the other of the warring parties but by a balance in tension between them – albeit with advantage to the propertied class. Just as the archer's bow is constituted by the

---

9 Oswyn Murray, *Early Greece* (Glasgow: Fontana, 2nd edn, 1993), p. 233.
10 Herodotus, *The Persian Wars*, transl. George Rawlinson, V.29.

tension between bow and string, which gives the deceptive appearance of motionlessness, so stability in society is not a state of rest but a constant tension of opposites held in precarious balance.

But even if Heraclitus himself did not associate social and cosmic orders in quite this way, there can be little doubt that Plato thought in such terms. Writing in democratic Athens, however, he could not have envisaged a Milesian resolution to the social conflicts of his day. Athens had already long ago passed through the kind of balance in tension which Solon, for instance, had sought to establish. The balance had long ago shifted too far towards the demos, and Plato could no longer imagine a stabilization of tension in the interests of the wealthy or the aristocracy. The demos now had to be unambiguously subordinate. His idea of social and political stability was uncompromisingly an order of motionless hierarchy, with lower elements in complete submission to the higher.

When the Stoics revived the *logos* of Heraclitus, they did so in conscious opposition to Plato's principle of order, at a time when the danger to property seemed very real, and dominant classes were certainly in fear of social revolution. Although it cannot be said that the early Stoics recommended an explicitly democratic order, they did reject the Platonic conception of *homonoia*, a concord based on rigid hierarchy. 'For Zeno', writes one commentator, '*homonoia* was not a relationship between classes that would not work, but a relationship among individual wise men; it was based not on suppression of recalcitrant elements, a potential source of conflict, but on their absence.'[11] If this utopian ideal fell short of democratic advocacy, how it identified the sources of conflict is significant enough. In any case, in the civil strife of Hellenistic Greece, Zeno's alternative idea of *homonoia* would certainly have been more attractive to supporters of democracy and far less welcome to their opponents than was Plato's uncompromising hierarchy.

It is not, therefore, unreasonable to emphasize the radical possibilities of the cosmological, psychological and epistemological monism of Stoic philosophy, at least in its original form. While it could be interpreted as an other-worldly doctrine with no practical implications for everyday social life, the doctrine of the all-pervasive *logos* certainly can have egalitarian consequences. The principle that, in this unitary cosmos, virtue is a unity and human beings who all share in the divine *logos* are free and equal, certainly was used to support the contention that slavery is contrary to nature, as is the inequality between men

---

11 Erskine, *op. cit.*, p. 31.

and women. It is, of course, possible to justify domination and subordination, inequalities of class and status or the relation between rulers and ruled, even in the face of natural equality. Even Plato defends the principles of rule and subordination less consistently on the basis of natural inequalities than on the grounds that there is a universal principle dividing ruling elements and ruled, reason and non-reason, and that a necessary division of labour in society will always mean that some people are rational and others are not. But it seems reasonable to draw certain radical political conclusions from Stoic philosophy, if only because the Platonic and Aristotelian dualism, which Stoics like Zeno deliberately rejected, applied the same principles to their political theories as they did to their theories of knowledge and nature.

It is significant, too, that later Stoics, especially those associated with Rome, who were more favourably disposed to empire and even slavery (if only on pragmatic grounds), felt compelled to modify the psychological monism of their predecessors. The Middle Stoics, Panaetius and Posidonius, for instance, harked back to Platonic and Aristotelian psychology. As for the truly Roman Stoics, they hardly bothered with such fundamental philosophical questions and were far more interested in ethics on its own terms, without any grounding in systematic theories of the cosmos or psychology.

To sum up, then, the social and political implications of Stoic cosmology, psychology and epistemology are in general not easy to read; and, in any case, their doctrines varied in different historical circumstances. When the early Stoics rejected the dualism that pervaded the cosmology, psychology and epistemology of their great predecessors, Plato and Aristotle, they also seem to have made corresponding judgments about slavery, freedom and empire. When the later Stoics retreated from the more radical positions of their predecessors, they were accommodating themselves to new social and political realities, most notably the rise of Rome and the conservatism of its ruling classes.

The dangers of Stoic egalitarianism became especially apparent in the context of the Spartan revolution. Military victories by the reforming king, Cleomenes, and especially the destruction of Megalopolis in 223 BC, were particularly alarming to propertied elites. To what extent the revolution was inspired by Stoic doctrine is a matter of conjecture; but the Stoic philosopher, Sphairos of Borysthenes, who wrote a tract on the Spartan constitution, was the tutor of Cleomenes and is said to have helped him institute his reforms.[12] At any rate, in the climate

---

12 See *Ibid.*, esp. Chs 6 and 7.

of the times, it is hardly likely that propertied classes would have welcomed any principle of natural equality or social justice that recognized no differences of class or status, any challenge to existing hierarchies, or any doctrine that might represent a threat to property (which for the Stoics is, in any case, a conventional, not a natural, institution, in a cosmos where all things are common), even if only by identifying property as the source of strife and instability. In the wake of the revolution and with the rise of Rome, its dominant aristocracy and growing empire, there emerged a Stoic current more congenial to the ruling elements.

The threats to property seemed that much more immediate when Rome's own resident radicals, the brothers Gracchi, came on the scene, with their ideas on agrarian reform and, perhaps, some kind of popular sovereignty. They certainly knew Greek and Greek philosophy, as did their opponents, who now mobilized Stoic arguments in defence of property, empire and even slavery. We shall return to these arguments, to the ideas of later Stoics such as Panaetius and the Romans who were influenced by them, notably Cicero. But something must be said first about the Roman context, as the new imperial power eclipsed its Hellenistic predecessors while absorbing the Greek world and its culture.

The Rise and Fall of Rome

Rome, like Athens, developed as a small city-state; and like the Athenian polis, the Roman Republic was governed by a small and simple state apparatus. By 265 BC, the republic was already governing most of Italy south of the Po, and its subjects outside Rome were 'citizens' only in very loose terms. Yet even then the ruling aristocracy, more powerful than its Athenian counterpart, was keen to maintain the state in its rudimentary form and long resisted the emergence of a professional state apparatus, preferring to govern themselves as amateurs. The aristocracy governed collectively, with individuals holding office for limited periods and every senator subject to principles of collegiality. But if this arrangement suited their purposes, it created problems of its own, requiring, again as in Athens, careful management of often tense relations between aristocracy and people and among rival aristocrats themselves.

In Rome, with its dominant aristocracy, the political form of the accommodation was not a democracy in the Athenian manner but a republic dominated by the aristocratic senate. Yet, while aristocratic dominance is a constant theme of Roman politics throughout both republic and empire, there was from the beginning a tension at the heart of the republic. It was a state built on private wealth, an instrument of individual ambition and acquisition for a ruling class of private proprietors who competed with one another for wealth and power but whose class position, in the absence of a superior state power, was sustained only by their own fragile collegiality. This form of state also implied an ambiguous relationship between the aristocracy and subordinate classes. Like Athens, Rome departed from the pattern of other ancient 'high' civilizations where a clear division existed between rulers and producers, monarchical states and subject peasant communities. In Rome, as in Athens, peasants and urban plebeians belonged to the community of citizens. While the balance of class forces between landlords and peasants in Rome, unlike Athens, had produced an aristocratic state, its dominant class was obliged to enlist the political and military support of its subordinate fellow-citizens, so that here, as in Athens, some of the characteristic legal and political arrangements of the republic are traceable to aristocratic conflicts and accommodations with popular forces – such as the office of tribune, in which a member of the elite was elected by the people to represent their interests (though tribunes were never regarded as 'magistrates', which meant that their office did not entitle them to sit in the senate).

In the early years of the republic, the Roman peasantry was relatively strong, but the history of the republic is a story of peasant decline and an increasing concentration of land and power in aristocratic hands. While the expansion of Rome into a huge territorial empire depended on the peasantry which manned what was to become the largest military force the world had ever known, their mobilization and deployment away from Rome made them more vulnerable to expropriation at home. As the army was effectively professionalized, peasants were turned into soldiers and the aristocracy benefitted on the home front too, while the agricultural labour force in the imperial homeland was increasingly given over to slaves, available in unprecedented numbers through conquest and trade.

As new lands were captured in Rome's imperial expansion, the issue of their distribution loomed very large on the political agenda, particularly the issue of land set aside as *ager publicus*, state lands available for colonization by citizens or for leaseholds at nominal rents. Some members of the aristocracy who served as tribunes of the people did seek to utilize the *ager publicus* to redress the balance between the rising aristocracy and increasingly impoverished peasants; but they were bitterly opposed by the ruling class in general, and the reforming agrarian laws seem to have had no lasting effect. The most famous

attempt to effect a more equitable land redistribution, the reforms of
the Gracchi, ended with the murder of the tribune Tiberius Gracchus
at the hands of the aristocratic opposition, and later the violent death
of Tiberius's brother Gaius, who had sought to continue and extend
his brother's reforms and seems, unlike Tiberius, to have had a radical
anti-senatorial political agenda.

With slaves and peasants (whether as tenants or as soldiers) creating
wealth for the landlords, and urban masses in the huge metropolis of
Rome living in appalling slums, overcrowded, unsanitary and dangerous,
the differences of income between rich and poor at their peak have been
estimated at 20,000 to 1, in contrast to the ratio of a few hundred to 1
in Athens after the Peloponnesian War. 'No administration in history',
as one distinguished historian of Rome has remarked, 'has ever devoted
itself so whole-heartedly to fleecing its subjects for the private benefit
of its ruling class as Rome of the last age of the republic.'[13]

By the time the republican era drew to a close, replaced by an imperial state (conventionally dated from the foundation of the principate
under Augustus Caesar in 27 BC), the Roman ruling class had amassed
private fortunes of staggering proportions, by means of exploitation
and corruption at home – from their landed estates, urban slum tenements, usury, trading in property, government contracts, and so on –
and even more spectacularly by systematic plunder of their expanding
empire. The administration of the empire provided the Roman aristocracy with unprecedented opportunities for looting and extortion.
Proconsular office in imperial domains was a sure means of lining the
pocket and for the most prominent Roman oligarchs to consolidate
their personal power by acquiring what increasingly amounted to
private armies. The empire also had the advantage of shifting the
burden of taxation – at least for a time – away from citizens, including
peasants, and onto imperial subjects. This undoubtedly lowered the
risk of popular unrest in Rome, but the price paid by peasants was
the increasing concentration of land in the hands of the aristocracy.

Yet the very success of the republic as an instrument of aristocratic
gain proved its undoing. The irony is that it was the triumph of the
aristocracy which eventually led to the fall of the republic, as the
weakness of the threat from below deprived the ruling class of any
unity it might have had in the face of a common enemy. The growth
of the empire aggravated the inherent weaknesses of the republican

---

13 Ernst Badian, *Roman Imperialism in the Late Republic*, 2nd edn (Oxford: Blackwell, 1968), p. 87.

state by enlarging the scope of oligarchic competition and raising the stakes. With an increasingly unruly oligarchy, the vast military apparatus of imperial expansion was bound to be deployed in the service of personal ambition and intra-oligarchic rivalry. The empire also placed intolerable strains on the administrative capacities of the republic and its principle of government by amateurs. With no strong state to keep the warring aristocracy in check the republic descended into chaos. It is not surprising that the fabric of republican government gave way under the strain.[14]

The most famous period of Roman history, the moment of Julius Caesar and Marcus Tullius Cicero, was the end of the republic: a time of unceasing intra-oligarchic conflict and violence, corruption, and breakdown of order, which spilled over into the vast expanses of the empire as ambitious aristocrats brought their proconsular armies into play. The time of troubles was brought to an end, and the cohesion and class power of the oligarchy preserved, only by the establishment of an imperial state in place of the city-state form of the republic. If the class interests of the oligarchy had created and sustained the republic, the acquisitive and expansionary logic of that same oligarchy had now driven it beyond the narrow bounds of the republican form.

What is most striking about the history of Rome, and what is most important for our understanding of its political and cultural life, is the Roman preoccupation with private property. The monumental scale of its land-grabbing project, both in the concentration of oligarchic property at home and in imperial expansion, was unprecedented and unequalled in the ancient world. It reflected a distinctive system of social relations and class reproduction, quite different from other ancient civilizations where centralized states ruled subject peasant communities and access to the surplus labour of others was typically achieved by direct possession of the state. State-appropriation in these other civilizations did not, as we have seen, necessarily preclude private possession of land, either for those who acquired it as a perquisite of office or for peasant-smallholders; but access to substantial wealth – that is, to the surplus labour of others on a large scale – tended not to be a function of property as such but rather of state power. In Rome, by contrast, landed property was the only secure and steady source of wealth.

---

14 The classic discussion of this period is Ronald Syme's *The Roman Revolution* (London and Oxford: Oxford University Press, 1960).

As in other pre-capitalist societies, juridical status and political power remained critical factors in the relations of exploitation. But in the absence of a centralized appropriating state superimposed on subject communities of producers, and without a clear monopoly of juridical privilege and political power for the ruling class, private property became an end in itself in unprecedented ways. Land-ownership became the major condition of surplus extraction, and there developed a compelling pressure to acquire land, even to dispos-sess smallholders. Since the citizenship of peasants precluded their juridical dependence, their exploitation – as tenants or casual labourers – depended on their economic vulnerability. If expropriated, they could be replaced by slaves as a labour force on large estates; and in the last century of the republic, in Roman Italy (agricultural slavery was less important in other parts of the empire such as North Africa or the east) one third of the population consisted of slaves. As the empire grew, the juridical and political status of the peasantry declined, while the burden of taxation increased.

The collective power of the aristocracy was sufficient (unlike that of ancient Athens) to achieve an unprecedented concentration of land in the hands of the oligarchy; and the principal career for the Roman ruling class was the acquisition and management of property. Even imperial service in the provinces was a way of looting subject popu-lations to obtain the means of investing in property. Public office was in general just a moment in that career; and, while imperial office was certainly a road to fame and fortune, aristocrats were not always keen to take it. The characteristic aspiration of the Roman aristocracy was *cum dignitate otium* (leisure with dignity), and their principal moti-vation for seeking release from public duties was quite simple: 'Their primary function and activity after all was the supervision and main-tenance of their wealth.'[15]

When the distinctive social property relations of Rome outgrew the republican state, they produced a new imperial system, an 'under-governed' empire. Although some parts of the empire were under more direct Roman rule than others, its administration of such far-flung territories could not have been achieved without a network of more or less self-governing cities (often newly founded and in largely rural areas), which amounted to a massive class federation of local aristoc-racies. This municipal system made possible what has been described

---

15 Chester Starr, *The Roman Empire, 27 B.C. to A.D. 476: A Study in Survival* (New York: Oxford University Press, 1982), p. 63.

as 'government without bureaucracy'. While the imperial state did, of course, have its share of centrally appointed officials, the empire 'remained undergoverned, certainly by comparison with the Chinese empire, which employed, proportionately, perhaps twenty times the number of functionaries.'[16]

This imperial system, with its diffuse administration, enhanced and extended the power of private property. The Roman Republic had established the rule of property as never before, and the empire pushed forward the frontiers of that regime. It constituted a historically unprecedented partnership between the state and property, in contrast to all other known civilizations in which a powerful state meant a relatively weak regime of private property. Even many centuries later, in late imperial China, for instance, with its long history of well-developed property in land, the imperial state consolidated its power by expanding the smallholder economy while discouraging large land-ownership, and centralized administrative power by co-opting large proprietors into the state. The result was a huge imperial bureaucracy, living off taxation of the peasants, while great wealth and power resided not in the land but in the imperial state, in an elite at the top of which stood the court and imperial officialdom. The Roman Empire was very different, with its distinctive mode of coexistence between state and private property.

But the strengths of the Roman regime were also its weaknesses.[17] The mode of administration, and the system of private property on which it was based, meant that the empire tended towards fragmentation from the start; and in the end, that tendency prevailed. The imperial bureaucracy grew, above all for the purpose of extracting more taxes – as always, largely to maintain the empire's military power. But the growth of the bureaucracy was a sign of weakness, not of strength. With no significant new and permanent conquests after the first century AD, the Roman army was overstretched in keeping control of the existing empire, while the bureaucracy and the tax-hungry state grew in order to sustain the army. The burden this imposed on Rome's imperial subjects simply hastened the decline. The so-called 'barbarian' invasions were less a cause than an effect of Rome's disintegration. In fact, it can be very misleading to speak of invasions at all, since Rome

16 Peter Garnsey and Richard Saller, *The Roman Empire: Economy, Society and Culture* (London: Duckworth, 1987), p. 26.

17 The rest of this paragraph and the following one are taken from my book, *Empire of Capital* (London: Verso, 2005), pp. 36–7.

had long had more or less friendly interactions with the 'barbarian' neighbours within its orbit, using them both as a source of military manpower and in commercial relations. By the time incursions across the imperial frontiers became a fatal threat and not just an annoyance, a crumbling state had long since become an intolerable burden to peasants and a dispensable nuisance to landlords.

It is a striking fact that the so-called 'fall' of the empire took place in the west and not in the imperial east, where the pattern of rule was more like that of other ancient empires: a bureaucratic state in which land remained largely subordinate to office. It was in the western empire, where state rule was diluted and fragmented by aristocracies based on huge landed estates, that the weaknesses of the empire proved fatal. As the imperial state imploded, it left behind a network of personal dependence binding peasants to landlord and land – a development encouraged by the state itself when, in a time of crisis, it tied many peasants to the land, no doubt for fiscal purposes. The simple opposition between freedom and slavery would be gradually replaced by a spectrum of dependence.

In the centuries following the 'decline and fall', there would be various attempts to recentralize this fragmented system under one or another dynastic monarchy, with successive cycles of centralization and repeated fragmentation, as one or the other element in the uneasy Roman fusion of political sovereignty and landed property prevailed. But the regime of private property had left its mark; and the fragmentation of the Roman Empire is still recognizable in European feudalism, a system of 'parcellized sovereignty' based on property, with political and economic power united in a feudal lordship dominating and exploiting a dependent peasantry without the support of a strong central state.

The Culture of Property: The Roman Law

The Roman property regime, and the particular form of Rome's class accommodations, shaped not only the political life of both republic and empire but also their cultural formation. Although the Romans would thoroughly appropriate Greek culture as their empire absorbed the Hellenistic world, they would never overtake their teachers in the characteristically Greek domains of philosophy and political theory. They certainly left their mark on their adopted cultural traditions – particularly, for instance, in Stoic philosophy; but their most distinctive contributions to the theorization of social and political worlds are to be found elsewhere: in the law and in Christianity, or at least the form of Roman Christianity that ultimately triumphed to become the 'universal' Church.

We can begin to appreciate the specificity of Roman political culture by considering more closely how the Roman resolution of its early social conflicts differed from the Athenian. The Athenians, as we saw, managed the conflicts between peasants and landlords, 'mass' and 'elite', largely on the political plane. The effect of their democratic reforms was gradually to dilute legal or status distinctions among free Athenians in the common identity of citizenship. The Romans to some extent also pursued the political course, and the citizen body also included both rich and poor; but, while property increasingly trumped heritage, even status distinctions among citizens, notably between patricians and plebeians, continued to play a role, with patricians enjoying privileged status and disproportionate representation in assemblies. The Romans did, to be sure, devise political institutions and procedures to regulate relations between different types of citizen – such as the particularly distinctive office of the tribune. But, while influenced at first by Greek law, the Romans constructed a much more elaborate legal apparatus, relying more than the Greeks on the law to manage transactions between mass and elite, between propertied classes and less prosperous citizens. Social relations between these groups were in large part played out not in the public domain of political life but in the sphere of private law – a distinctively Roman category; and the regulation of property would constitute by far the largest part of Rome's civil law.

The founding moment of the Roman law, the enactment of the Twelve Tables in the middle of the fifth century BC, was understood by Romans looking back at their legal history as a response to plebeian grievances about the old system of customary law, which had been interpreted and applied by patrician judges. But the Twelve Tables probably did not fundamentally transform the substance of traditional law or its aristocratic bias, and certainly did not dilute the distinction between patricians and plebeians. Instead, plebeians had to make do with the commitment of the law to a written code, which explicitly outlined their rights. While many adjustments and additions would later be required, especially as the republic grew into a massive empire, the system of private law which emerged from this early written code would remain the basis of the Roman law.

Both in its origins and in its substance, the Roman law was rooted in the old relations between patrician landlords and plebeian farmers, many of whom may, in the early years, have been in a dependent condition, occupying and working surplus land allowed them by landlords in exchange for political and military support. This traditional relation of *patronus* and *cliens* would soon change its form, and the division between patricians and plebeians would no longer entail the same relation between landlords and dependent peasants; but patronage would continue to denote a relationship between men of unequal status, in which a member of the Roman elite would offer help and protection to social inferiors (or sometimes, in a public capacity, to groups and even cities), who became his clients, in exchange for their loyalty, deference, political support and various kinds of service. The distinctively Roman conception of patronage and the relation between patron and client, which had no Athenian analogue, would continue to shape Roman conceptions of social and political dependence.

Even in the absence of the personal relation between patron and client, social relations between classes continued to play themselves out in the private sphere, where the law regulated property and all the various rights and obligations associated with it. This bespeaks a concept of the public realm very different from the Greek. The Greeks made various distinctions between state and non-state spheres. In the previous chapter, we encountered such a distinction, for instance, in Sophocles's play, *Antigone*. But a reminder of what was at issue in that play may also help to clarify the ways in which these Greek distinctions differed from the Roman antithesis of public and private. Although *Antigone* is often read as a clash between the individual conscience and the state, it has more to do, as we saw, with the opposition between two conceptions of *nomos*, Antigone representing eternal unwritten laws, in the form of traditional, customary and religious obligations of kinship, and Creon the laws of a new political order. The play also deals with two conflicting loyalties or forms of *philia*: on the one hand, the ties of blood and personal friendship and, on the other, the public demands of the civic community, the polis whose laws are supposed to be directed to the common good. In neither of these cases is the non-state realm adequately described as *private*, since both polis and non-polis principles concern communal obligations.

The Greeks come closest to a public–private dichotomy in the distinction between *oikos* and polis. As Thucydides makes clear in his account of Pericles's Funeral Oration, Athenians certainly distinguished between a citizen's domestic concerns, or an individual's own business, and the common affairs of the polis. But in Greek political theory, the distinction between *oikos* and polis, as elaborated most clearly by Aristotle, has to do with two forms of association and the different principles that govern them – in particular, the inequality of household relations and the civic equality of the polis, or the *oikos* as the realm of necessity and the polis as the sphere of freedom. A man denied access to the political sphere because of his bondage to necessary labour was, for Aristotle, not so much a private individual, as against a citizen, but rather a 'condition' of the polis, as against a 'part' of it. Democrats would have disagreed with Aristotle about the political consequences of social inequality, or whether a life of necessary labour disqualified people from politics; but they would have shared his view that the distinctive characteristic of the political sphere was civic equality – which is, of course, why democrats and antidemocrats disagreed so fiercely about access to that privileged sphere for the poor and labouring classes.

The Romans, by contrast, elaborated some fairly clear distinctions between public and private, yet these had little to do with the criteria which, for the Greeks, distinguished *oikos* from polis. For the Romans, for instance, inequality was formally present in the political sphere and was not therefore the criterion that marked off public from private. It was certainly not a question of distinguishing between a domestic sphere in which superior ruled inferior and a civic sphere in which social unequals met as political equals. In Rome, relations between social unequals in the private sphere of property were reflected in the public sphere of hierarchical citizenship. The Romans created a new and probably unprecedented kind of private sphere; and their distinction between public and private represented a new form of dichotomy, which is clearly visible in the distinction between public and private law that lay at the heart of the Roman legal system.

The only extant elaboration of the distinction defines it like this: 'Public law is concerned with the Roman state (*status rei Romanae*), while private law is concerned with the interests of individuals, for some matters are of public and others of private interest. Public law comprises religion, priesthoods, and magistracies.'[18] Private law was by far the greater concern of the Roman legal system, and the apparatus of law to deal with matters of public administration was fairly rudimentary by comparison. The primacy of private law is in itself significant, as is the mere fact that the Romans felt the need to draw such a clear line between public and private. The determining factor cannot have been simply the growth of the state. The republic had a

---

18 This formulation is by the Roman jurist, Ulpian (d. 228 AD). The compilation of the Roman law under the emperor, Justinian I (*c.* 482–565) – the *Digest* of Justinian – is said to owe something like one third of its content to Ulpian and begins with this distinction between public and private law.

minimal, virtually amateur state, while even the empire was 'under-governed'; and other ancient civilizations had far more elaborate states. What set the Romans apart from all other high civilizations was their property regime, with its distinctive legal conception of property; and with it came a more sharply delineated private sphere in which the individual enjoyed his own exclusive dominion.

The contrast with Greece is here particularly striking. It has often been remarked that the Greeks had no clear conception of ownership, indeed no abstract word for it at all. An Athenian might claim a better right than someone else to some piece of property but certainly nothing like the exclusive claim entailed by the Roman concept of *dominium*. In disputes over property, the difference in practice may not have been as great as it seems in theory, but its significance should not be under-estimated. It tells us a great deal about how the Romans conceptualized the social world. The word *dominium* 'and the actual law relating to ownership', writes one commentator on Greek law, emphasizing the contrast with Rome, 'serve to underline the strongly individualistic character of Roman ownership, which comes out forcibly in the plain-tiff's words in a *vindicatio* [the ancient legal action in which a Roman citizen asserted a more or less exclusive right of ownership over some-thing]'[19]: 'I claim that this thing is mine by the *ius Quiritum*', that is, by the legal right of private exclusive individual ownership which only Roman citizens could enjoy. In this way, 'The Roman citizen asserts a claim against all the world, based on an act of his own will.'[20] The concept of *dominium*, then, marks out the private sphere with an unprecedented clarity, and the private is inseparable from property.

The idea of an exclusive private and individual sphere of mastery contained in the concept of *dominium* would develop in tandem with the concept of a distinctly public form of rule. The *imperium*, which designated military command and also the right of command attached to certain civil magistrates, would evolve to encompass the rule of the emperor, eventually approaching something like a notion of sovereignty,

---

19 A.R.W. Harrison, *The Law of Athens: The Family and Property* (Oxford: The Clarendon Press, 1968), p. 201. It may be misleading to call Roman property 'absolute', but perhaps no more misleading than is the concept of 'absolute' property itself. If 'absolute' means completely inviolable, without restrictions on its use, or without any obligations (such as taxation) attached to it, there has never been a truly absolute form of property. But it would be a mistake not to acknowledge the distinctively *exclusive* quality of Roman property, the degree to which it belonged to the individual to the exclusion of others, even if certain obligations might be associated with it.

20 *Ibid.*

which distinguished the Roman idea of the state from the Greek conception of the polis as simply a community of citizens. The partnership of *dominium* and *imperium*, then, sums up both the distinction between public and private and the alliance of property and state that was so distinctively Roman.

To say that the Romans devised a conception of property more individualistic and exclusive than ever before, or that they differentiated private and public in historically unprecedented ways, is not to say that they anticipated modern liberal individualism. Their concern was not, for example, the protection of individual rights from incursions by the state. Indeed, they scarcely had a conception of the state, or of individual rights, of the kind that would be required to think in these terms; nor were their social relations and institutions of a kind to generate such ideas.

Rome was not a capitalist society, nor a 'liberal democracy'. It is certainly true that, unlike any other ancient civilization, the Romans created a regime with two distinct poles of power, in which a well-developed central state coexisted with strong private property; and it is no doubt also true that, as the imperial state grew, there were tensions between propertied classes and an increasingly burdensome state. But there never existed in Rome a system of appropriation, like capitalism, which depended on intensive growth, rooted in profitably competitive production, rather than on the extensive growth of property in a massive grab for land. Territorial expansion in the empire was an extension of land concentration at home; and the public power of the state, its coercive force, played a more immediate role in the acquisition of private wealth.

Roman ideas of property and its relation to the public sphere expressed this distinctive partnership of property and state. The emblem of the Roman state, SPQR, *Senatus Populusque Romanus*, the Senate and the Roman People, does not convey a formal, abstract concept of the state so much as a snapshot of the relations between dominant and subordinate classes, as well as alliances and rivalries within the ruling class itself. It is significant that *Senatus* is distinguished from, and placed ahead of, *Populus*, in a formula that denotes the dominance of the propertied classes in the senate and their limited accommodation with the people, a 'mixed constitution' containing popular elements but governed by an aristocracy. The absence of any abstract notion of the state is particularly clear in the republic, with its amateur government by members of the propertied elite taking time out from the management of their private wealth. In that context, the distinction between private and public represented not an antithesis between two poles of power but rather the dominant class in its two different aspects.

The clear delineation of public and private spheres, then, was not, in the main, intended to protect the private from public intrusion. It was more a matter of managing the private sphere itself. In the first instance, especially in the form of private law, it contributed to the regulation of relations between classes by recognizing the sanctity of property while spelling out the rights and obligations associated with it. Later, the ruling class's descent into self-destructive conflict would add a new dimension to the management of the private sphere, as we shall see in the work of Cicero; and as republic gave way to empire, the relation between public and private would inevitably change. Yet even when the polarities increased with the growth of the imperial bureaucracy, the state remained a distinctive collaboration between property and state, as private appropriation continued to depend on imperial power, while the imperial system relied on a network of alliances among landed elites.

The Roman law also mapped the social world in other significant ways. The distinction between the *ius civile*, the law specific to Roman citizens, and the *ius gentium*, which applied to other peoples, contains a wealth of information about the Roman world. This distinction between the Roman civil law and the law of nations in the first instance set Roman citizens apart from others, while at the same time acknowledging the need to provide some means of regulating the transactions between Romans and non-Romans, in a growing system of international trade and an expanding empire. The idea of the *ius gentium* both acknowledged that other peoples operated according to their own laws and customs and also sought to find principles common to all which could form the basis of transactions among them and be applied in Roman courts. This applied not only to principles having to do with relations among nations, such as the inviolability of treaties, but also to a wide range of private law matters concerning the performance of contracts, conditions of buying and selling, and so on.

The exclusiveness of the civil law became increasingly irrelevant as the Roman citizenship expanded, but the *ius gentium* continued to serve other purposes. The identification of certain universal principles accepted by all peoples had opened the way to a concept of *natural* law, a *ius naturale*, deriving from natural reason. At the same time, the idea of the *ius gentium* as simply the observable commonalities among social practices in various nations also allowed for the kind of Roman pragmatism that could, for example, regard slavery as an essentially unnatural institution while treating it as legitimate just on the grounds that it was (allegedly) a universal practice accepted by many particular systems of custom and law.

The 'undergoverned' Roman Empire, composed of diverse and loosely connected fragments and relying on an alliance of propertied elites spread over a huge territory, depended for its cohesion not only on a vast military force but on cultural ties and universalistic ideologies that could help to bind the imperial fragments together. The part played by the Roman law in maintaining the cohesion of the empire had at least as much to do with its cultural and ideological effects as with its role in governance. Even at the height of imperial dominion, Roman law never completely overshadowed the particularities of local law and custom; but the spread of the empire was accompanied by an increasing assertion of universalism against legal, political and cultural particularisms of various kinds, a universalism expressed in the natural law or the *ius gentium* no less than in Stoic cosmopolitanism and, finally, in Christian doctrine and the 'universal Church'.

The Culture of Property: Stoic Philosophy in Rome

The topography of a social world shaped by a distinctive property regime is visible also in Roman philosophy, particularly in its variants of Stoicism. Let us remind ourselves of the changes that Stoic doctrine underwent as Roman hegemony spread. In general, the most obvious transformation as Stoic philosophy came within the Roman orbit was a decreasing interest in cosmological, psychological or epistemological questions and a growing preoccupation with ethics alone. But before Stoicism became a truly Roman phenomenon, there were already moves away from the doctrines of the early Stoics and even from their cosmological and psychological foundations. Posidonius of Apameia (135–51 BC), with whom Cicero studied, not only modified Stoic ethical doctrine but also challenged the psychological and cosmological monism that underlay the ethics and politics of Stoicism; and the evidence suggests that this was already true of Posidonius's teacher, Panaetius of Rhodes (*c.* 185–109 BC), who first brought Stoicism to Rome and who greatly influenced Cicero. In their hands, Stoicism became a philosophy more congenial to the interests of the Roman ruling class. While early Stoic doctrine could be read as a challenge to slavery, empire and even, perhaps, to property itself, this 'Middle' phase of Stoicism provided the philosophical means to defend them. But even short of that, the modifications in ethics made Stoicism more adaptable to the values of Roman elites.

Panaetius came to Rome during the late republic after studying with Stoic philosophers in Greece, where he had met the Roman general, Scipio Africanus the Younger, also a student of Stoicism. He would later return to Greece to head the Stoa in Athens. But while in Rome, he remained close to Scipio and introduced Stoic ethics to the so-called Scipionic circle of intellectually inclined conservative aristocrats, who played a major role in disseminating Panaetius's ideas.[21]

What made his teachings especially attractive to men of this kind was that he adapted the ethical doctrine of Stoicism to the particular virtues most highly prized by them in their aspirations to honour and glory, placing an emphasis 'on such active virtues as greatness of soul or magnanimity, on generosity or liberality, on decorum and propriety, and on energy and industriousness, as against the traditional Stoic stress on fortitude and justice'.[22] More fundamentally, Panaetius eased the rigidity of Stoic ethics, making the doctrine more adaptable to ethical ambiguities and compromises of the kind that would be regularly encountered by Rome's aristocracy, in a world made up not of sages but of ordinary people; and he attached greater value to lesser goods, which fell short of the highest Stoic ideals. Stoicism had always allowed for a distinction between moral goods and goods that were morally indifferent but which could be rated in respect to preferability on other grounds. Material wealth was a typical example of the morally indifferent but preferable good. Now, such secondary goods were given higher status than the Early Stoics had granted them.

Justice, in this view, had more to do with positive legality than with higher moral laws – as one might expect in a society so imbued with legalism. This meant that strict moral principles might have to give way to existing Roman practices, to the requirements of contracts and the exigencies of everyday life in business and politics, as long as they remained within the law. But once this legalistic notion had replaced the old Stoic conception of an absolute and universal justice above man-made law, it was possible to temper legal justice by supplementing it with less exalted moral principles of equity. This would have significant implications for some of republican Rome's most important political controversies.

---

21 Some scholars regard the Scipionic circle as a fiction – which appears, for instance, in Cicero's *De Amicitia* (*On Friendship*). But whether or not there existed any such more or less formally organized 'circle', there can be no doubt that there was a significant conservative sector of the Roman aristocracy, of which Scipio was a prime example, which was influenced by the ideas of the Middle Stoa.

22 Neal Wood, *Cicero's Social and Political Thought* (Berkeley and Los Angeles: University of California Press, 1988), p. 48.

The role of the Scipios in Rome nicely illustrates the political significance of these changes in Stoic philosophy. In 134, Tiberius Sempronius Gracchus, cousin of Scipio Africanus the Younger and himself a successful general, was elected to serve the following year as tribune of the people. With the help of his brother, Gaius, he proposed a radical agrarian law to redistribute public lands in the interest of impoverished farmers. The opposition to the Gracchan reforms was led by their cousin, Scipio Africanus; and, in the hostility aroused by Tiberius's tribunate among the Roman aristocracy, he was murdered in a riot by senators and their supporters, led by P. Scipio Nasica.

In the debates surrounding Tiberius's agrarian law, Stoic principles may have been invoked on both sides. The earlier Spartan revolution, with its radical programme of land redistribution and debt cancellation, had been informed by the egalitarian ideas of Early Stoicism, together with its principle that, in a cosmos regulated by a single common *logos*, all things were fundamentally common; and these ideas may also have inspired Tiberius. But in the wake of the Spartan revolution the modification of Stoic principles, especially by Panaetius, had weakened the threat they posed to property. If the case for the Gracchan reforms could be supported by Stoic ideas on equality, social justice and the principle of commonality, the opposition could, and did, appeal to the modified Stoicism that identified justice with existing law but also tempered law with notions of fairness or equity. On the basis of those later Stoic principles, no higher standard of universal justice had any decisive bearing on the question of agrarian reform; and, while its legality was certainly an issue, because nothing could be just that was illegal (just as nothing that was lawful could be called unjust), beyond legality there were also requirements of equity.

It is striking that principles of equity were invoked by Rome's leading thinkers not in support of, but in opposition to, land redistribution. In *De Officiis* (*On Duties*), a work that on the author's own testimony is profoundly influenced by Panaetius, Cicero comments on the damage done by both the Spartans and the Gracchi, as examples of the consequences that flow from violating equity in the redistribution of property. Having said that 'it is the peculiar function of the state and the city to guarantee to every man the free and undisturbed control of his own particular property', Cicero goes on to castigate the 'ruinous' measures adopted by land reformers who 'do away with equity'. '[H]ow is it fair', he asks, 'that a man who never had any property should take possession of lands that had been occupied for many years or even generations, and that he

who had them before should lose possession of them?'[23] Cicero seems
to share the view of his teacher, the Stoic Posidonius, student of
Panaetius, who maintained that, while there was nothing illegal about
what Tiberius did, he deserved the punishment he got.

It would, of course, be possible to argue that the practical ethics
of the Middle Stoa serve no particular social or political interests but
provide for ethical standards that can be met by ordinary people and
not just sages, or at least by Roman grandees faced with the imperfect
realities of everyday political and economic life. The moral rigidities
of Early Stoicism, it might be said, are not particularly congenial or
even humane; and surely principles of equity are good for everyone.
If Stoic arguments were used in defence of ruling class interests, can
the philosophers themselves be held responsible; and what is the point
of spelling out the immediate political sources and consequences of
these ideas? The least that can be said in response to such objections
is that, even if we leave aside the known associations of a philosopher
like Panaetius and his close connection to Roman leaders with a clear
political agenda, there is something to be learned from identifying the
particular historical conditions that placed certain urgent questions
on the political agenda and shaped the ways in which those questions
were answered. At the same time, it is not simply a matter of exploring
historical contexts to help understand ancient texts. To historicize, as
we said in Chapter One, is to humanize; and there is something deeply
troubling about analyses of political theory that are insensitive to the
pressing social issues to which it is addressed.

If we acknowledge the historical circumstances in which the ethical
doctrine of the Middle Stoa was rooted, and even the specific social
interests that it served, we can nonetheless accept that its social and
political implications are not necessarily one-sided and that its softening
of Stoic rigidities has a wider appeal. But Panaetius did not confine
himself to easing the requirements of Stoic ethics. The surviving evidence
suggests, for example, that he accepted slavery in a way his predecessors
had not. This might be expected of an ethical doctrine that allowed for
adaptations to normal if less than ideal Roman practices; but there is
also evidence of a more fundamental shift in psychology and cosmology
designed to provide a philosophical foundation for the defence of social
hierarchy and even slavery. Apparently dividing the soul between a
controlling reason and subordinate appetites, he revived the old dualism
which had underpinned the hierarchal philosophies of Plato and

---

23 Cicero, *Off.* II, 78–80, Loeb Library translation.

Aristotle. In relation to slavery, it was now again possible to argue, as Plato had done, that subordination of some men to others was good for both, if it accorded with the principle of rational control over baser elements. It was even possible to maintain, as Aristotle had done, that slavery was good for both parties in the relationship, as those fit only to obey can only benefit from subjection to a superior master.

Similar doctrines were applied in defence of Roman imperialism. Whether Panaetius himself made such an argument is unclear, but Cicero in his *Republic* deploys it in justification of both slavery and empire. In this dialogue, which purports to take place in the garden of Scipio Africanus the Younger, Cicero gives a speech to Laelius, one of the most important members of the Scipionic circle and clearly of Stoic persuasion, about the dominion that Rome has achieved 'over the whole world'. 'Do we not observe', says Laelius, 'that dominion has been granted by Nature to everything that is best, to the great advantage of what is weak? For why else does God rule over man, the mind over the body, and reason over lust and anger and other evil elements of the mind?' There is, to be sure, a difference, he says, between the kind of rule exercised by a king over his subjects, or a father over his children, and the rule of master over slave. The first – and this also applies to various other kinds of political arrangements – governs in the way that the mind governs the body, while the second is like the rule of reason over lust and 'other disquieting emotions', in that its object is to restrain and overpower slaves, just as reason, 'the best part of the mind', restrains 'the evil parts of the mind . . . with a stricter curb. . . . ' Since the empire is the product of just wars in defence of Rome's allies, we are given to understand that, while imperial domination may have elements of the first kind of rule, it also belongs, justly, to the second, in which lesser beings or nations are forcefully subjected to their superiors for their own benefit.[24]

---

24 *Rep.* III, 36–7, Loeb Library translation. The translator remarks that these fragments 'are part of the argument for the justice of slavery and imperialism, in which it is maintained that certain nations and individuals are naturally fitted for and benefited by subjection to others.' He points out that St Augustine later explained the meaning of these passages in *The City of God*, XIX, 21. The relevant passage in St Augustine reads ' . . . the rule over provincials [according to Cicero's *Republic*] is just, precisely because servitude is the interest of such men, and is established for their welfare when rightly established; that is, when licence to do wrong is taken away from wicked men; and that those subdued will be better off, because when not subdued they were worse off. In support of the reasoning a striking example is introduced, as if drawn from nature, and stated as follows: Why, then, is it that God commands man, the soul commands the body, the reason commands lust and the other vicious parts of the soul?' (Loeb Library translation).

That Cicero was putting into Laelius's mouth ideas derived from Panaetius is suggested near the beginning of the dialogue, when Laelius refers to conversations those present used to have 'with Panaetius . . . in company with Polybius – two Greeks who were perhaps the best versed of them all in politics'.[25] Doubts may remain about Panaetius's rejection of Early Stoic monism, or about his application of a psychological dualism to social and political relations; but the evidence for a restoration of Platonic dualism, between a ruling rational element and the irrational subjected to it, is clearer in the work of his pupil, Posidonius, described by his contemporaries as a great admirer of Plato and Aristotle. Posidonius also refers to historical cases of domination that seem to be examples of inferiors being subjected to superiors, for the good of the subject. In any case, the theory of empire which emerges from the various scraps of evidence concerning Panaetius's view, and/or the views of those strongly influenced by him, is, at the very least, that imperial domination is justified if it works to the benefit of its subjects. This may not go as far as Aristotle's notion that some men are natural slaves and so can only benefit from enslavement to superior masters; but the conception of what is beneficial to the subject is itself clearly coloured from the start by the Platonic and Aristotelian idea – inconsistent with the Early Stoic notion of a universal *logos* in a unitary cosmos – that there is a natural division between ruler and ruled and that some men are better off ruled.

Cicero

No one gave voice to the Roman culture of property better than the statesman, orator and thinker, Marcus Tullius Cicero. His political ideas may not have been deeply original; but his synthesis of the prevailing currents, including Stoicism, was brilliantly adapted to the conditions and interests of the Roman senatorial class, at that particularly turbulent moment in the late republic. By this time, when the republican form

---

25 *Rep.* I, 34. The historian Polybius (*c.* 203–122 BC), though a Greek, had become close to the Scipios and a supporter of Roman imperial rule. His grand history, which seeks to explain how Rome achieved its conquests, gives much of the credit for Roman success to its mixed constitution, the equilibrium and interdependence of classes created by the collaboration of consuls, Senate and multitude. Outlining the various forms of constitution, their origins and, in the manner of Plato, their process of degeneration, he seems to be making a case for Roman imperial rule addressed to a Greek audience. (See Peter Green, *Alexander to Actium: The Historical Evolution of the Hellenistic Age* [Berkeley and Los Angeles: University of California Press, 1993].)

was no longer able to maintain the delicate balance within and between social classes, the chief social problem confronting the dominant elites was no longer the threat from below but, above all, their own self-destruction. In his political theory, as we have already seen, Cicero certainly guarded his flank against popular threats, including the redistribution of property; but his principal concern was to restore the unity and stability on which the property regime depended. The challenge he took on was to defend the primacy of property and the dominance of propertied classes while counselling the ruling class to self-restraint.

Cicero was born in 106 BC, the son of a fairly prosperous and prominent, though not senatorial, landed family. As a member of the equestrian rank and a 'new man', he was no doubt subjected to snobbery; but his family was well connected, and he enjoyed all the benefits of a gentlemanly life, including the best education. As a young student of law, he came into contact with the type of Roman statesmen who would be his political models throughout his career, upholders in his eyes of the ancestral constitution and austere exemplars of the republican virtue which was waning in his own turbulent time. His education also encompassed philosophy, and he spent some time in Athens, studying oratory and rhetoric. He came away from his philosophical education with a great admiration for Plato, yet also with a mild philosophical scepticism, based on the teachings of Philo of Larissa, and an element of Stoicism – its ethics rather than its epistemology or metaphysics – none of which he regarded as antithetical to Plato.

Returning to Rome to practise law, he entered so actively and successfully into politics that he went through the sequence of offices with remarkable speed, becoming *quaestor* at the age of thirty, performing financial and imperial duties assisting the provincial governor of Western Sicily. This also entitled him to enter the senate, and he was eventually elected – at the earliest possible age of forty-two – to the consulship, the highest office the republic could offer him. By now, he was well established as a defender of conservative republicanism, an opponent of agrarian and democratic reforms and regarded by conservative senators as an effective counter to popular leaders like Caesar and Catiline, aristocrats who – as their critics perceived them – pandered to the multitude. One of Cicero's main accomplishments was to defeat the agrarian reforms of the tribune Publius Servius Rullus; but by far his most famous political act was his defeat of Catiline, who was allegedly plotting to seize power with the support of the urban masses and dispossessed or indebted peasants.

This notable success may also, however, have contributed to Cicero's undoing. He dealt with the conspirators with a ruthlessness and disregard for the law which antagonized even conservatives. In any case, the political winds in Rome were shifting towards his enemies. He was driven into exile and the comforts of philosophy. He returned to Rome in 58 BC and in 51 was sent to Cilicia to fulfil the duties of proconsul, which were required of every former consul. In charge of the civil and military administration of this imperial province, he did a creditable job, extracting less profit from his post than was usual among Roman proconsuls. Although we should have no illusions about Cicero's attitude to wealth, including his own personal property (he was, among other things, an enthusiastic slum landlord[26]), by Roman standards he undoubtedly performed his duties with admirable rectitude, and even had one modest military success in his province. On his return to Rome, he found his beloved republic in a state of civil war, the opposing sides led by Caesar and Pompey with their respective private armies. Cicero sided with Pompey, regarding Caesar's victory and dictatorship as the end of the republic, and indeed the Roman state. But he never suffered at the hands of the triumphant Caesar, who, on Cicero's own testimony, treated him with the utmost courtesy. On the assassination of Caesar, Cicero allied himself with the assassins and became for a short while effectively ruler of Rome. When his allies were, in turn, defeated by Caesar's lieutenant, Marc Antony – whom Cicero had ferociously attacked – the new triumvirate proscribed their predecessors, including Cicero, and he was finally murdered by their soldiers in 43 BC.

Cicero is certainly not a systematic thinker, and even less a methodical philosopher in the manner of Plato or Aristotle. But certain principles emerge fairly unambiguously not only from major works such as the *Pro Sestio* (*In Defence of Sestius*), *De Re Publica* (*The Republic*), *De Legibus* (*The Laws*), and *De Officiis* (*On Duties*), but also from other speeches and letters. In what follows, we shall not try to follow a detailed line of argument in any single work, as we did in the case of Plato and Aristotle; but an effort will be made to assemble

---

26 Cicero's letters to his friend, Atticus, reveal an avid interest in his own properties and a keen eye for profit. It is hard not to be amused, for instance, at the following passage from one of his letters: 'Two of my shops have collapsed and the others are showing cracks, so that even the mice have moved elsewhere, to say nothing of the tenants. Other people call this a disaster, I don't call it even a nuisance. Ah Socrates, Socratics, I can never repay you! Heavens above, how utterly trivial such things appear to me! However, there is a building scheme under way, Vestorius advising and instigating, which will turn this loss into a source of profit' (*Att.* XVI.9, 1).

a more or less coherent political theory, tracing the connections among the essential principles laid out in his various works and considering their sources, significance and implications.

Although Cicero's political thought is commonly neglected now, it has been remarkably influential in the Western tradition, if only because of its enormous popularity in the seminal early modern period. European and American thinkers, especially from the sixteenth to the eighteenth century, found in his work, especially *On Duties*, a whole range of congenial ideas, some of which have led commentators to credit Cicero with an implausible modernity, despite his firm roots in antiquity. These ideas have been summed up as follows:

> ... the principles of natural law and justice and of universal moral equality; a patriotic and dedicated republicanism; a vigorous advocacy of liberty, impassioned rejection of tyranny, and persuasive justification of tyrannicide; a firm belief in constitutionalism, the rule of law, and the mixed constitution; a strong faith in the sanctity of private property, in the importance of its accumulation, and the opinion that the primary purpose of state and law was the preservation of property and property differentials; a conception of proportionate social and political equality, entailing a hierarchy of differential rights and duties; a vague ideal of rule by a 'natural aristocracy'; and a moderate and enlightened religious and epistemological skepticism.[27]

Cicero was not, of course, alone among ancient Greek and Roman thinkers to believe in some kind of moral equality, or to advocate liberty, the rule of law or the mixed constitution; and he was certainly not alone in his conception of social and political hierarchy or a species of 'proportionate' equality and rule by a natural aristocracy. What is more distinctive is his conception of natural law, which allows him to combine advocacy of aristocratic rule and political hierarchy with a principle of universal moral equality. This apparent contradiction would become a staple of Western political thought, especially in the early modern period, when ideas of natural human equality and the equal moral worth of all individuals were (as in the case of John Locke) accompanied by political hierarchy, and sometimes even used paradoxically (most notably by Thomas Hobbes) to justify not only hierarchy but absolute rule. Cicero, while certainly influenced by

---

27 N. Wood, *op. cit.*, p. 4.

Stoicism, developed the concept of natural law as the Stoics never did and is perhaps the first major thinker to elaborate this paradox. There are significant contrasts on this score between the Roman thinker and his classical Greek predecessors, Plato and Aristotle.

We have seen how Plato, writing in the context of Athenian democracy, challenged the democratic polis by positing a natural principle of inequality. This may not have meant that, in his view, natural inequalities among men were enough to account for the division between ruler and ruled; but that division itself was for him a natural and necessary principle, based on the partition of the soul between 'better' elements and 'worse', which is reproduced in the inevitable division of labour between those who work for a livelihood and those who govern them. Aristotle too insists that there is a universal and natural division between ruling elements and ruled, and in his ideal polis that division is reflected in the distinction between the 'conditions' and 'parts' of the polis.

Cicero has a different approach to the question of inequality. He certainly shares the views of Plato and Aristotle on the necessity of political inequality. He even has a notion of the bipartite soul, which, as we saw in Laelius's speech in the *Republic*, he explicitly translates into a principle of political and imperial hierarchy. As he makes particularly clear in *On Duties* and elsewhere, he certainly believes in a social division of labour which subordinates men in base and vulgar occupations to those who live a gentlemanly life. At the same time, he follows the Stoics in their conception of a cosmos permeated by a universal principle of reason, which not only governs the universe but resides in every human soul. This divine rational principle takes the form of absolute, universal, immutable and eternal laws, which regulate the cosmic order and establish the ethical norms of human behaviour. All human beings are, in principle, innately capable of knowing these natural laws, since they all partake of the same cosmic reason; and this innate and universal reason constitutes a universal community, a cosmopolis, to which all human beings, in all times and places, belong.

We have, of course, already encountered the kind of cosmopolitan principle that is able to coexist, perhaps even to reinforce, the distinction between rulers and ruled. But, especially when combined, as it is for Cicero, with both the bipartite soul ruled out by early Stoic theories of the cosmic order, and an unambiguous commitment to an inegalitarian political order, the Roman Republic dominated by an aristocracy, this principle appears paradoxical enough to require explanation. It could simply be dismissed as an irreducible inconsistency; but, since Cicero, more statesman than philosopher, is at pains to elaborate the concept of natural law in a way the Stoic philosophers themselves never did, it is at least worth exploring what purposes it served in the pursuit of his political aims.

Moral Equality, Political Inequality

Let us first place the question in a longer historical perspective. Western political theory did not invent the notion of human equality. Ancient Chinese philosophy, for example, has its own forms of natural egalitarianism. But Western political theory, at least at certain seminal moments in its history, confronted the very specific problem of finding ways to explain and justify domination *on the basis* of natural equality. Or, to put it another way, given the assumption of equality, it had to find ways of explaining and justifying domination as such. The notion of natural equality became a troublesome issue when and because it was coupled with a challenge to the very idea of rule and domination. As long as the principle of domination was more or less unchallenged on its own terms – whether as the mandate of heaven or even simply on the basis of tradition – it was perfectly compatible with fundamental human equality. But once the principle of domination itself was thrown into serious question, it was a very different matter. The burden of justification fell much more heavily on human inequality, as a natural basis for social inequality and domination; and in those circumstances, a notion of natural equality could represent a serious threat to dominant elites. When people questioned authority by invoking natural equality, theoretical and ideological strategies had to be devised to overcome that threat and to turn democratic ideas against themselves.

The history of this strategy begins in ancient Greece. The principle of domination was, as we saw, challenged there, in theory and practice, in particular ways that distinguished it from other high civilizations. In the community of citizens that constituted the ancient Greek polis, the principal political relation was not between rulers and subjects but among citizens. This did not mean that citizens were socially or economically equal; but landlords and peasants belonged to the same body of citizens, sharing a civic equality. This produced a new political sphere, in which deep social divisions, and class conflicts in particular, played themselves out in political terms, not just in overt struggles for power but in the daily deliberations and debates of assemblies and juries. This also meant that, probably for the first time in history, there could be a significant tension between economic inequality and political equality.

This is the context in which notions of equality presented new problems for those wanting to justify domination; and much of ancient Greek philosophy, as we have seen, was motivated by the need to deal with those problems. In challenging democracy and trying to defend a principle of social hierarchy, Plato, for instance, opted for the strategy of finding a new, supra- if not supernatural principle of hierarchy which transcended any natural equality. This seemed the safest strategy in a context where democracy was a real challenge to dominant elites. Yet the separation of civic equality and class inequality had opened up new possibilities. Until then, it had always been clear that the state represented domination, even, or especially, where men were assumed to be naturally equal. But now, the state itself – in fact, the state above all – represented equality. In spite of all existing social inequalities, all citizens were equal in their new political identity. This meant that relations of domination could be disguised in wholly new ways, if only they could be clothed in the mantle of citizenship and civic equality. This was not, of course, a simple matter; but, as we saw, something like this strategy was adopted by Alexander the Great and his successors, as they claimed the values of the polis, and even of democracy, in defence of the new imperial cosmopolis.

Propertied elites in republican Rome confronted some of the same problems as their Greek counterparts. Here too they were obliged to reach political accommodations with the lower classes to preserve social order and safeguard their own property, and here too landlords and peasants shared a political identity as citizens. But there were also significant differences between the Roman Republic and Athenian democracy, which allowed, or required, different ideological strategies. The republic was clearly dominated by the senatorial aristocracy, its dominance acknowledged even in the civic sphere; the Romans never developed a notion of one citizen, one vote but counted only group votes; the identity of citizenship did not dissolve or overshadow the division between patricians and plebeians, patrons and clients, the Senate and the Roman People; private property not only had a clearer legal definition but also a more decisive political priority; and Rome's vast territorial empire was very different from the loose network of Athenian alliances and dependencies.

As the republic disintegrated in the time of Cicero, the most urgent issue facing the senatorial aristocracy was not a threat from below but its own self-destruction. Cicero's political theory was clearly a response to this crisis of the Roman aristocracy. His perception of the crisis and its causes undoubtedly shaped his theoretical responses and may, among other things, give us some insight into his conception of natural law.

Cicero traces the republican decline to the moment of the Gracchi, as he explains in *In Defence of Sestius*. A staunch opponent of redistributive agrarian reforms and members of the ruling class who advocate them, he regards this as the moment when the golden age of the republic ended. From then on, the senatorial elite was fatally divided between those who wanted to preserve senatorial authority and ancient traditions, the *mos maiorum* or customs of their ancestors, and those who pandered to the multitude by supporting the tribunate, agrarian reforms and the rights of popular assemblies in opposition to the senate. This division between *optimates* and *populares*, which reached a peak in the Catilinarian conspiracy, remains, in Cicero's eyes, a mortal danger to civic peace and stability; and the responsibility lies squarely with the *populares*.

Cicero sets his major work on the fundamental principles of the state, the *Republic*, in the time of the Gracchi, though it is clearly a comment on his own day. The work is perhaps also, as some commentators have suggested, a response to Lucretius's *De Rerum Natura*, which was being widely read in elite circles, because Cicero seems to regard its Epicurean principles as a threat to civic life and the *mos maiorum*. In the dialogue, Cicero unambiguously aligns himself with the distinguished participants who are well-known enemies of the Gracchi. These are men whom Cicero venerates as personifications of the old traditions and the *mos maiorum*; and he holds them up as models in his own time of strife, in which the senatorial elite is driven instead by insatiable greed for power and wealth, without the constraints of tradition, noble purpose or civic duty. Cicero hopes to restore a republic marked by *cum dignitate otium*, peace or leisure with dignity – a slogan that suggests both his wish for a dignified civic harmony in which every man receives what he deserves according to his worth, and also the aristocratic aspiration to a life of leisure with dignity.

Under the circumstances as Cicero perceives them, how might the Roman ruling class be persuaded to return to the ways of its ancestors? How might they be persuaded to adopt the *mos maiorum* as their guiding principle and to restore a republic marked by civic peace and dignity, a harmonious state in which rights and rewards are properly distributed among men according to their worth, on the principle of proportionate equality, and where both the state and its ruling citizens enjoy *cum dignitate otium*?

Certain principles are obviously necessary to his purpose. What Cicero has to say about the state and property is strategically indispensable. We saw in our discussion of the Stoics that, in his view, 'it is the peculiar function of the state and the city to guarantee to every man the free and undisturbed control of his own particular property'; and we also saw how redistributive land reforms – in which 'a man who never had any property should take possession of lands that had been occupied for many years or even generations, and that he who had them before should lose possession of them' – violate the principles of equity. These passages are significant not only because they display his commitment to the sanctity of property, his dedication to the interests of the landed classes, and his strong opposition to reforms and reformers; but also because of what they suggest about Cicero's conception of the state. What is striking is not only that he attaches such importance to the protection of property as an, if not the, essential purpose of the state, but the very fact that he offers a formal definition of the state in a way that no Western philosopher had done before.

As we have seen, Rome's well defined conception of exclusive property was accompanied by a particular distinction between public and private. This invited a definition of the public sphere, specifically the state, in a way that Greek experience did not. Just as the Greeks never elaborated a clear idea of property, they never went beyond the notion of the public sphere, the polis, as synonymous with the community of citizens. The Roman Republic, and the Roman law, encouraged a perception of a clearly defined public sphere and a conception of the state as a formal entity apart from the citizens who comprised it, even distinct from the particular persons who governed them at any given moment. Cicero takes on the challenge of defining the state in a manner befitting the Roman conception of property and the relation between property and state. He does this for fairly obvious reasons. His ideal ruling class is one that combines the enjoyment and enlargement of their estates with the demands of civic virtue, and so he sets himself the task of conceptualizing the relation between public sphere and private in such a way as to maintain the sanctity of private property while stressing public duty.

At the heart of his definition is his characterization of the state as 'a union of a large number of men in agreement in respect to what is right and just and associated in the common interest'.[28] Justice and the common interest are inextricably linked in Cicero's formulation, which requires that, in all matters private and public, we should give each person his due, his *dignitas*, while preserving the common interest. To give each person his due means that everyone should refrain from injuring another without due cause, keep promises and contracts, and

---

28 *Rep.* I, 39.

respect all property, private and public. But what is due to any person depends on his worth; and Cicero leaves us in no doubt that, whatever else may determine the value of a man, wealth and birth are critical, and the life of a gentleman is worth more than that of a labourer. These principles of justice are dictated by natural law, contrary to philosophers, notably Epicureans and Sceptics, who have suggested that justice is merely conventional. There is such a thing as natural justice, argues Cicero; and it must also be reflected in customary and statutory law. If man-made laws do not conform to the dictates of natural law, they are not true law; and a state governed by such laws is not a true state.

The hierarchy of law, descending from the law of nature, is at the centre of Cicero's political theory. Law, he writes,

> is not a product of human thought, nor is it any enactment of peoples, but something eternal which rules the whole universe by its wisdom in command and prohibition. Thus they have been accustomed to say that Law is the primal and ultimate mind of God, whose reason directs all things either by compulsion or restraint. Wherefore that Law which the gods have given to the human race has been justly praised; for it is the reason and mind of a wise lawgiver applied to command and prohibition.[29]

In the *Republic*, having insisted on the universality and immutability of true law, he goes on to warn that 'We cannot be freed from its obligations by senate or people'.

By placing natural justice at the heart of his conception of the state, Cicero has certainly ascribed some kind of moral purpose to the state. Yet that purpose is impossible to dissociate from his notion of the common interest, which has less to do with any higher moral goal than with the mundane interests of property, peace, security and material well-being. In that respect, his view of the state and its purpose appears to have more in common with Protagoras than with Plato, being less concerned with the fulfilment of some higher human nature than with the normal comforts of everyday life. In the *Laws*, his praise of human rationality includes an appreciation of the practical arts not so very different from that of Protagoras; and there is even a certain similarity between Cicero's conception of justice as an innate and universal human sense, which enables people to live together in comfort

---

29 *Laws* II, 8.

and harmony, enjoying the benefits of reason and the arts, and
Protagoras's conception of the innate and universal sense of justice
and respect for others which make possible the civilized, comfortable
life of the polis.

But Cicero's political conclusions are different from those of
Protagoras. He comes down on the side of Plato and his antidemocratic
judgments on the political capacities of shoemakers and smiths. In his
speech, 'In Defence of Flaccus', this great admirer of Greek culture
reveals his strong dislike of Athenian democracy, attacking 'those
cobblers and belt-makers', those 'craftsmen, shopkeepers and all the
dregs' in the Assembly, who were the ruin of democratic Athens and
represent a salutary lesson to the Roman Republic's own brand of
demagogues. In the *Laws*, as well as other works and speeches, he
makes very clear his disdain for those engaged in menial occupations
and his utter contempt for the poor, as if they were criminals, while
heaping praise on occupations appropriate to gentlemen, such as war,
politics or philosophy, and farming or commerce on a large scale. The
ideal gentleman and political leader is the substantial landed proprietor,
and even the profits of commerce should ideally be invested in land.

It is not surprising, then, that when, in the *Republic*, Cicero surveys
the various types of constitution, he concludes that, of the simple
types – kingship, aristocracy and democracy – democracy is clearly
the worst. Democratic equality, even when the demos governs wisely,
violates the principles of justice and equity by denying men their just
– unequal – deserts: 'For when equal honour is given to the highest
and the lowest – for men of both types must exist in every nation –
then this very "fairness" is most unfair; but this cannot happen in
states ruled by their best citizens.'[30] The best type of state is a mixed
constitution, striking a balance in the class conflict between rich and
poor, which, while granting some degree of *libertas* to every man,
distributes it unequally according to the unequal *dignitas* among its
citizens. As in the Roman Republic, there is a hierarchy of social orders,
and with it a hierarchical order of political rights.

Cicero thus manages to combine what appear to be democratic
principles of arithmetic equality with an aristocratic notion of
'proportionate' equality, attributing to all men a sense of justice in
the manner of Protagoras, while identifying justice with social and
political hierarchy in the manner of Plato. Cicero sees no contradictions
between his own political principles and Plato's and presents himself

---

30 *Rep.* I, 53.

as following in the Athenian philosopher's footsteps, even down to the titles of his two major works in political theory. But he distinguishes himself from his great predecessor on the grounds that Plato's philosophy was too abstractly utopian, while his own intentions are very explicitly political and practical. It is also possible that the egalitarian dangers of the cosmopolitan idea seemed less immediate to a defender of the propertied elites in republican Rome, where their supremacy was effectively unchallenged, than a principle of equality seemed to propertied classes in democratic Athens.

It may be useful here to recall the role played by 'unwritten law' in Athenian democracy. While democrats – philosophers, dramatists or ordinary citizens – might remain wedded to the idea of universal laws, such as obligations of kinship or reverence for the gods, the relation between such laws and the *nomoi* of the polis had become an urgent practical issue in ways that put unwritten laws in question altogether, whether they were man-made or decreed by nature. We witnessed the tensions between unwritten, timeless laws and civic law in Sophocles's *Antigone*; but they were particularly visible when, after the oligarchic coup of the Thirty Tyrants, the conflicts between democrats and oligarchs prompted the restored democracy to prohibit the invocation of unwritten law because of its deeply oligarchic associations. For supporters of democracy, it was not simply a question of committing laws to writing in order to make them known to all citizens and protect them from aristocratic judges. More fundamentally, the notion of unwritten law had come to be identified with oligarchic principles of natural inequality, the idea that men were unequal by *physis*, which, in the eyes of democrats, had been rightfully challenged by civic equality. Plato, of course, was the principal philosophical exponent of this oligarchic view, especially in his identification of justice with inequality, on the basis of a higher principle of cosmic order. For his democratic opponents, unwritten law represented injustice, not justice, and men had to turn to the laws of the polis to get their just deserts. The polis and its *nomoi*, as we saw in Greek drama, had also replaced the endless chaos of blood vengeance and irrational violence. In that sense it was civic law, not unwritten laws of nature, that represented the triumph of reason and 'Holy Persuasion'.

In Cicero's conception of natural law we see something quite different. It is certainly true that his natural law included norms of behaviour that would have been congenial to democrats no less than oligarchs, as would his conception of a universal moral equality among all men. But inscribed in his universal law of nature and the transcendent laws of reason is a fundamental human inequality, which means that the principles of oligarchy are divinely ordained and superior to civic law. It is not for nothing that he regarded himself as a follower of Plato. His notion of natural law can, at least in this respect, indeed be understood as a translation of Plato's ethereal philosophy into the idiom of mundane Roman politics.

The combination of natural law and proportionate equality, as Cicero presents it, seems to come down to this: equality of obligation, inequality of rights. With his specific political project in mind, it is not surprising that the burden of natural law is 'restraint', 'prohibition' and 'compulsion' – which applies to all classes, calling upon elites to act with restraint and the people to stay in their place. In the immediate historical and political circumstances confronted by the Roman statesman, the advantages of his formula are clear. It underwrites precisely the kind of 'mixed constitution' he favours, granting all citizens a certain moral and even political status, while vesting rule in an aristocratic elite. It also has the virtue of calling an unruly aristocracy to order, reining in its excesses while respecting its property and its political dominance. Finally, although Cicero has remarkably little to say about the empire he served and from which he benefitted personally, his political formula has its uses in defending Roman imperialism, giving philosophical support to the Roman idea of a benevolent empire, in which the superior rule the inferior in the interests of both, according to the law of nature.

In this defence of empire, as in its Hellenistic predecessors, the idea of the cosmopolis is combined with, or rather derived from, the civic ideology descended from the polis. On the one hand, the Roman Empire depended in large part on the so-called municipal system, an alliance of ostensibly self-governing units dominated by local aristocracies. And, on the other hand, just as Alexander had defined his imperial rule as cosmopolitan, the idea of the cosmopolis could be translated into the 'universal' Roman Empire, which would extend Roman citizenship far beyond the borders of metropolitan Rome. Citizenship, of course, no longer meant what it had done in the democratic polis, but it was an effective ideological instrument of imperial hegemony. Eventually, that ideology would transmute the Roman imperial cosmopolis, together with the natural law that governed it, into the 'universal Church' of Christianity.

Roman Christianity: From Paul to Augustine

At least to the secular imagination, the roots of Christianity in the specific conditions of the Roman Empire seem all but self-evident. The peculiar blend that is Christian theology could hardly have been born anywhere else, amalgamating Judaic monotheism, Greco-Roman paganism, the Greek philosophical tradition, the legacy of Hellenistic kingship (and Alexander's self-deification) in the Roman imperial idea, together with Rome's universalistic aspirations and the Roman law.

The emergence of the specifically Roman Christianity that would from then on shape the tradition of Western political theory can be best understood by tracing the transformation of the Christian faith from an essentially tribal sect into a universal(ist) religion, and from a rebellious Jewish faction into an ideological bedrock of empire. The story of that transformation begins with Paul of Tarsus and culminates in Augustine of Hippo. Its essence is the creation of a distinctive universalism which allows the supreme omnipotent authority of one God to coexist with the more or less absolute temporal powers of emperors and kings, and the equality of all humanity before God with the most extreme social inequalities and rigid earthly hierarchies – not unlike the delicate balance we have already encountered in the modified cosmopolitanism of Roman Stoicism and Cicero's concept of natural law.

The doctrinal balance effected by Roman Christianity had very particular social, political and cultural conditions. It certainly presupposed the distinctive imperial blend perfectly embodied in Saul of Tarsus/St Paul, Hellenized Jew and (perhaps) Roman citizen.[31] But, while the capital of empire would move from west to east, from Rome to Constantinople, with the establishment of Christianity as the imperial religion by the Emperor Constantine in the fourth century AD, the triumph and elaboration of Pauline Christianity depended on the increasing divergence of Eastern and Western empires, which saw the emergence of a distinctively Latin theology rooted in the western provinces and reaching fruition in Romanized North Africa.

Christianity developed in tandem with the imperial state. The development of Christian doctrine, its conception of divinity and the relation of humanity to God, is inextricably bound up with the Roman imperial idea, which underwent significant changes in the first few centuries of the Christian era. As imperial state displaced the old republic and developed according to a logic of its own, the early imperial myth of the *princeps* governing in tandem with the senate

---

31 There has been considerable debate about the Roman citizenship attributed to Paul in *Acts*. But even those who question it are prepared to accept that, at the very least, he would most likely have belonged to a kind of *politeuma*, a community granted certain autonomous rights by the Roman Empire, which, if not actually amounting to Roman citizenship, enjoyed some analogous freedoms and privileges.

inevitably gave way to the emperor conceived as absolute *dominus*. At
the same time, the republican notion of empire as the product of legitimate conquests by the city-state of Rome would be replaced by a
more cosmopolitan idea of a 'supra-national world empire', in which
all peoples were equally ruled by one absolute ruler no longer centred
just in Rome.[32] It is surely not fanciful to see the Christianization of
the empire as the cultural completion of this transformation.

The Empire went through a crisis in the mid-third century, its
unity threatened by fatal fragmentation and its frontiers collapsing.
When it re-emerged for a time with new vigour, it was thanks to a
military and bureaucratic revolution, which would be completed by
the Christian emperor, Constantine, and buttressed ideologically by
his conversion of the empire to Christianity. But the consolidation
of the state bureaucracy did not mean a weakening of the imperial
aristocracy. On the contrary, it produced a new and larger ruling
class, an 'aristocracy of service', whose military and official functions
gave its members unparalleled access to wealth.[33] At the same time,
the western provinces, where the gulf between rich and poor was
growing ever wider, were increasingly dominated by the landed
aristocracy, which had amassed wealth estimated on average at five
times that of the first-century senatorial class. This also meant a
significant change in the urban culture of the empire, as the public
life of ancient civic communities gave way to inward-looking
domesticity, and aristocratic civil benefaction gave way to lavish
displays of private wealth.

Both the consolidation of the imperial state and the ascendant
aristocracy, especially in the west, shaped the evolution of Christian
theology. While changes in the imperial idea can persuasively be represented as the triumph of the Hellenistic East over the Roman West,
and eastern notions of kingship over Roman republicanism, there is
another thread in the process which belongs specifically to Western
Christianity. Byzantine 'Caesaropapism' emerged in the east, a unity
of religion and state in which Christianity acknowledged its subordination to political authority, leaving a spiritual residue of mysticism
outside the state. By contrast, the West would eventually produce its
distinctive notion of two equal powers, temporal and spiritual, each

---

32 Wolfgang Kunkel, *An Introduction to Roman Legal and Constitutional History*,
2nd edn. (transl. J.M. Kelley) (Oxford: Clarendon Press, 1973), pp. 50–1, 62–3.

33 Peter Brown, *The World of Late Antiquity: From Marcus Aurelius to Muhammad*
(London: Thames and Hudson, 1971), pp. 24–7.

with its own earthly institutions and hierarchies. The idea of two equal powers may always have been as much myth as reality, but it points to certain underlying features of the Western empire which decisively shaped its theological formation.

The sources of Western Christian dualism may be found in social and cultural conditions we have already encountered in our discussion of the Roman property regime and the distinctive public/private dichotomy that it engendered. The Romans, in their very specific social conditions, elaborated a conceptual apparatus which lent itself particularly well to apprehending distinct but coexisting structures of authority – as in their conceptions of property and state, or *dominium* and *imperium*. The same distinctions could be used to modify the principles of universality and commonality, such as those established by the Stoics, allowing the particular and private to intrude upon the universal and common.

So, for instance, Seneca (*c.*3 BC–AD 65) explicates Stoic doctrine by demonstrating how all things can be considered common, at least to wise men, while still remaining individual and private property. He draws a significant analogy with the rights of the emperor: 'all things are [Caesar's] by right of his authority [*imperio*]'; yet at the same time the sense in which everything is his by right of 'imperium' must be distinguished from the way things belong to him as his own personal property by right of inheritance, 'by actual right and ownership', or *dominium*. Seneca then goes on to apply the analogy to the gods, allowing us to trace the conceptual logic that joins the idea of divine authority to Roman conceptions of property: 'while it is true that all things belong to the gods, all things are not consecrated to the gods, and . . . only in the case of the things that religion has assigned to a divinity is it possible to discover sacrilege.'[34]

Here, then, was a way of thinking about property and spheres of authority that made it possible to insist on one universal cosmic *logos,* a universal and common natural law, the equality of all human beings, and even the exclusive supremacy of one omnipotent God; while still declaring the sanctity of private property, the legitimacy of social inequality and the absolute authority of earthly governments, including those that by any reasonable standard could be judged as defying the ethical principles of divine or natural law. It was a way of thinking that reflected the historical realities of a cosmopolitan empire, which appealed to universalistic principles to sustain its legitimacy, while

---

34 *On Benefits*, VII, vi–vii.

coexisting with, and supporting, a regime of private property of an unprecedented kind: a distinctive union of a powerful state and strong private property quite different, as we have seen, from other ancient high civilizations. Much of Roman Stoic philosophy, to say nothing of the Roman law, was dedicated to maintaining this distinctive balance, defending the claims of the state's *imperium* while consolidating the sanctity of private *dominium*. It required only minor conceptual adjustments to translate this dualistic logic, with its distinctive division between two spheres of authority, into the particularly Western Christian division of secular and spiritual realms.

The Bible attributes to Jesus himself the principle that we should 'Render unto Caesar the things which are Caesar's, and unto God the things that are God's.' Stated in this simple form, the principle is nicely consistent with Seneca's modified Stoicism. While certainly not questioning the supremacy of God, the universality of His divine law or His 'ownership' of everything in this world and beyond, it nonetheless finds room for Caesar's realm of absolute authority. God's cosmic *imperium* coexists with Caesar's earthly *dominium*, just as Caesar's temporal *imperium* coexists with the private *dominium* of the Empire's propertied citizens.

It was Paul, the founder of Christianity as we know it, who, in his defence of absolute obedience to earthly powers, began the process of translating into systematic Christian theology the doctrine of universal divinity and the spiritual equality of all human beings before God, combined with the earthly inequalities of property, social hierarchy and absolute political authority. He establishes his universalistic principles by dissociating Christianity from Jewish law, replacing the particularism of an essentially tribal religion with a transcendent moral doctrine that applies equally to all human beings, Greeks or Romans no less than Jews, and slaves no less than masters. The 'righteousness of God', he writes, manifests itself apart from any law. In this, he belongs to Hellenistic and Stoic traditions of cosmopolitanism, which he may have learned not only from Stoic philosophy but from the *Septuagint,* the Hellenistic Greek translation of the Old Testament, where the Hebrew Bible's Jewish exclusiveness is modified by a certain cosmopolitan opening to gentiles.[35] Yet Paul's universalism is a two-edged sword. On the one hand, it asserts the equal moral value of all human beings. On the other hand, it leaves completely unchallenged,

---

35 For a discussion of Paul and the *Septuagint*, see Calvin Roetzel, *Paul: The Man and the Myth* (Edinburgh: T. & T. Clark, 1999), esp. pp. 16–17.

indeed supports, the social inequalities of the temporal sphere, enjoining their acceptance, and emphatically asserts the absolute authority of the secular state:

> Let every soul be in subjection to the higher authorities, for there is no authority except from God, and those who exist are ordained by God. Therefore he who resists the authority, withstands the ordinance of God; and those who withstand will receive to themselves judgment. For rulers are not a terror to the good work, but to the evil. Do you desire to have no fear of the authority? Do that which is good, and you will have praise from the same, for he is a servant of God to you for good. But if you do that which is evil, be afraid, for he doesn't bear the sword in vain; for he is a servant of God, an avenger for wrath to him who does evil. Therefore you need to be in subjection, not only because of the wrath, but also for conscience's sake. For this reason you also pay taxes, for they are servants of God's service, attending continually on this very thing. Give therefore to everyone what you owe: taxes to whom taxes are due; customs to whom customs; respect to whom respect; honor to whom honor.[36]

This declaration of the emperor's divinely ordained authority can be interpreted in more than one way. The ideology supporting the first Christian emperor, Constantine, as spelled out by the Bishop Eusebius in his famous oration in praise of Constantine (which is hard to match in its obsequious grandiosity), would identify the emperor as God's representative, even his partner, the earthly embodiment of the divine *logos*. But as far-reaching in its consequences as this doctrine certainly was, there is in Pauline theology another theme, which would be fully elaborated only in the Christian West, in specifically western conditions: the emperor not as God's representative on earth or personification of the divine *logos* but as the (to be sure, divinely ordained) secular ruler of a fallen humanity.

It may be useful to consider the context in which Paul wrote his Epistle to the Romans and the significance his contemporaries would have attached to his assertion of universalistic, cosmopolitan principles against the particularism of the Jewish law. Apart from any other implications of Pauline doctrine, and whether a conflict between universalist 'Hellenists' and particularist 'Hebrews' ever actually took place

---

36 Romans 13.

among the early Christians, Paul's universalism had some very obvious advantages for the pagan Roman authorities and imperial elites. Christianity may have begun as a movement of the urban poor; but Paul's message to the prosperous classes was decidedly more reassuring than were, for instance, the convictions of other early Jewish Christians who, following Jesus, preached an egalitarianism not confined to the moral or spiritual sphere, repudiating materialistic values and calling upon Christians to give up their wealth to their community. Even Paul's emphasis on salvation by faith rather than works had clear advantages to those who stood to lose from strict adherence to the social Gospel.

Slavery itself was compatible with Paul's doctrine of universal equality. He calls upon servants to 'be obedient to them that are your masters according to the flesh, with fear and trembling, in singleness of your heart, as unto Christ . . . knowing that whatsoever good thing any man doeth, the same shall he receive of the Lord, whether he be bond or free.'[37] Pauline principles oblige the master to recognize his servant's moral equality by treating him well, but they represent no challenge to the institution of slavery.

Paul's most basic theological principles would also have been far more congenial to Roman state authorities than were Judaism or Jewish Christianity. At a time when rebellious Jews were resisting Roman hegemony and refusing to acknowledge the divinity of the emperor, while Jewish Christians pointedly denied the divinity of Caesar by asserting the lordship of Christ, Paul's universalistic attack on Jewish particularism, and his replacement of Jewish monotheism with a cosmopolitanism which at the same time renders unto Caesar the things that are Caesar's, nicely undercut any such challenge to imperial authority. It gave support to the secular universalism of the Roman Empire, replacing, among other things, the temporal pretensions of the Jewish law with a universalistic monotheism that, unlike the Jewish version, left Caesar's authority intact.

Pauline Christianity, in other words, effected an adaptation of universalism analogous to the changes in Stoic doctrine, which blunted its egalitarian implications and its potential challenge to existing authorities, making the doctrine more congenial to Roman elites. It might be said that, like the Roman Stoics, Paul – who was familiar with and influenced by Stoic philosophy – achieved this effect by reintroducing a kind of dualism that allowed a separation between, on the one hand,

---

37 Ephesians 6: 5–9. See also Paul's Epistle to Philemon, in which he asks a wealthy Christian to receive humanely the escaped slave whom Paul is sending back to him.

the moral or spiritual sphere, in which the cosmic *logos* dictated a universal equality, and, on the other hand, the material world in which social inequalities and even slavery prevailed and political authority was entitled to impose an absolute and universal obedience, just as masters could compel their slaves.

But Christianity required its own distinctive means of dividing the spheres of authority. For the Stoics, it was enough to acknowledge that, in the real world, not all human beings are wise, so that the ordinary earthly life of ordinary earthly men and women must be governed by some kind of practical ethics and a legalism tempered by equity. The Stoic case for Roman property, political hierarchy and empire was obviously strengthened by attempts to replace the Early Stoic monism with something like Platonic principles of rule and subordination. But for the most part, Roman Stoics, as we saw, contented themselves with concentrating on the field of ethics unencumbered by deeper speculations on psychology, cosmology or metaphysics. Christianity required something more.

There would, of course, emerge a Neoplatonist strand in Christianity, which adapted Plato's conception of a transcendent realm beyond empirical reality and posited the One, the ultimate unitary and unknowable divine reality from which all other levels of reality emanated. Platonic philosophy could, to be sure, supply a cosmic principle of rule and subordination, which could be used – as some Stoics did use it – to justify earthly hierarchies; and perhaps the idea of the One from which descending orders of reality all emanated could be invoked in support of the emperor's absolute power, for instance in the manner of Eusebius and his invocation of the divine *logos* personified in Constantine. The old Platonic opposition of sensible and intelligible worlds could also lend support to a Pauline Christian dualism. But Christian Neoplatonism was not particularly well suited to give positive support to existing social and political arrangements. It tended rather to devalue earthly existence and the material realm, and encouraged Christians to seek mystical release from it, always striving to attain the spiritual realm and assimilate the human soul to God as much as possible. This could no doubt encourage a passive acceptance of worldly injustice and in this way support existing authorities at least by default; but it did little to bolster the claims of property and state. For Christians a defence of the Roman social, political and imperial order posed a very particular challenge, in the face of a theological universalism, governed by one omnipotent God; and Western Christianity met that challenge in very particular ways.

In the final analysis, the whole Pauline structure of dual authority depended on the concept of sin. It is a striking fact that the emphasis on sin was a distinctly Western phenomenon; and while it would be foolish to explain this solely in relation to the ideological requirements of Roman hegemony, it would be no less foolish to ignore the role of sin in buttressing the principle of 'render unto Caesar'. Earthly governments and total obedience to them are necessary, according to this version of Christianity, because and only because human beings are sinful by nature. It is true that, for Paul, Christ represented salvation from the universal taint of sin, but in this life, if not the next, there was no escaping human sinfulness; and that made Caesar's authority an unavoidable necessity. The principle that human sinfulness legitimates earthly authorities, already present in Paul, would reach its full development in Augustine; and here begins a long tradition in Western political theory, which attributes the necessity and legitimacy of private property as well as earthly government to the fallen condition of humanity.

At the same time, among the earthly institutions that organize this fallen world, there is the Church – and here too the distinctiveness of Western Christianity is manifest. The focus on the role and structures of the Church belongs to the West no less than does the emphasis on sin and personal salvation. In the development of Christianity from the Eastern Roman Empire through Byzantium, the state effectively became the Church. The empire was the Church on earth, as the emperor was its head. The Western approach was different. Here, the Church was responsible for organizing the personal salvation of Christians, who could have no hope of seeing true harmony and justice in this world and who were obliged to rely on Caesar – not as sacred representative of God on earth but as profane political authority – to regulate their fallen lives.

The Church, in fact, became a parallel structure, a mirror image of the Roman state, in which religious functions were conceived as offices. Even the outlines of the Western Roman social hierarchy were mirrored in the Church, with bishops playing the part of the landed senatorial aristocracy. Indeed, the ecclesiastical aristocracy tended to be drawn from the same social source; and the episcopacy would become one of the landed aristocracy's principal institutions, a relocation of aristocratic power at a time when secular authority was crumbling.[38] Western bishops were, in fact and in conception, the product of Rome's distinctive social order, the unique autonomy of landed property and the predominance of aristocracy. They would

---

38 Patrick Geary, *Before France and Germany: The Creation and Transformation of the Merovingian World* (New York and Oxford: Oxford University Press, 1988), pp. 32ff.

continue to represent as much a secular as an ecclesiastical power; and the particular development of Western Christianity would, as we shall see in the next chapter, continue to mirror the destiny of landed aristocracies, sometimes reflecting their dominance and at other times manipulated by kings engaged in centralizing projects against aristocratic autonomy.

It is one of history's many ironies that, while the empire collapsed in the west, as the imperial state gave way to a fragmented order dominated by the landed aristocracy, it was the west that preserved Roman imperial structures and institutions, in the hierarchy of the Church. While the seeds of these developments are already present in Paul's *Epistles*, a truly Roman, Latin theology emerged only at the end of the second century. For a long time, the culture of educated Christian elites was practically indistinguishable from that of their pagan fellow citizens, with an emphasis on literature and rhetoric, in contrast to the philosophical concerns of the east.[39] It should by now be no surprise that the first major figure in the development of a distinctively Western theology, the son of a Roman centurion based in Carthage, was trained in Roman law and that, in the absence of any Latin theological tradition, he drew on the concepts and language of the Roman law. Tertullian's legalistic temperament and training may also help to explain his particular emphasis on sin; and his doctrine of original sin (he has even been credited with inventing the term), as inherited by every human individual from Adam, made each member of humankind the bearer of guilt – a doctrine perhaps particularly well suited to a theology that conceived of the cosmic relationship between God and humanity in general in legalistic terms, on the analogy of secular crime, judgment, and punishment or pardon. At any rate, Western Christianity would thereafter continue to develop under this legalistic influence. Tertullian's legalism can hardly be just the accidental consequence of his personal experience. He was surely a creature of the Western Roman Empire; and against the background of Pauline doctrine and its place in imperial history, there is nothing surprising about the reflection of Roman institutions and the Roman law in the organization and teachings of the Church.

The imperial model of church organization was also most fully spelled out in Carthage, when, in the third century, Cyprian, bishop of Carthage and a Roman citizen of noble birth, elaborated the most authoritative Latin doctrine on the hierarchy of the Church in his *De*

---

39 *Ibid.*, p. 31.

Catholicae Ecclesiae Unitate (*On the Unity of the Catholic Church*). But by far the most important product of the western empire – yet again based in North Africa – was Augustine, bishop of Hippo.

Augustine of Hippo

Augustine's masterpiece, the *City of God*, is conventionally taught in English-speaking universities as a classic of medieval political thought; but, while it profoundly influenced medieval Christianity, it is very much a product of the late Roman Empire. It is precisely his engagement with imperial realities that compelled him to break new ground, not only in theology but in political theory. In his interrogation of the relation between Christianity and empire, which took to new extremes the dualism of St Paul and his doctrine of obedience to even the most sinful of temporal powers, Augustine departed from the classical conception of the state and its moral purpose and in so doing opened new questions about political obedience and obligation.

Augustine was born in North Africa in 354, to a Christian mother and a pagan father of the curial class – the prosperous, if not aristocratic, class from which local magistrates were drawn and who were responsible for funding various public functions. After studying and teaching, first in Rome and then in Milan, and having flirted with Manichaeism and Scepticism, he finally underwent his own conversion to Christianity, which was powerfully influenced by Neoplatonism. He was particularly affected by its idea of God as spirit and the conception of evil as withdrawal from God rather than an independent malign force, but also by the belief in the possibility of attaining virtue in this life through philosophical contemplation – a belief he would later abandon. Throughout his life, he enjoyed the friendship and patronage of the Romanized aristocracy; and, after spending much of his youth in the fleshpots of Rome, he became bishop of Hippo in his native North Africa in 395.

This was the granary of the empire, a land of huge estates, worked not by slaves but by peasants, many of them dependent. Augustine's life in the late empire was a time of acute economic and social strife in the region, plagued by agricultural decline, rural unrest, popular revolts against Roman colonial rule, a polarization of the population and depopulation as peasants fled the land. Estates in Augustine's part of North Africa were increasingly dependent on itinerant labour, the social type that would, many centuries later, be described as 'masterless men' by social critics fearful of the disorder engendered by footloose labourers.

The social unrest that accompanied economic decline was aggravated by the Christianity of the African peasantry and schisms like the Donatist Church, which included some members of the educated classes and their clients but whose base of support was among the lower orders. An extremist fringe of Donatism, the Circumcellions, probably drawn from Libyan-speaking landless peasants, some renegade slaves and migratory labourers, represented not only a theological or political danger but also a social one.[40] While there has been much debate about whether the motivations of this movement were primarily social or religious, there seems little doubt that Romanized landed elites perceived it as a threat to their very way of life.

While the Donatist schism and the Circumcellion threat were part of the larger context for Augustine's hardening views on heresy and the necessity of state suppression, the immediate occasion of his *City of God* was that of barbarian raids and the sack of Rome by Alaric, king of the Visigoths, in 410. North Africa was spared Alaric's attack by a storm that turned back the invaders, and Carthage became a haven for aristocratic refugees from Rome. Among them were wealthy educated pagans who blamed the disaster on the abandonment of ancient ways, above all the repudiation of paganism in favour of Christianity. Augustine set out to demonstrate to such imperial elites that Christianity was not their enemy, that it was not inconsistent with earthly government, social order or duty to the state – or, indeed, to property and social inequality. In the process of making his case for the exoneration of Christianity, he succeeded in arguing a brief for absolute obedience to even the most unchristian of worldly rulers.

The essence of Augustine's doctrine is, again, the fallen condition of humanity and the stain of original sin. He underpins this doctrine with a particularly harsh conception of predestination. Not only are some predestined to enjoy God's grace and salvation, whatever their own acts on earth, but the separation of others from God's grace and their eternal punishment is also predestined, not a function of their own uniquely sinful acts – an extreme version of predestination that would later be adopted by Calvin but by very few others. Augustine denies that it rules out free will; and it is certainly true that the doctrine of predestination, precisely because it makes grace and punishment independent of specific human actions, has no necessary implications

---

40 See Neal Wood, 'African Peasant Terrorism and Augustine's Political Thought', in *History from Below: Studies in Popular Protest and Popular Ideology in Honour of George Rude*, ed. Frederick Krantz (Montreal: Concordia University, 1985), pp. 279–99.

for individual free will. But the fundamental purpose of the doctrine is not to resolve the conflict between the principles of individual freedom and determinism but rather to construct a foundation for his conception of two 'cities', the City of God and the earthly city.

In his earlier years, Augustine essentially shared the view of other Christians concerning the role of the Roman Empire as God's providential instrument for the Christianization of the world, in the manner proposed by Eusebius in praise of Constantine. But the disasters experienced by the western provinces, both from external threats and internal disorder, posed a challenge to such Christian optimism and put in question the position of Rome as God's chosen earthly medium of salvation. Had Augustine written the *City of God* in different historical circumstances, at a time when Constantinian triumphalism may have seemed more convincing, it might be plausible to suggest, as some commentators have done, that Augustine's most important accomplishment in that work was to 'relativize' the empire by challenging its universalistic claims. But history had already made a mockery of Rome's presumption, whether pagan or Christian; and in that context, Augustine's argument was less a challenge to Rome's imperial pretensions than, on the contrary, a new way of buttressing imperial authority without appealing to an implausible divine election.

Western Christianity, in contrast to the Byzantine East, faced very specific difficulties because of its relation to the Roman Empire. The empire in the West preceded Christianity, and after its conversion – in many eyes, because of it – seemed on the verge of destruction. The East faced no such complications. Imperial Christianity and the eastern empire were born together under Constantine, and the east did not face the same barbarian threat. There are no doubt many reasons for the theological divergences between Western and Eastern Christianity, but we should not underestimate the doctrinal consequences of their divergent relations with secular empire. While the East was able to assume the unity of empire and Christianity, Church and state, and even the subordination of the Church to the secular state, Western Christianity was obliged to deal not only with the rupture between imperial paganism and Christianity but also with the near-collapse of empire after its conversion. That precluded any easy assumptions about relations between Church and state. This affected not only teachings with immediate consequences for the understanding of divine and secular authority but even the most arcane of Christian doctrines, such as interpretation of the Trinity. Much of Augustinian theology was an attempt to come to terms with a secular authority whose Christian foundations were ambiguous and a Christianity which seemed to endanger secular order.

An essential element in Augustine's defence of Christianity against the charge that it was responsible for the calamities facing the empire was a consideration of Cicero's definition of the state, in the speech attributed to Scipio in the *Republic*, which we have already encountered: the state, says Scipio, is 'a union of a large number of men in agreement in respect to what is right and just and associated in the common interest'. Augustine rejects this definition, on the grounds that it does not conform to historical experience. Neither the Roman Republic, nor the Roman Empire (despite its many contributions to the welfare of humanity), nor indeed any other pagan state could ever fit this definition, since justice cannot exist except under the rule of God. But Augustine's objective is not to delegitimate the pagan state. On the contrary, the effect of his argument is to make it clear that the pagan state is no less a state and no less entitled to obedience than any other state on earth. It is striking that, while his discussion concentrates on pagan states and the City of God, no special status is granted to the Christian state – which, when all is said and done, is prey to all the evils of humanity's fallen condition. His purpose is not to maintain that Christian states are more entitled to obedience than pagan rulers but simply to insist that Christians cannot be blamed for the corruption of the Roman commonwealth. On the one hand, Rome was never a commonwealth in Cicero's sense because it never enjoyed true justice, so Christianity cannot be blamed for destroying the Roman commonwealth; and, on the other hand, in the transformation from paganism to Christianity, it retained the qualities of a genuine state despite the absence of true justice in both cases. There is nothing, then, in Christian doctrine which can be used to advocate disobedience to the imperial state or to promote civil disorder.

To explain the evils facing Rome, while at the same time justifying obedience to its earthly authority, required something very different from a conception of the Roman Empire as the fulfilment of God's purpose on earth. Augustine repudiated altogether the notion of Rome's Christian mission. By now, he had also given up some of his earlier Platonism, in particular his youthful optimism about the attainment of virtue by means of Platonic contemplation. Just as he lost faith in the empire's divine purpose, his hopes for human virtue were replaced by a preoccupation with humanity's innate sinfulness. Augustine also now rejected his earlier Platonist belief in the rational order of the cosmos descending from the heavens to earth, and any conception of natural law in which human law is an earthly reflection of a divine cosmic order. In place of such ideas, he proposed his doctrine of two cities.

The Augustinian idea of two cities is not easy to grasp. Although it undoubtedly owes much to the tradition of Roman dualism and its Christian adaptations, it is nothing so simple as a distinction between earthly and heavenly realms, or secular and spiritual authority. Augustine invokes various dichotomies to characterize the antithesis of divine and earthly cities: the one represents the saintly, holy, elect, pious and just; the other designates the impure, impious, unjust and damned. But, while the two are antithetical, they exist inextricably together; and both run inseparably through every human society. Augustine even rejects the distinction between the sacred and profane as two discrete spheres – so that the Church itself, while holy, is for him an earthly institution plagued like all others by the conflict between holiness and sin.

Even those who belong to the City of God must pass through the earthly city and share its tribulations; and the conflict between the two forces will go on until the end of history, when the City of God will finally triumph. In the meantime, the earthly City remains dominant, and history will remain a tragic spectacle, in which true harmony and justice can never prevail. The best that can be hoped for until the end of historical time is the maintenance of earthly peace and social order, which are no less necessary to the City of God as it passes on its earthly pilgrimage than they are to the damned while they live on this earth. Every person and all institutions, the holy no less than the transparently unholy, must therefore subject themselves to the earthly powers whose purpose is to maintain peace and order in this world – not a just or rightful order but a measure of security and physical comfort, to ameliorate the disorder that inevitably follows from the essential nature of the earthly world and the flawed human beings who populate it.

At the root of this pessimism is, of course, the notion of humanity's fallen condition and the power of sin. In this, Augustine was a true and explicit follower of Paul; and like Paul, he concluded from this that Caesar's earthly power, while not fulfilling any truly divine mission, was nevertheless providentially ordained by God. But Augustine takes the doctrine much further, systematically elaborating the reasons for obedience to a pagan emperor like Julian the Apostate, no less than to Constantine the Christian, even after the Christianization of the empire, which Paul, in the early days of Roman Christianity, could hardly have foreseen. If anything, the burden of Augustine's argument is virtually all on the side of obedience to imperial authority; and this explains even his hardening attitude, as bishop, to heresy, which has led some commentators to accuse him of fathering the Inquisition.

It may, at first glance, seem inconsistent to adopt such a repressive line towards heresy while taking as limited and pessimistic a view of what the Church can do in this world and identifying the Church itself as an inevitably flawed secular institution. The very notion of 'heresy', in fact, is, on Augustinian assumptions, theoretically problematic. But there is no mystery about it if we consider that Augustine's principal aim is to sustain the power of existing authorities and the imperial state. The effect of his doctrines was not only to uphold the authority of an imperfect Church, whose right to obedience did not depend on the personal virtues of its clergy, but also to underwrite obedience to the secular state. His notorious campaign against the Donatists, for instance, was directed against their challenge both to the Church and to the imperial power. Their doctrine of a 'pure' Church represented a threat both to a corrupt and sinful clergy and to the ecclesiastical authority of the emperor. Augustine was keen both to preserve the inviolability of the Church hierarchy and to circumvent the problem of relations between secular and ecclesiastical authority, effectively declaring the supremacy of imperial power in the absence of any possible justice on earth. By identifying the Church as a secular institution, not a distinct sphere that must be rendered unto God, he ensured that the principle of 'render unto Caesar' could not be understood as *limiting* the emperor's authority.

To understand the role of predestination in this argument, let us consider the task faced by Augustine. Here is a Christian bishop who is seeking to assert the supremacy of secular authority, as well as to preserve the social arrangements based on the rights of property conferred by the authority of kings and emperors. These secular authorities, which Christians are enjoined to obey, may include non-Christians and even the unholiest of tyrants; yet their authority applies equally to saints and to sinners. Now, it is much easier to justify the subjection of all humanity, regardless of virtue or vice, to the same worldly tribulations, or to insist on the absolute obligation to obey ungodly authority, instead of resisting it on holy principle, if grace and punishment are set apart from any human choice or action. No human being can be compelled to disobey authority or to challenge unjust institutions on the grounds of higher moral principles if such moral resistance is as futile on earth as it is inconsequential in heaven.

This was the crux of the dispute between Augustine and Pelagius, another victim of his anti-heretical zeal, who not only insisted on human free will but utterly rejected the idea of original sin and the necessity of divine grace. Adam, according to Pelagius, was certainly a bad example, but he was not the bearer of a universal guilt imposed on all humanity, just as Christ was a good example but not a necessary source of redemption from original sin. Human beings, obliged to live a virtuous life, were intrinsically capable of living without sin. The issue between these two theologians had less to do with free will itself – a problem which, as we have seen, Augustine sought to finesse – than with the underlying concept of original sin and its implications for human conduct in this world. The Pelagian heresy may seem very harsh in the demands it makes on free human beings, imposing on the individual the responsibility of a holy and ascetic life; but it challenges the realities of Roman society and the values of the imperial aristocracy in a way Augustine's theology does not. While Augustine gave comfort to a wealthy and predatory ruling class, making demands on their thoughts but not on their deeds, Pelagius exposed the immorality of wealth and was a uniquely harsh critic of Roman society. Augustine's campaigns against Donatists and Pelagians, argues his biographer, Peter Brown, together represent 'a significant landmark in that process by which the Catholic Church had come to embrace, and so to tolerate, the whole lay society of the Roman world, with its glaring inequalities and the depressing resilience of its pagan habits.'[41]

The doctrine of original sin, especially with the burden Augustine places on it, makes great demands on every aspect of Christian theology. It can, for instance, be argued that it allows no ambiguity about the full divinity of Christ. The tradition of 'heresies', such as Arianism, which denied that full divinity, might well be understood as a challenge to any strict notion of original sin, if only because they make it harder to understand how an excessively human Christ could be exempted from the universal taint. Augustine, in particular, clearly felt the need to respond to these heresies by elaborating an interpretation of the Trinity according to which the Holy Spirit 'proceeds' from both God and the Son, instead of from God alone, who conferred it on the Son. He strongly opposed the version of the Trinity more common among early Greek Christians, which seemed to suggest not only that Christ received the Holy Spirit from God but that ordinary mortals participated in the Holy Spirit in much the same way as did the Son, 'begotten' of God. The Augustinian version of the Trinity drove a wedge between ordinary mortals and a direct experience of the Holy Spirit and made

---

41 Peter Brown, *Augustine of Hippo* (London: Faber and Faber, 1967), p. 350.

them more dependent on intercession by the Church.[42] At the same time, it buttressed the doctrine of original sin which had as its corollary the obligation to obey the temporal powers of both Church and state.

It is surely significant that the schism between Eastern and Western Christianity would later come to a head over the so-called 'filioque' controversy, concerning the addition of the clause 'and the Son' to the Nicene Creed, so that the Holy Spirit was seen to proceed not only from God but from the Son. Eastern Christianity never faced the same political dilemmas as confronted the West and perhaps for that reason was not so compelled to resort to doctrines of original sin or all the theology supporting them. When Charlemagne, as we shall see in the next chapter, provoked the separation between Rome and Byzantium by insisting on the 'filioque' clause, following Augustine, he certainly had immediately opportunistic reasons for asserting the theological superiority of Rome over Byzantium; but we should not overlook the deeper political significance of such arcane doctrines in sustaining temporal powers in the West.

Augustine provides a powerful, and Christian, justification for both ungodly rule by non-Christian rulers and ungodly or unchristian behaviour by Christian emperors and kings. He not only finds a way of reconciling Christian morality with amoral earthly rule but even establishes Christianity as a way of *justifying* immoral earthly rule.

---

42 Elaine Pagels, in her book, *Adam, Eve, and the Serpent* (New York: Random House, 1988), has argued that the transformation of Christianity into an imperial religion by the conversion of Constantine was accompanied by 'a cataclysmic trans-formation in Christian thought' effected by Augustine, who replaced the early Christian doctrine of moral freedom with an ineluctable bondage to original sin, providing a justification for Christian submission not only to ecclesiastical authority but to imperial power. Christian attitudes on sexuality were part of this transformation. But these transformations were surely already present long before the conversion of Constantine, in the doctrines of St Paul, whose attitudes on sin and sexuality, no less than submission to imperial authority, prefigured Augustine's. Paul may not have transformed Christianity into an imperial religion – a change that awaited the Constantinian conversion – but he certainly made Christianity compatible with submission to imperial power, on the grounds of humanity's inevitable sinfulness. Augustine's version of the Trinity, however, was truly distinctive and took Christianity even further in the direction of submission to both ecclesiastical and secular power. Eugene Webb has argued that, by interpreting the symbols of Father, Son, and Holy Spirit in a way that made impossible the Christian's experience of participation in the filiality of Christ, Augustine took a final step in transforming Christianity into a doctrine of command and coercion. ('Augustine's New Trinity: The Anxious Circle of Metaphor', *Religious Innovation: Essays in the Interpretation of Religious Change*, ed. Michael A. Williams, Collett Cox and Martin S. Jaffee (Berlin: Mouton de Gruyter, 1992), pp. 191–214).

What makes the paradox even more paradoxical is that Augustine has put a Christian theory of political immorality in place of the old Greco-Roman pagan theories of civic virtue.

Augustine departs from the ancient traditions of Greek and Roman political theory not only in his answers but also in his questions. Greek political theory, as we saw, emerged in response to the dissolution of traditional relations between rulers and ruled and the emergence of a new form of political organization, a civic community. Its central category was citizenship, not rule and obedience, and it conceived of politics not as a relation between rulers and ruled, or masters and servants, but as a transaction among equal citizens. Antidemocratic philosophers like Plato and Aristotle, who sought to restore a relation between rulers and ruled, still felt obliged to operate within these civic categories. Plato did much to re-establish the principle of rule as the central category of political thought; and the idea of a universal cosmic hierarchy was certainly used by him and his successors (including Aristotle) to justify a permanent division between rulers and ruled. But that division was presented less as a political relation between those who ruled and those who were obliged to obey them than as a relation between a political sphere and those outside it. Plato, for instance, in the *Statesman* distinguishes between the royal art of politics and other, subordinate arts which serve the political without partaking of it. For Aristotle, the relations that characterized the polis, as distinct from other forms of association like the *oikos*, were relations among equals, while relations among unequals – between, for instance, 'parts' and 'conditions' of the polis – were not political.

The civic categories of Greek political theory persisted in Rome, even when empire replaced republic; and political theory was slow to take up the challenge posed by the renewed relations between rulers and ruled. The fact that these questions re-emerged in a context where traditional principles of domination and obedience had long been undermined by the civic relations of polis and republic, where there could be no easy assumptions about an inevitable division between rulers and ruled or about a correspondence between class inequality and political hierarchy, meant that the Roman Empire had distinctive ideological requirements in constructing a case for obedience to rule. It is true that Western political theory would not produce systematic theories of political obligation until the early modern period, when arguments had to be found to impose the obligation to obey authority on men who were naturally free and equal. But the Roman Empire broke new ground in justifying inequality and domination. We have seen how thinkers like Cicero sought to meet the requirements of justifying inequality; but no one before Augustine was so systematically preoccupied with questions of rule and obedience – and it was Christianity that provided the necessary conceptual tools.

The development of Western Christianity was, as we have already seen, shaped in very particular ways by the specificities of Greco-Roman political life. We have also seen how the special conditions of the Roman Empire encouraged a theology of sin. Augustine was preoccupied with the immediate question of Rome's decline and how, in those conditions, to explain the need for obedience to a secular authority which could no longer be plausibly regarded as the privileged agent of God's mission on earth. But obedience and obligation posed more general problems in a political culture imbued with Greco-Roman civic principles.

Imperial rule, which required obedience to one supreme ruler, meant that it was no longer enough simply to divide the social world between a political community of citizens and those outside it, as Plato and Aristotle had done. In any case, the equality of human beings before God was an essential principle of Christianity, so political rule could not be justified in Christian terms by dividing humanity between those who belonged to a civic community and those outside and subordinate to it. Within those constraints, the most effective way to justify a secular imperial authority was to abolish the civic sphere altogether. Even the passive variety of Roman imperial citizenship is emptied by Augustine of any residual substance. If the old Greek principles of political community presupposed some kind of human capacity for self-government – whether innate in all men, as assumed by Protagoras, or confined to a few, as in Plato's political theory – those civic principles could best be challenged by denying any such capacity for civic virtue or self-rule. Nothing was more aptly suited to that purpose than the Augustinian doctrine of sin.

THE MIDDLE AGES

From Imperial Rome to 'Feudalism'

'[T]here seems little doubt,' writes the eminent medieval historian, Rodney Hilton,

> that peasantries were the basis of the ancient civilizations out of which most European feudal societies grew . . . In fact, viewed from the standpoint of this most numerous class of rural society, the difference between late Roman and early medieval civilization may not have been all that easy to discern.[1]

Yet, despite this fundamental continuity, some conventions of Western culture have produced a sense of profound rupture between classical antiquity and 'feudal' society, as the western empire descended into the 'Dark Ages' after the 'decline and fall'. Enlightenment conceptions of progress and classical political economy, for instance, tended to view the Middle Ages as an interruption in the progressive development of Western civilization from its roots in classical antiquity, a hiatus that delayed the inevitable triumph of rationalism and/or 'commercial society' after their promising beginnings in the ancient Mediterranean. The natural course of history, it seems, resumed only with the Renaissance.

Feudalism, in these conventions, often appears to come out of nowhere, or at best from outside, imported into the imperial territories by barbarian invaders. When the feudal order has been presented as a synthesis of Roman and barbarian elements, the Roman past still seems to be a hollow memory rather than a living social legacy. More

---

1 Rodney Hilton, *Bond Men Made Free: Medieval Peasant Movements and the English Rising of 1381* (London: Temple Smith, 1973), p. 10.

recent scholarship has done much to correct this disconnected view of history. But the legacy of old conventions has been hard to uproot, not least because the continuities are more visible from the vantage point of peasants, and history has seldom been recorded from the standpoint of the peasantry. Even historians who are more sceptical of the 'decline and fall' as rupture, or question 'Germanic' influences, or reject the idea of a medieval hiatus by finding the roots of modernity in the Middle Ages, have sometimes tended to emphasize the void left by a dying Roman Empire, which was to be filled by a thoroughly new feudal order, whether transmitted by barbarian invasions or born out of the wreckage of empire, the chaos of social disorder and war.

The history of political thought may seem immune to these ideas of historical rupture, because the legacies of ancient thinkers, the Roman law and Christianity are so obvious in medieval culture. But the continuous history of philosophy and 'canonical' political theory, which is particularly circumscribed by the experience of dominant classes and cultural elites, is perhaps even more inclined to obscure the underlying social continuities in relations between landlords and peasants.

To emphasize the continuities is not at all to deny the social transformations that took place in the dying years of the empire and thereafter. On the contrary, the point is to observe the development of feudal society precisely as a transformation and not an alien intrusion. What is at issue here is not immobility but change as a continuous historical process. To be sure, the intruding 'barbarians' brought with them practices and institutions that would shape the feudal order; but their institutions merged with already existing social relations. Medieval social and political forms are inexplicable without reference to the specificities of Roman society or its distinctive forms of property. Nor does stressing the continuities require us to excavate a history of Western political thought derived from the utterances of peasants, a history that is simply not there to discover, even in the records of peasant rebellion. It is enough to acknowledge that landlords are what they are because of their relations to the property and peasants over whom they exercise their lordship, and medieval agrarian relations were firmly rooted in their Roman antecedents.

The concept of feudalism is often said to be of questionable value, and there has certainly been much variation in its usage. Yet there can be little doubt that developments in the western empire produced distinctive social forms without which the later history of Europe is inexplicable, and some kind of shorthand designation seems all but indispensable. For the sake of convenience, unless and until a generally accepted designation is found to replace it, we can apply the term 'feudalism', or perhaps feudal society, to these social forms, while acknowledging that there was no single feudal order unvarying throughout the West.[2]

Between the sixth and tenth centuries, the period commonly identified as the era of feudalization, the Roman Empire was replaced by what has been called the 'parcellization of sovereignty'.[3] Persuasive arguments have recently been made that the process was much more sudden than medieval historians have conventionally suggested and that there was a 'feudal revolution' only at the end of this period;[4] but whether the process was gradual or revolutionary, the imperial state gave way to a patchwork of jurisdictions in which state functions were vertically and horizontally fragmented. Domination by an overarching imperial state was replaced by geographic fragmentation and organization by means of local or regional administration, perhaps in the form of contractual arrangements within the ruling class, between kings and lords or lords and vassals – though these arrangements could take many different forms, and the very existence of vassalage has been put in question.[5] This administrative, legal and military patchwork

---

2 For an important discussion of feudalism and specifically differences between England and France, see George Comninel, 'English Feudalism and the Origins of Capitalism', in *The Journal of Peasant Studies*, July 2000, pp. 1–53.

3 Perry Anderson, *Passages from Antiquity to Feudalism* (London: Verso, 1974), pp. 148ff.

4 There have long been fluctuations between histories of feudalism that insist on continuities and those that emphasize more revolutionary transformations. A case for a 'feudal revolution' was made by T.N. Bisson in *Past and Present* in 1994 ('The "Feudal Revolution"', *Past and Present* 142, February 1994, pp. 6–42), which generated a debate among several historians in subsequent issues (152, August 1996, and 155, May 1997). Among the participants was Chris Wickham, who, with some reservations about Bisson's argument, judiciously and persuasively defended the idea of a 'feudal revolution'.

5 Susan Reynolds, in particular, has argued that the concept of vassalage is virtually meaningless, while even the concept of 'fiefs' is too vague and variable to be very useful (*Fiefs and Vassals: The Medieval Evidence Reinterpreted*, New York and Oxford: Oxford University Press, 1994). The argument here, as will be explained in what follows, in no way depends on the existence of vassalage or, indeed, on the notion of fiefs. Reynolds has also taken issue with arguments that, in her view, attribute too much importance to intellectual constructs, including the revival of ancient Greek philosophy, in constituting social and political relations in the Middle Ages. She emphasizes 'traditional bonds of community' and communal practices established long before, and independently of, such ideas. It should already be clear that this criticism cannot apply to the concept of feudalism employed in this chapter.

was generally accompanied by a system of conditional property, in which property rights entailed jurisdictional and military service.

This is not the place to consider whether, or to what extent, feudalism was a product of Germanic influences – even if it were possible to identify any single 'Germanic' entity or culture. It is, however, misleading to imagine invasions of the Roman Empire by more or less pristinely 'Germanic' tribes, emerging more or less untouched from the forests of the north. The interactions between the Romans and the 'Germans' go much further back than the late mass migrations commonly regarded as 'barbarian invasions'. These included long-standing relations of exchange, which served to aggravate social differentiation within the German tribes and to destabilize relations among Germanic communities themselves, provoking constant warfare and increasing militarization. By the time their incursions into Roman territory became a decisive factor in determining the fate of the empire, the Germans were already deeply marked by their long interactions with Rome.

There has been considerable debate about whether relations between landlords and peasants should be included in the definition of feudalism. At one extreme is the argument that relations between seigneurs or manorial lords and their dependent labourers cannot be called feudal, because feudalism has to do not with domination and dependence but with contractual relations among juridical equals – at least among people of lordly status, even if some owed service to others. At the other extreme is a definition of feudalism entirely based on relations among landlords and peasants, which is sometimes applied not only to the specifically Western medieval forms of peasant dependence but to any type of agrarian exploitation by means of rent-extraction. Both these extremes seem unhelpful.

On the one hand, it should go without saying that feudal lords, however we define them, depended for their very existence on their relations with peasants. Wherever there were lords, there were peasants whose dependent labour sustained them. On the other hand, a diluted definition of 'feudalism', which embraces any kind of relationship between landlord and peasant, obscures the specificities of agrarian relations in the medieval West. What is distinctive about the Western case is the exploitation of peasants by lords in the context of parcellized sovereignty – with or without the relations of vassalage. The concept of 'feudalism' is useful because, and to the extent that, it draws attention to this distinctive formation.

In the very particular unity of economic and extra-economic power that emerged in medieval 'Europe', economic relations of appropriation were inextricably bound up with political relations, as they had been in ancient bureaucratic states. But, in sharp contrast to those ancient civilizations where subject peasants were ruled by monarchical states, the feudal state was fragmented by parcellized sovereignty; taxation by the state gave way to levies collected by lords and appropriation in the form of rent; and lordship combined the power of individual appropriation with possession of a fragment of state power. Lordship, which constituted a personal relation to property and command of the peasants who worked it, took over many of the functions performed in other times and places by the state. The effect was to combine the private exploitation of labour with the public role of administration, jurisdiction and enforcement. This was, in other words, a form of 'politically constituted property', a unity of economic and extra-economic power, which presupposed the uniquely autonomous development of private property in ancient Rome.

In the preceding chapters, there was some discussion of property relations in ancient Greece and Rome, emphasizing their distinctiveness when compared to other 'high' civilizations. Property in land was more thoroughly separated from the state than in the 'bureaucratic' kingdoms where it tended to be closely bound up with state service. In such kingdoms, peasant producers were subject to surplus extraction less in the form of exploitation by individual private proprietors than in the form of collective subjugation to an appropriating, redistributive state and its ruling aristocracy, typically in the form of taxation and compulsory services. In Rome, private property developed as a distinct locus of power in unprecedented ways; and peasant producers were more directly subject to individual private appropriators, who extracted surplus labour in the form of rent. These developments, as we have seen, were reflected in the Roman law, which formally recognized the exclusiveness of private property and elaborated a distinction between two forms of domination, the ownership of property and the power of state rule, the powers of *dominium* and *imperium*. The conceptual elaboration of these two distinct foci of power would have enormous implications for the development of political theory.

When a massive imperial state did emerge, with its own bureaucracy and system of taxation, it was already fundamentally different from the other imperial or monarchical states of antiquity. Even at the height of the empire, the primary form of appropriation by dominant classes was not through state office by means of taxation but the acquisition of land and direct exploitation of the labour that worked it, whether peasants or slaves. Landlords and peasants confronted each other more directly as individuals and classes, as distinct from rulers and subjects, while imperial governance itself depended on a network of local landed aristocracies, especially in the western empire. This mode of imperial rule had the effect of strengthening property, in contrast to other ancient states which impeded the full and autonomous development of private property or propertied classes independent of the imperial bureaucracy. When the empire adopted the expedient of paying for military services by grants of land, this property in land preserved the attributes of Roman ownership.[6]

The existence of two poles of power, the state and private property, meant that there was a tendency to fragmentation at the very heart of the imperial state. When the empire disintegrated – precisely in the west, where state rule existed in tension with aristocracies based on huge landed estates – aristocratic autonomy would continue to grow, even when some form of public power continued to exist. The devolution of public functions to local lords occurred even where monarchical powers succeeded, at least for a time, in their attempts to recentralize the state. Monarchies typically depended, to varying degrees but always unavoidably, on territorial aristocracies which exercised functions – judicial, administrative and military – formerly belonging to the state.

---

6 An interesting but, in my view, flawed argument has been proposed by an eminent historian of late Rome and the Middle Ages, Chris Wickham, who has more recently modified his view but without completely replacing what seem to me its most problematic aspects. In his original formulation, he invoked the notion of the 'tributary system', in which surplus extraction takes place by means of taxation, and contrasted it to feudalism, in which surplus extraction takes the form of rent instead of tax. ('The Other Transition: From the Ancient World to Feudalism' and 'The Uniqueness of the East', originally published in 1984–5 and both republished in *Land and Power: Studies in Italian and European Social History, 400–1200* (London: The British School at Rome, 1994). The tributary system includes the bureaucratic redistributive kingdom as I have described it here; but in Wickham's view, it also includes the 'ancient' form exemplified by Greece and Rome, in which the city rather than a central monarchical state is the tax-extracting entity. The Greco-Roman case was distinctive, he argues, also because the tributary form coexisted with 'feudalism'. The transition occurred, he suggests, when the tensions between these two coexisting modes of production led to the decline of the tributary element (in particular, the imperial state) and the growing predominance of the feudal form. I find this account problematic for several reasons: each category, the 'tributary' and the 'feudal', is far too undifferentiated and explains very little – especially because any relations of rent-extraction between landlords and peasants are called 'feudal', which tends to obscure the particularities of Western landlord/peasant relations, while any form of taxation appears to partake of the 'tributary' form. The approach is more taxonomic than historical, positing two modes of production with no historical beginning and no internal dynamic that might help to explain the transition – the 'feudal' form is simply there and, in its tension with the 'tributary form', there is no apparent reason for its eventual predominance; and above all, this approach fails to capture the specificity of the 'ancient' form. It is not enough

Even when, in the eighth century and thereafter, the Franks, especially under Charlemagne, restored some kind of unity and order to the chaotic remnants of the Western empire, creating their own large imperial dominion, the Frankish realm was administered by regional counts, while newly conquered territories were controlled by local military strongmen. This fragmented administration continued even after Charlemagne's coronation in 800 as *Imperator* in the Roman manner, which appeared to revive the universal empire. The so-called Holy Roman Empire which ensued would, in the centuries that followed, even aggravate the conflicts of fragmented jurisdiction, adding yet another claim to temporal authority, in an already combustible mix of lordly, royal and papal authority.

Kingship in the medieval West was always characterized, in varying degrees, by a tension between monarchical power and lordship, between centralized and local authority. This tension would produce uniquely Western conceptions of rule, in which a resolution between competing

---

to say that the tributary form here was different because the city was the tax-extracting entity or even to say that it coexisted with 'feudalism'. The point, at the very least, is that the city and even the empire, with their systems of taxation, were themselves already shaped by the uniquely autonomous development of private property. The city-state of the Roman Republic was constituted by specifically Roman relations between landlords and peasants, and the empire that grew out of it presupposed the development of a historically unique landed class.

More recently, Wickham has replaced his distinction between tributary and feudal *modes of production* with a distinction between two types of *polity* or state: one based on taxation and the other on land. This distinction has certain advantages over the other, but it is still far from characterizing the specificities of the Roman tax-based state and the differences between it and, say, a tax-based state like imperial China, where the relation between state and landed property was significantly different. For that matter, it is difficult to do justice to the divergences between the Western and Eastern Roman empires without acknowledging such differences in their state/property relations. In the east, the imperial state was typically superimposed on already existing and highly developed state structures. In the west, where no such structures had existed, the development of aristocratic landed property – and its centrifugal effects – went much further, and it was here that the empire disintegrated. In any case, except in some ahistorical taxonomy, there probably has never existed a simple land-based state, in opposition to a tax-based state. Wickham's model for the land-based form seems to be the fragmentation of the state or 'parcellization of sovereignty' based on a hierarchy of landed property which emerged in feudal Europe (he cites the great historian of feudalism, Marc Bloch, as the scholar who has best analyzed it); but that feudal form surely presupposes the distinctive development of Roman property and Rome's landed aristocracy, as well as the Roman imperial state, with its system of taxation. Wickham's own magisterial and persuasive analysis of the early Middle Ages confirms this, yet his conceptual framework tends to obscure it.

claims to authority was sought not by asserting the simple and unambiguous predominance of central over local power but rather by invoking some kind of mutuality, an agreement between two legitimate forces conceived in contractual or, eventually, constitutional terms.[7] It is hard to imagine how such a dispensation could have emerged without the distinctively Western development of property as an autonomous force in tension yet in tandem with the state.

After the end of the ninth century, there was, in effect, no sovereign state, if the hallmark of state sovereignty is legislative power (as distinct from the application of existing law). Some public institutions, particularly certain kinds of courts, continued to exist; but there was effectively no legislation at all for two centuries, except for changes in customary law. The disintegration of Western Frankish rule in the tenth century left local castle lords in command, while the east, particularly Germany, was controlled by powerful duchies. By the early eleventh century, even the functions of public courts fell into the hands of local lords, with regional counts appropriating jurisdictions not as public offices but as private property. If any legal and political order existed in these regions, it has been said, the only sector of the population that remained subject to any social discipline was the peasantry, under the control of individual lords. [8] Aristocratic autonomy now truly became the parcellization of sovereignty.

To put it another way, the public or civic sphere completely disappeared. This was so not only in the sense that the state apparatus effectively disintegrated but also in the sense that public assemblies in which free men could participate, of a kind that survived throughout the Carolingian realm, no longer existed.[9] Clear distinctions between free men and slaves gave way to a complex continuum of dependent conditions. The category of 'free' man effectively disappeared in the former Frankish empire, where even owners of free land might be subject to seigneurial jurisdiction and feudal obligations, while the

---

7 See Janet Coleman, *A History of Political Thought: From the Middle Ages to the Renaissance* (Oxford: Blackwell, 2000), p. 18, for a discussion of the peculiarly Western resolution of tensions between local and central authorities.

8 It is argued, in *The Cambridge History of Medieval Political Thought: c.350–c.1450* (Cambridge: Cambridge University Press, 1988) that the coincidence of lordship and ownership, which made peasants both tenants and subjects at once, applied throughout the West, including England (p. 195). As we shall see, however, the English case was exceptional, because the coincidence of lordship and ownership did not take the form of parcellized sovereignty in the way that it did on the Continent.

9 I owe this point to George Comninel.

concept of slavery was overtaken by a spectrum of dependence, in relations between lords and 'their' men.

By the thirteenth century, more firmly established feudal monarchies restored effective systems of administration. This was also a period when the Holy Roman Empire, now led by German kings, achieved its greatest power as a central European state, while the papacy was asserting its own authority in the temporal domain. Yet even then, although the feudal subjection of peasants to lords was eased to some extent, the autonomous powers of lords, with their administrative and jurisdictional challenges to royal authority, would remain defining features of the medieval order. When a public realm and spheres of civic participation re-emerged, it typically took the form of corporate entities, internally self-governing yet bound by charters defining their corporate relation to superior authorities. Far from resolving the old jurisdictional conflicts, the new configuration of power in the later Middle Ages created even more virulent contests, with seigneurial and corporate claims to autonomous jurisdiction vying with, and intensified by, the powers of emperors and popes.

There were, to be sure, patterns of social order in Europe other than the characteristically 'feudal' relations between landlords, peasants and kings, even at the height of feudalism. Where urban concentrations had survived the collapse of the Roman Empire, and where landholding patterns produced a larger proportion of free peasants as distinct from serfs, the seigneurial system was comparatively weak. This was true in northern Italy, where towns had remained relatively strong, and the legacy of the Roman municipal system was more persistent. Just as towns had been the social and political domain of Romanized local elites, who effectively governed the surrounding countryside, the city continued to be the administrative centre of the secular and ecclesiastical authorities that carried on the legacy of Rome. A typical pattern was administration by bishops who preserved something of the Roman Empire and its municipal government, though this relatively unified civic administration increasingly gave way to a more fractured system of governance by various corporate entities and guilds. While the imperial elites had been overwhelmingly landed classes, in medieval Italy – especially from the beginning of the eleventh century – there emerged a powerful urban patriciate. Some of the urban communes became prosperous commercial centres, with dominant classes enriched by commerce and financial services for kings, emperors and popes. Collectively, they dominated the surrounding countryside, the *contado*, extracting wealth from it in one way or another, not least to sustain the public offices that, directly or indirectly, enriched many members of the urban elite.

Much confusion has been generated by historical accounts of feudalism that identify commerce with capitalism, treating money and trade as inimical to feudal relations. Yet money rents were a prominent feature of relations between landlords and peasants, while commercial transactions – typically, in luxury goods – were very much a part of the feudal order.[10] The thriving commercial centres of northern Italy may have stood somewhat apart from the seigneurial system, but they served a vital function in the larger European feudal network, acting as trading links among the segments of that fragmented order and as a means of access to the world outside Europe.

Nor did these cities escape the parcellization of sovereignty. While other parts of Europe were experiencing feudalization, municipal administration was undergoing its own fragmentation. The communes became and remained, in varying degrees, loose associations of patrician families, parties, communities and corporate entities with their own semi-autonomous powers, organizational structures and jurisdictions, both secular and ecclesiastical, often in fierce contention with each other and in battle among warring civic factions. A lethal ingredient in this mix was the intrusion of papal and imperial powers. Even while civic communes were to a greater or lesser extent autonomous from larger temporal authorities, they were often fierce battlegrounds in those wider power struggles, which played themselves out as vicious factional rivalries within the civic community – what would come to be known as the conflict between Guelf (papal) and Ghibelline (imperial) factions; typically, but not necessarily, corresponding to divisions between merchant classes and landed *signori*.

Interpretations of medieval 'republicanism', especially conceived as a foretaste of political modernity, can be misleading not only because cities with effective civic self-government were essentially oligarchies, but also because they never constituted a truly united civic order, with a clearly defined public sphere detached from private powers of various kinds. In moments of more effective republican government, greater efforts were made to unite the civic community; but no medieval Italian commune ever succeeded in transcending its inherent fragmentation or the fusion of public power with private appropriation. The triumph

---

10 The view that capitalism emerged when and because the expansion of trade destroyed feudalism was decisively challenged in the so-called 'Transition Debate', sparked in the early 1950s by a debate between Maurice Dobb and Paul Sweezy, followed by a discussion among several other Marxist historians. (*The Transition from Feudalism to Capitalism*, introduction by Rodney Hilton [London: New Left Books, 1976]).

of more despotic oligarchies did not represent a major rupture with republican forms but belonged to the same dynamic of what we might call urban feudalism. Nor did their attempts to extend and consolidate their own rule truly overcome the feudal fragmentation of governance. Even the most centralized of 'Renaissance' states in post-medieval Italy would continue to be divided by party, privilege and confused jurisdictions.

The most notable exception to the feudal breakdown of state order in the West was England, with significant implications for later European development and for the history of political theory. Although the collapse of the Roman Empire in Britain seems to have produced a breakdown of material and political structures more catastrophic than anywhere else in the West and a more drastic discontinuity with Roman forms, in Anglo-Saxon times a process of state-formation was already well advanced, with kings, landlords and church hierarchy working in tandem to produce an unusually centralized authority. While France was disintegrating, the English forged a unified kingdom, with a national system of justice and the most effective administration in the Western world. There also began to emerge a new kind of national identity – 'the Anglo-Saxons', and later 'the English'.

Anglo-Saxon kingdoms were certainly administered with the help of local aristocracies who had considerable powers; yet local lords governed – in principle and even in practice – not as autonomous regional counts but as partners in the royal state from which their administrative authority derived. In England there would emerge a distinctive relation between central government and the lesser nobility. Local elites, with considerable local authority, would govern not as feudal lords but in effect as delegates of the royal state, and not in tension with the central state but in tandem with the rise of a national Parliament as an assembly of the propertied classes ruling in partnership with the Crown.

In the eleventh century the Normans would bring with them elements of Continental feudalism, but the feudal parcellization of sovereignty never took hold in England as it did elsewhere. The Norman ruling class arrived, and imposed itself on English society, as an already well organized and unified military force and consolidated the power of its newly established monarchical state by adapting Norman traditions of aristocratic freedom to Anglo-Saxon traditions of rule.

It is certainly true that lords of the manor in England had substantial rights and jurisdictional powers over their tenants; but the centralized power of the monarchy remained strong, and a national system of law and jurisdiction emerged very early, in the shape of the common law, the king's law. The development of the English monarchy was, and continued to be, at bottom a cooperative project between monarchs and landlords.[11] Even when open conflict and, indeed, civil war erupted between king and aristocracy, the stakes had less to do with a contest between centralized government and parcellized sovereignty than attempts to correct imbalances in the partnership between monarchs and lords. The baronial challenge to monarchy in the documents that make up Magna Carta, for example, can certainly be construed as an appeal to reinstate some kind of feudal right; but, while barons may have been demanding that they should have the right to be tried by their peers in their own courts, they were not asserting their own jurisdiction over other free men. Unlike their counterparts in France, where seigneurial and royal jurisdiction would long continue to be regarded as in conflict with each other, English barons were claiming their rights at common law, that is, as rights deriving from the central state. The barons took that state for granted hardly less than did the king himself; and this would continue to be true in every episode of conflict between the monarchy and propertied classes, up to and including the Civil War and the Glorious Revolution of the seventeenth century.

The relative strength of the centralized state in England, however, did not mean the weakness of the landed aristocracy. In significant ways, the contrary is true. There emerged a cooperative division of labour between the central monarchical state and the landed class, whose power rested not on fragmented sovereignty but on its command of property. It is true that the Roman system of property, like the Roman state, suffered a more complete disruption in England than elsewhere in the former empire; but, just as effective central administration was re-established in England more quickly than elsewhere, a strong and exclusive form of property would emerge in England as it did nowhere else.

English property law would, on the face of it, become the most 'feudal' in Europe. This was so in the sense that here, as nowhere else in feudal Europe, there were no exceptions to the principle of 'no land without its lord', and there was no allodial land. Yet the paradox of English 'feudalism' is that the condition for the complete feudalization

---

11 For a discussion of relations between aristocracy and monarchy in the process of feudal centralization in England, in contrast especially to France, see Robert Brenner, 'The Agrarian Roots of European Capitalism' in ed. T.H Aston and C.H.E. Philpin, *The Brenner Debate: Agrarian Class Structure and Economic Development in Pre-Industrial Europe* (Cambridge: Cambridge University Press, 1985), esp. pp. 253–64.

of property was the centralized monarchy, together with its law and courts – not parcellized sovereignty but, on the contrary, its absence. If all land had its lord, it was only in the formal sense that the monarch was conceived as the supreme landlord. Yet, in practice, tenements held directly, in common law, under the jurisdiction of the king – including certain types of humble property held by tillers and free-holders who owed no military service and were free of lordly jurisdiction – constituted private property more exclusive and less subject to obligations to an overlord than anything that existed on the Continent, despite (or in some ways because of) the growing dominance of the common law in preference to the Roman law.[12] Monarchical rule and exclusive private property, in other words, were developing together.

For all the feudal trappings of English property, and the departures of the common law from the legal traditions of Rome, private and exclusive property would develop more completely in England than in any of the Continental states where Roman law survived and where the parcellization of sovereignty prevailed. In England, the total breakdown of the Roman imperial order may have had the paradoxical effect that, when the Roman legacy was reintroduced from the Continent – not only by the Norman Conquest, but even before, by Anglo-Saxon kings availing themselves of Continental legal expertise – the regime of exclusive private property was more forcibly implanted and rigorously imposed.

---

12 It should be emphasized here that the development of the common law in England and its relation to the establishment of exclusive rights of property was not, as is often suggested, the simple transition from feudal relations of mutuality under feudal law to individual and exclusive property rights in common law, defensible in a common, national court. (See, for instance, Coleman, *op. cit.* p. 616). The common law had its roots in Anglo-Saxon England and thus preceded 'feudalism', so that when the Normans brought feudal law from the Continent, it was implanted in the context of an already established common law. It is also important to recognize that the possibility of defending property rights before a national court, as existed elsewhere in Europe too, did not in itself represent a negation of feudal property. In France, for example, when peasants had the right to defend their property in royal courts, property was still held on feudal principles, with attendant obligations, and each seigneurie continued to have its own system of law and its own autonomous jurisdiction. Nor did the fact that the land might be alienable change the feudal obligations associated with it or the right of the seigneur to interpose himself in the transaction. It is misleading to suggest that, by the late Middle Ages, property both in England and on the Continent was well on the way from feudal to capitalist, simply because property rights were increasingly defensible at law, before a national court. Quite apart from the misleading conflation of absolute property with capitalism, the fact remains that property in England developed in ways quite distinct from other European cases, and even with its feudal trappings was more 'absolute' and exclusive than anywhere else.

Nonetheless, despite this significant exception, parcellized sovereignty continued to be a dominant theme in medieval European history. It is true that, by the end of the twelfth century, more or less stable political administrations began to re-establish themselves in various parts of Europe, either in the form of monarchical states or as autonomous urban communes. The classics of medieval political philosophy belong largely to this later period, and are preoccupied not so much with tensions between feudal lords and monarchical states as with conflicts among kings, popes and Holy Roman emperors. Nevertheless, even as kings contended with ecclesiastical and imperial hierarchies, monarchs would continue to rely on, and compete with, the lordly jurisdictions of landed aristocracies; and corporate entities of one kind or another continued to assert their autonomy against various claims, secular and ecclesiastical, to a higher unified sovereignty.

In all these cases, the question of legal and political sovereignty was always inseparable from tensions between the authority to govern and the power of property; and political conflicts were often conducted through the medium of controversies on property rights. In the feudal unity of property and jurisdiction, institutions claiming legal or administrative powers of any kind were inevitably obliged to confront competing rights of property; and questions about the relation between *imperium* and *dominium* were bound to pose themselves with special urgency.

Church, State and Property

Christianity added its own distinctive features to the complexities of feudal governance. The division of labour between Church and state which had emerged in the Roman Empire would be shaped by the disintegration of the imperial state and the medieval tensions between seigneurial and royal power. The effects of parcellized sovereignty are strikingly apparent in the development of Christian doctrine.

The classic statement of the division between secular and spiritual power was written in the late fifth century by Pope Gelasius. Although it was intended to deal with a very specific problem at a particular moment of schism between East and West, it would continue throughout the Middle Ages to be the *locus classicus* of Western Christian doctrine on the relation between the two spheres. In a letter to Emperor Anastasius in Constantinople, conventionally entitled *Duo Sunt*, Gelasius defended the Roman Church against the imperial claims of Byzantium by insisting on the superiority of the spiritual over temporal power:

There are two powers, august Emperor, by which this world is chiefly
ruled, namely, the sacred authority of the priests and the royal
power. Of these that of the priests is the more weighty, since they
have to render an account for even the kings of men in the divine
judgment. You are also aware, dear son, that while you are permitted
honorably to rule over human kind, yet in things divine you bow
your head humbly before the leaders of the clergy and await from
their hands the means of your salvation. In the reception and proper
disposition of the heavenly mysteries you recognize that you should
be subordinate rather than superior to the religious order, and that
in these matters you depend on their judgment rather than wish to
force them to follow your will.[13]

This manifesto nicely reveals the paradoxes at the heart of Western
Christianity in its relation to secular power. Its assertion of spiritual
superiority could be, and certainly was, invoked to support the temporal
authority of popes. Yet it not only presupposes the duality of power
but, like Pauline doctrine, it can also – and perhaps even more readily
– be understood as leaving the secular power essentially in command
of this world, while relegating the Church to an elevated sphere beyond
the daily practices of governance. The message seems to be that the
'two swords' which govern the world should be wielded by two different
hands, and the sword of temporal power should be rendered unto
Caesar. But, as the empire disintegrated, Christianity was obliged to
adapt to new conditions. The relation between secular and ecclesiastical
authority became more complicated, especially when the institutions
and doctrines of the Church were elaborated by the Franks as a supplement to state administration.

   An essential element of the Carolingian strategy for dealing with
an extensive empire in the absence of a central state power adequate
to the purpose, and dependent on regional lords to administer order,
was to mobilize Christian religion as a unifying force and a discipline.
Charles Martel's principal strategy in consolidating his rule was to
use the Church hierarchy and episcopacy, with all its property and
perquisites, as a means of countering the challenge of aristocratic
autonomy by creating a friendly aristocracy of his own. He also
established an alliance with the papacy, largely in order to detach
Christianity from local loyalties (including reverence to local saints)
which had helped to sustain regional lords opposed to his centralizing

---

13 J.H. Robinson, *Readings in European History* (Boston: Ginn, 1905), p. 72.

project. This alliance between papacy and monarchy or empire would later, of course, become deeply problematic and the conflict between them a central theme of Western political thought; but at this stage it was congenial to both these temporal powers.[14]

Charlemagne would continue to mobilize the ecclesiastical apparatus to sustain his own rule. This meant, above all, that Christian conversion was imposed and enforced by the sword, and that he sought to make religion uniform throughout his realm. His religious strategy required, among other things, a literate clergy; and this requirement was not the least important motivation in the cultural renaissance conventionally attributed to his reign. It also meant that Christian dogma and ritual were made to encompass all aspects of life with increasingly complex liturgical forms, placing an increasing emphasis on sin and on the correctional, disciplinary role of religion.

Charlemagne's reign was responsible for entrenching certain fundamentally Augustinian doctrines in Western Christianity, and in so doing, bringing about the final schism between East and West. This is not the place to canvass the debate on the arcane question of the 'filioque' clause (discussed in the previous chapter); nor can we judge to what extent the Frankish insistence on including this clause in the Nicene Creed was, as is often suggested, simply an opportunistic move in the struggle between the Franks and the Byzantine East, branding as effectively heretical the Eastern Greek interpretation of the Trinity, in support of a strategy to establish the Frankish empire as the true Rome. But it is at least worth considering that, for Charlemagne as for Augustine before him, the filioque clause might have had the added advantage of reinforcing the doctrine of original sin and the necessity of obedience to prevailing authority.

The state administration was supplemented by the Church bureaucracy, from bishops, the Church aristocracy, down to lowly priests who were conceived as a means of transmitting the royal will to peasants.[15] The clergy was just as much a part of the state's administrative hierarchy as were regional counts. It is not surprising, then, that Carolingian rule is often described as theocratic, not only because its claims to legitimacy relied on its association with the Church and

---

14 For a discussion of this strategy, see Patrick Geary, *France Before Germany: The Creation and Transformation of the Merovingian World* (Oxford and New York: Oxford University Press, 1988), esp. pp. 212–20.

15 On the distinctive role of the Church in the Carolingian state, see the *Cambridge History, op. cit.*, esp. pp. 220–1.

mutual obligations in the community of faith but also because the state apparatus was so dependent on the clergy. Yet it seems fruitless to ask whether Carolingian kingship was more 'theocratic' than 'seigneurial' or 'feudal' and more useful simply to acknowledge the complexities of the medieval order in the West, the inevitably tense collaborations between monarchs and lords, and the role of the Church in the contests between them.

However much relations between Church and state would fluctuate throughout the Middle Ages and beyond, the doctrinal effects of Christianity's administrative and correctional function would remain deeply ingrained in Christian theology. At the same time, the fragmentation of secular authority and jurisdiction would be aggravated by the parallel structures of ecclesiastical power and property. Although Carolingian rule represented a partnership between Church and secular state, it was bound eventually to increase tensions between them, precisely because it confirmed the Church itself as a temporal power. These tensions would be felt throughout our period. When, in the later Middle Ages, monarchical states consolidated their rule, they were increasingly challenged by ecclesiastical authority, especially by the growth of papal government and papal claims to a 'plenitude of power'. The division of labour between secular and spiritual spheres, which may have seemed a relatively simple matter in relations between the Roman Church and Caesar, was implicated, in ever more intricate ways, in the complex contestations between kings, emperors, popes, and various other autonomous powers.

As conflicts between royal or imperial and ecclesiastical authority became more intense, the doctrine of Gelasius was developed accordingly, with wide-ranging implications not only for ideas on Church and state but also for other aspects of political theory. Successive popes went beyond the Gelasian division of labour between secular and spiritual authority to assert the temporal superiority of ecclesiastical power far more unambiguously than Gelasius himself had done. At a particularly critical moment in the eleventh century, Pope Gregory VII set out to deprive kingship of any remaining sacral or theocratic elements, bolstering papal claims to a plenitude of power by asserting that kings were simply secular, and above all removable, officials. He skilfully turned Germanic notions of elective monarchy against the German emperors themselves, insisting that the suitability of candidates for royal office was a matter for papal approval, with the ultimate sanction of excommunication.

Later popes would go even further in consolidating the Church as a governmental power, with jurisdiction not only in spiritual matters but in the public domain. It is significant that this issue played itself out in theories of private property, elaborated by civil and canon lawyers as well as philosophers. The spiritual role of the Church had to do with the inner being, the soul, of every Christian, while ecclesiastical authority in the public sphere, its jurisdiction over mundane and material matters, was identified with its control of wealth and property. The vast wealth of the Church could become the basis of a claim to temporal authority on the grounds that it was held on behalf of the whole Christian community. It was a short step from this assertion of temporal power over the material well-being of the Christian community to the claim that ecclesiastical authority trumped that of the secular state. Defenders of papal authority would, for instance, argue that *dominium* or ownership of the Church's temporal goods resided in the Christian community as a whole and that therefore the ecclesiastical establishment which administered the vast wealth of the Christian community – that is to say, exercised jurisdiction over it – was in effect a governmental power, wielding coercive force on behalf of the faithful in pursuit of the common good, just as secular governments purported to do on behalf of their own subject communities. Ecclesiastical jurisdiction thus challenged the jurisdiction of secular powers on their own terrain. Claiming to be acting in the common good of the whole Christian community, for both its spiritual and temporal benefit, the papacy could claim superior authority.

The final conceptual step was taken by Pope Boniface VIII, at the beginning of the fourteenth century, in conflict with Philip IV of France over the very temporal matter of taxation. Declaring the pope's plenitude of power in the most uncompromising way, his papal bull, *Unam sanctam*, proclaimed the unambiguous superiority of papal authority over every temporal power, the spiritual sword over the secular. Pope Boniface clearly overstepped the mark and lost his battle with the French king. Others might have been more circumspect in asserting papal authority; but, once relations between secular and ecclesiastical powers had been cast in the terms of competing jurisdictions, it would have been only a matter of time before one pope or another made something like this conceptual move.

We should not take it for granted that the battle between ecclesiastical and secular powers was bound to take this jurisdictional form, nor should we assume that conflicts between competing authorities inevitably implicate conceptions of property. That such conflicts expressed themselves in these terms in medieval Europe speaks to the very particular relation between state and property in Western development and conceptions of power defined by the duality of state and property. The preoccupation with, perhaps even the conception of, jurisdiction presupposes the kind of boundary disputes generated by parcellized sovereignty and the overlapping claims associated with it. Parcellized sovereignty, in turn, presupposes the autonomous development of property in classical antiquity and the emergence of aristocratic power grounded in landed property, as against the public power of the state. The various overlapping and contending jurisdictions of feudalism were all shaped by that original duality of power. A bureaucratic state in which authority is delegated from the centre and the boundaries of office are well defined – imperial China comes to mind – may generate its own conflicts between emperors and local officials. But these disputes are of a different kind and need not produce a legal apparatus designed to negotiate contesting and overlapping jurisdictions or, indeed, the discourse of jurisdictional disputes. This kind of legal and discursive apparatus is distinctively Western.

The feudal parcellization of sovereignty, then, produced a very particular need to negotiate jurisdictional disputes in theory and practice; but the idea of jurisdiction in the West would not have taken the form that it did without the legacy of Roman property, and the history of Western political theory would continue to be shaped by the relations between property and state inherited from Rome. In the empire, as we saw, the distinction between *imperium* and *dominium* was relatively clear, representing two distinct forms of power, public and private, in varying degrees of tension depending on the claims asserted by the imperial state against the rights of private property. The legacy of Roman property survived the parcellization of sovereignty; but as the imperial state gave way to fragmented jurisdictions, there were corresponding changes in the concept of *dominium* and its relation to governmental power, changes already underway in the complex relations between the imperial state and 'barbarian' kingdoms. While feudal lordship certainly presupposed the autonomous development of property and landed aristocracies in ancient Rome, the complete and exclusive ownership suggested by *dominium* could not accommodate the conditional property of feudalism. Nor could the distinction between *imperium* and *dominium* adequately capture the unity of appropriation and governance in the 'politically constituted property' of feudal lordship. Changes were needed on both sides of the duality.

On the one hand, the line between *dominium* and possession could no longer be so clearly drawn. The Roman law in classical times had provided for rights in property short of absolute ownership, so that possession or usufruct could be separated from legal ownership. Medieval adaptations of the Roman law were obliged to go further in blurring the line between ownership and possession to allow for conditional and overlapping rights in property. On the other hand, the feudal unity of private property and public power meant that the sphere of public governance could no longer be easily defined in the terms of the Roman *imperium* or the distinction between public sovereignty and private property, or for that matter, in terms of the dichotomy of public and private at all. In conditions of parcellized sovereignty and politically constituted property, the powers of government did not belong only to public officers of a central state. Jurisdiction could be exercised by authorities without *imperium*, or authorities apart from, and indeed opposed to, the secular state; or it could even be vested in the property rights of lordship in which private rights and public powers were united. Jurisdiction could belong to landlords or popes no less than to emperors or kings. The distinction between *dominium* and *jurisdictio* did not require a clear separation of private property and public power; yet, while it allowed for the unity of property and government, it did not rule out a distinction between *dominium* and administration or control – so that, for instance, the ecclesiastical establishment could exercise jurisdiction over Church property, which in principle belonged to the *dominium* of the whole Christian community.

The question of property opened a series of disputes across the whole range of political theory and practice. The confusions of possession, use and ownership involved in feudal property inevitably raised questions about the relations among them, in particular whether people with acknowledged rights of use could claim, simply by virtue of use, the kind of mastery implied by *dominium*. If effective ownership could be derived from use, did this mean that property was a kind of natural right, independent of law and convention? Or was property a right conferred by civil government, entailing only such rights acknowledged by law, and their attendant obligations?

Property rights were an issue for secular rulers seeking ways to assert their public authority over claimants to autonomous powers without denying them their rights of private property. For the Church, matters were even more complicated; and it was here that debates about the nature of property were most systematically pursued. The Church's own vast properties, as well as the private possessions of the faithful, had to be defended. Ecclesiastical authority also had to be asserted against secular power; and, as we saw, the concept of property could be mobilized to that end. Yet the Church was also confronted with internal opposition to its own great wealth, which stood out in provocative contrast to the poverty of Christian multitudes.

This was particularly true with the rise, in the twelfth and thirteenth centuries, of 'heretical' sects who denounced the ostentatious wealth and corruption of the Church. This, in turn, gave rise to the new mendicant orders whose self-imposed poverty was meant, among other things, to defend Catholic orthodoxy against such heresies. The poverty of the mendicant orders then required explanation: did it represent a challenge to property itself, or was there a way of reconciling 'apostolic' poverty with rights of property? Since mendicants made use of material goods to sustain themselves, were they effectively asserting rights to property; or was use, in this case as in others, distinct from ownership? Beyond that lay questions about the moral order ordained by God: must Christians assume that the existing disposition of property and power on this earth, whatever its apparent evil, is divinely ordained and, in that sense, 'natural'; or can there be a conflict between temporal realities and a divinely ordained moral order?

In ancient Rome, there had been varying views on the right of property, but in general Roman jurists regarded property as a convention established by states and enforced by civil law. In the late empire, the Church fathers, notably St Augustine, had proposed a resolution that would continue to be influential throughout the Middle Ages and beyond. Both government and property, according to this doctrine, were necessary evils after the Fall. This meant that, while property was a human convention created and enforced by the state, its function in maintaining peace and social order, like the function of government itself, was sanctioned by divine authority. It followed that apparently inequitable dispositions of property and power could command the acquiescence of Christians, just as Caesar could command their obedience.

In the later Middle Ages, the Franciscan order required something more to sustain its commitment to apostolic poverty. St Francis, the son of a merchant family, appeared to take a fairly extreme view, making no allowance for individual property among the brethren and repudiating commercial transactions. Such an extreme separation from the commercial economy that surrounded them at least in medieval Italy, and on which their survival depended, could hardly be sustained; and Franciscan thinkers found ways of demonstrating that use could be separated from ownership. The theologian and philosopher Duns Scotus (1266–1308) in particular argued that, in the state of innocence, all things had been used in common. This meant that common use was ordained by natural law. But common use did not entail common ownership, since everyone was only entitled to use what was necessary without excluding use by others. It followed that use and ownership were separate; and no form of ownership, let alone private property, could be regarded as natural – even if the complex relations of civil society required the institution of property in order to maintain the peace and civil order.

The Franciscan doctrine of poverty generated debate both about the question of property and, more generally, about relations between ownership and jurisdiction. This, as we have seen, had wider implications for relations between Church and state, papal authority and secular power. The Franciscans adopted the view that, since God gave the world to humanity for its common use, no one, neither individual nor corporate entity, could claim rights of ownership grounded in nature. Both ecclesiastical and secular powers could never do more than administer property as stewards. In the first instance, this principle could be construed as giving an advantage to ecclesiastical authority, if only because, since both ownership and jurisdiction derived from God rather than from any temporal power, the pope, who represented Christ on earth, could effectively claim to act on behalf of the true owner and to exercise superior jurisdiction, while other authorities, both secular and ecclesiastical, enjoyed only jurisdiction delegated by the pope. For all, or most, practical purposes, then, the jurisdiction of the papacy amounted to *dominium*.

The Dominican order would take issue with the Franciscan argument. On the one hand, Dominicans (most notably Thomas Aquinas) argued that use could not be separated from ownership, and that a transfer of use amounted to a transfer of ownership. On the other hand, they insisted on the separation of ownership and jurisdiction and denied that there was any sense in which either secular or ecclesiastical authorities could claim effective ownership or *dominium* over the property that they administered. We shall look at the Dominican argument more closely in our discussion of Thomas Aquinas, and at the Franciscan case as elaborated by William of Ockham. For the moment, it suffices to say that, while the Franciscan position seemed at first more congenial to papal authority, by the early fourteenth century it would be treated as a threat and even a heresy. The commitment to apostolic poverty, and all the arguments constructed to sustain it, came to be seen as a challenge to the Church establishment, with all its vast wealth. Dominican counter-arguments would then find papal favour, and Thomas Aquinas would eventually be canonized.

The strongest argument against the Franciscan position was laid out in Pope John XXII's papal bull, *Quia vir reprobus*. The pope maintained that God's *dominium* over creation was analogous to human *dominium* over earthly possessions, that this was true before the Fall as well as after, and hence that property was indeed natural. Furthermore, use and ownership could not be separated. Only ownership could justify the consumption of goods – that is, in effect, their destruction – because only owners had the right to destroy their own possessions; and even the use of non-consumable goods required a *right* to use.

Medieval debates about the right of property would continue to shape the development of Western political theory. In the fourteenth century and thereafter, the issue would be complicated by the various crises of feudalism, from the plague to peasant rebellions, which would bring about 'transitions' from feudalism to other economic and political forms. Yet we must resist the temptation of thinking that efforts to clarify the conception of property in the late Middle Ages represent a transitional moment from feudal property relations to capitalism. If anything, it was the realities of feudalism itself that demanded a systematic clarification of property. The need was more urgent precisely when and where the complexities of feudal jurisdiction were most powerfully at work: where there was a consistent blurring of lines between property and public power, or between ownership and possession, to say nothing of the needs of the Church in administering its massive wealth.

It is even arguable that precisely where feudal relations of parcellized sovereignty were weakest – that is to say, in England – the feudal idea of property could be preserved, at least in formal law. English property law may have been, in formal principle, the most 'feudal' in Europe, but it comfortably adapted itself to forms of private property that were unusually exclusive and free of feudal obligations. In much the same way, a systematic theory of sovereignty in later centuries would emerge first in France, where a centralizing monarchy was doing battle with parcellized sovereignty, not in England, where the reality of central sovereignty was already well established and there seemed no pressing need to devise a formal doctrine.[16]

---

16 When Jean Bodin in the sixteenth century elaborated his conception of absolute sovereignty in *Six Books of the Commonwealth*, he was not expressing the reality of a clearly sovereign monarchy in France but confronting the challenge posed to monarchical centralization by the autonomous powers of the nobility and corporate bodies. These were very evident in the Wars of Religion when provincial nobles mobilized Huguenot doctrines in support of their powers against the king.

Religion, Philosophy and Law

Ecclesiastical institutions inherited from imperial Rome belonged to the essential fabric of the medieval legal and administrative order, and the disciplinary doctrines of the Church were an indispensable tool in maintaining social order where the institutions and coercive force of public authority were not enough. But if the legacy of antiquity remained alive in medieval Christianity, Christian doctrine posed its own specific problems in the reception of ancient philosophy. The Greco-Roman legacy was transmitted not only by Roman Christianity and the traditions of the Roman law but, in the wake of Muslim conquests, by the Islamic revival of ancient Greek philosophy. Inevitably, the transactions between philosophy and theology took different forms in the various religious traditions; and this meant that the reception of the classical legacy was determined by the distinct and sometimes mutually exclusive doctrinal requirements of the three monotheistic faiths, Jewish as well as Christian and Islamic.

For all three of them, the central issue in negotiating relations between religion and philosophy was the status of law. Their most striking commonality was, as one commentator has put it, 'a divinely-revealed religion, the appearance of Greek political philosophy within a community that is constituted – either wholly or in its highest aims – by divinely-revealed Law, and the disagreement or conflict between the demands of the divine Law and the political teaching of the philosophers.'[17] All three religions would also accept the classic distinction, most notably outlined by Aristotle, between practical and theoretical sciences, and, in general, the superiority of the theoretical. But their conclusions about the connections between divine and secular law, and hence between theology and philosophy, inevitably differed. To be sure, there were many variations on this score among Christian thinkers themselves, as there were among Muslims and Jews. Yet in one crucial respect, Western Christianity as a whole differed in its very essence from the other two. This difference, which grew out of the very particular experience of Christianity as a product of the Roman Empire, would be elaborated in medieval theory and practice, adapted to the multi-layered fragmentation of authority in feudalism.

Both Islam and Judaism were distinguished from Christianity by their belief in a single divinely revealed system of law, encompassing

---

17 Eds Ralph Lerner and Muhsin Mahdi, *Medieval Political Philosophy* (Ithaca: Cornell University Press, 1972), p. 1.

the whole range of human practice, secular as well as religious. Christianity, by contrast, had been transformed from an essentially Jewish cult into a 'universal' Church and an imperial religion precisely by distancing itself not only from the old Law of Judaism but from the very idea of a single all-embracing religious law applied without distinction to both matters of faith and the mundane practices of everyday life. The 'universal Church', in other words, was born out of the distinction between Caesar and God and a conviction that each had his own proper sphere. The effect, perhaps indeed the purpose, of this distinction was to legitimate Caesar's claims – that is, the claims of the secular state – as the dominant temporal authority and as a source of law. At the same time, it gave theology its own exalted status, as, at least in principle, the highest form of knowledge, uniquely grounded in divine revelation.

Christian doctrine was capable of underwriting the obligation to obey even the most irreligious and sinful secular power, while still imposing rigid demands in the domain of faith. This did not necessarily preclude the invocation of religious principles to *oppose* this or that secular power; but, however much the boundaries between the spheres would be disputed in medieval Europe, the defining principle of Western Christianity remained the rendering unto Caesar and God their respective domains of law and obedience. Indeed, in the absence of that principle, which recognized both the support that each sphere derived from the other and the ever-present tensions between them, there would have been no such boundary disputes. The battles, theoretical and practical, among multifarious claims to temporal power in the medieval West cannot be understood without it.

Christianity's distinctive dualism had significant theoretical consequences. It meant, among other things, that theology as a distinct form of knowledge, sustained and enforced by its own institutional base in the Church, encountered very specific dilemmas when confronting classical political philosophy. It is certainly true that the early doctrines of the Church were already shaped by the classical legacy, from Platonic cosmology and Aristotelian epistemology to Ciceronian ethics; but classical political philosophy, and especially its Aristotelian revival in the thirteenth century, posed its own particular challenges. The Church was obliged to consider not only whether there were doctrinal incompatibilities between theology and philosophy but whether philosophy was intruding into its own theological domain, whether boundaries of authority were being dangerously crossed, and whether – or when – the principles of faith obliged them to draw an inviolable line. Various answers were, to be sure, compatible with Christian doctrine. It was possible, for instance, to construct a philosophy, as Thomas Aquinas notably did, that combined theological reflections with theories about human political organization and law, even raising questions about the connections between divine and civic law, or where the boundaries between them lay. Yet, however capacious Christian doctrine may have been, it remains significant that the question of connections and boundaries was there to be asked.

Islam, which had no institutional power comparable to the Christian ecclesiastical establishment and no such autonomous power specifically devoted to policing theology, seems to have found it easier to accommodate philosophy without drawing lines between its proper sphere and the realm of theology. To be sure, the unity of the law could lead to the complete delegitimation of philosophy and all the secular sciences. Yet it was also possible, while remaining true to Islam, to acknowledge that reason and faith could reach the same truths by different means, without provoking boundary disputes. Since there was only one law and only one source of legal authority, there was no reason to regard philosophy as a dangerous temporal rival. It could be treated as another route to the same eternal truths revealed by religion, the latter accessible to anyone, the former only to an intellectual elite. Philosophy and the secular sciences could be pursued on their own merits.

At any rate, because there was no possibility of conflict between two legal authorities, the relative virtues of philosophy and religion did not take the form of a jurisdictional dispute; and the question of incompatibility between philosophical teachings and Islamic law was a matter for jurists, not for theologians protecting their own authoritative turf. There were certainly Islamic thinkers who insisted on the dangers of philosophy; but philosophy could be defended on equally Islamic grounds, even to the point of giving it priority – as was famously done by the great Arab philosopher, Ibn Rushd (Averroes) whose commentaries on Aristotle were a, if not the, major resource for Christian thinkers like Aquinas.

A distinguished and high-ranking legal scholar and jurist, as well as a physician and philosopher, Ibn Rushd (1126–98) was born in Cordova. Apart from a period of disfavour and banishment (later revoked), he served the Almohad dynasty in North Africa and Moorish Iberia. In his *Decisive Treatise* he lays out the relation between the religious law and philosophy, arguing his case as if before a court of law, and using the Islamic law as his standard of judgment. He not only concludes that the two are compatible, and that the attacks on philosophy current in his day have no basis in Islamic law, but even hints that philosophy is inherently superior as a means to the truths at which religion aims. But since the rational and demonstrative methods of philosophy can only be understood by the few, religious methods of persuasion are the best means of approximating the truth for the benefit of the multitude. Religion and philosophy, then, can and must coexist in fruitful alliance.

It is significant that Ibn Rushd, while he was certainly taking issue with a strong Islamic current, was not speaking as an anti-Islamic outsider but as a defender of the Almohad rulers' patronage of philosophy. Although this argument is sometimes dismissed as a tactical ploy on the part of a fundamentally anti-religious rationalist and defender of philosophy, it seems more useful to acknowledge its fundamental compatibility with Islam. A not dissimilar argument had been made earlier by al-Farabi (870–950), often called by Muslims the founder of philosophy in the Islamic world, who distinguished between those who arrive at truth through their own intellect by means of demonstration (as in philosophy) and those, the 'vulgar' multitude, who are given access to the truth by means of persuasion and imaginative representation, the methods of religion. Ibn Rushd's argument can perhaps be understood as giving the last word to philosophy when religious principles are found to be incompatible with demonstrable truth, and this might be taken as an attack on religion. But, whether or not we accept at face value his insistence on accommodation between the two approaches to truth, the important point here is that for Islam, theology did not have the same exalted claims to superiority, even infallibility, conferred on Christian dogma by a powerful ecclesiastical establishment; so there was no reason embedded in Islamic doctrine to regard theologians as better interpreters of truth, even of religious truth, than philosophers.

Ibn Rushd has been credited with an almost modern secularism and rationalism; but we cannot capture the flavour of medieval Islam and the contrasts with Christianity without acknowledging the ways in which the Muslim religion itself encouraged the reception of classical philosophy, as it promoted science. To treat Ibn Rushd's approach as simply secular, opposed to Islamic religiosity, may be to impose on Islam a distinctively rigid Christian dichotomy: it is as if, when philosophy crosses jurisdictional boundaries, it can only be justified by rejecting religion altogether. In fact, even the concept of Averroism as applied to those, including Christians, who believed in a 'double truth' and the separation of philosophic and religious worlds, is based on a dichotomy that certainly does not appear in Averroes himself and is arguably alien to Islam. No such dichotomy was required by Islamic doctrine.

However much today's Islamic fundamentalism appears to rule out the kind of open-mindedness available to medieval Muslims, it is a striking fact that Islamic religious doctrine could in some important ways afford a greater intellectual flexibility than did Christianity. The other side of the same coin may be that Christianity, precisely because it so jealously guarded the sphere of theological authority in the division of labour between state and Church, produced its own negation in a kind of anti-clericalism that was alien to Islam. But as attractive as the anti-clerical mentality may be to committed secularists (including the author of this book), we have to be aware of the contrasts between Christian theological rigidities and the freedom of Islamic thought in the Middle Ages.

It may be that philosophy appeared less threatening to Islamic authority at least partly because the Arabs had only limited access to classical *political* thought, while other aspects of philosophy did not challenge the law so directly. It is also possible that the Platonic political philosophy available to them was better suited to Islamic purposes. Although Ibn Rushd was a great admirer and interpreter of Aristotelian ideas on science and philosophy, his exposure to Greek political theory, like that of Arab scholars in general, was mainly through Plato; and he wrote a commentary on the *Republic*, which he felt able to recommend to his fellow Muslims without much reservation. Perhaps he would have taken a different view of Aristotle's *Politics*, which was not available to him. In that classical text, the civic culture of the polis figured more prominently than it seemed to do in Plato's deeply anti-democratic work; and that might have made the *Politics* less congenial than Platonic texts, where the division of rulers and producers was so sharply defined.

It is even possible (though there is no evidence to support such a presumption) that, quite apart from the contingencies of availability, the more obvious dangers of Aristotle's civic philosophy help to explain the absence of the *Politics* from the Islamic canon. Perhaps the Platonic conception of rule conformed better to the aspirations of the caliphate, while the feudal parcellization of sovereignty made it easier for Western Christianity to absorb, or at least to finesse, the civic principle inherited from classical philosophy. Perhaps the clear Platonic division between ruler and ruled was less important in the medieval West, where the ostensibly settled relation between ruling elements and their subordinates took second place in political thought to conflicts among the various claimants to rule; or maybe the Aristotelian notion of 'political' rule was more easily adapted to an idea of secular kingship subject to secular law than to a notion of rulers descended from a divinely inspired prophet.

At any rate, the approach to the relation between religion and philosophy in medieval Latin Christianity was deeply rooted in the institutional dualism of feudal society. The same dualism is reflected in the distinction between civil and canon law, which has no analogue in Islam or Judaism; and it is characteristic of medieval political thought that much of it was conducted within and between these two legal discourses, by their respective experts. The Latin Christian duality, as we shall see in our discussion of Thomas Aquinas, was also at work in the concept of natural law, which plays a central role in Western political theory but is completely absent from Islamic political philosophy.

Redefining the Political Sphere

Up to this point, we have dealt with medieval ideas about government, property and jurisdiction without systematic discussion of any major political thinkers. The complexities of medieval governance, as we have seen, meant that such ideas were discussed in a variety of discourses, especially legal and theological, other than political philosophy as the ancient Greeks and Romans had understood it. This was especially true at the height of feudal fragmentation of the state. The reconsolidation of government in the later Middle Ages was certainly a spur to political philosophy; but even then, while there was a wealth of innovative legal and theological reflection on matters of power, authority and jurisdiction – reflections in some ways more immediately engaged with the concrete practicalities of governance than Greek and Roman political theory had been – it is significant that there were very few, if any, original contributions to specifically *political* theory on the order of the ancient or early modern classics. Medieval thinkers, especially with the translation into Latin of Aristotle's *Politics* in the thirteenth century, certainly adopted the classical tradition of political philosophy with great enthusiasm and inventiveness; but what was most inventive was their adaptation of that tradition, with its well defined political subject, to a very different setting, not easily captured by the political discourse of classical antiquity.

It was not simply a matter of extending ancient political theory to encompass a wider variety of political forms, city-states, kingdoms and empires distinct from the ancient Greek polis. The point is rather that medieval social arrangements were so different from ancient forms that they were not readily comprehended in the theoretical language of Aristotle's political philosophy. It can, indeed, be argued that one of feudal society's defining characteristics was the virtual disappearance of a clearly distinct political sphere of the kind conceptualized by Aristotle. Even in the later period, when centralized states were establishing firm roots, the complexities of legal and administrative order, the confusions of parcellized sovereignty and complex spheres of jurisdiction, the elaborate network of consensual or contractual relations, meant that the boundaries of the 'political' were ill-defined and fluid. The laborious reasoning of canon and civil lawyers was better suited to accommodate these complexities than was classical political philosophy.

To say this may seem to run counter to some widely accepted views about the strength of the civic principle in medieval Europe. It certainly raises questions, as has already been suggested, about the tendency to treat the political theory of the medieval commune as the precursor of modern republicanism – an interpretation we shall submit to closer scrutiny when we consider Marsilius of Padua, whose *Defensor Pacis* is often read as a pioneering republican tract. For the moment, let us consider a more general suggestion put forward by a distinguished historian of political thought, who argues that medieval political theory and practice, at least when compared to ancient Rome, were more, rather than less, attuned to active citizenship and the civic community:

> Medieval political theorists and practitioners were to take literally and then transform the maxim of late Roman law that 'what touches all should be approved by all' (*quod omnes tangit ab omnibus tractari et approbari debet*), wrenching it out of the context in Justinian's *Codex* where they found it, and thereby emphasizing a deliberative participation by the 'people' in consenting to the laws. Furthermore, the people would be declared capable of electing removable public officials as the executive government . . . This was something of which the ancient Romans . . . would never have approved because 'the people' for them were never considered to be a deliberative body.[18]

'[M]edieval jurists', the argument continues, 'gave preference to the substance of citizenship rather than simply to the abstract principles of Roman legal rules'; and this preference derived from 'the peculiar contractual genesis of medieval city communes, where the citizen was an active rather than a passive member of the city.'[19]

The contrast suggested here between medieval conceptions of active citizenship and the passive variety devised in ancient Rome does point

---

18 Coleman, *op. cit.*, p. 6.
19 *Ibid.*, p. 8.

to certain significant differences between them. The Romans certainly invented a new conception of passive citizenship when they conferred a civic identity on their imperial subjects, and even the Roman people themselves never exercised the deliberative functions of the Athenian demos. Whatever doubts we may have about the medieval civic community (which will be explored in what follows), it is certainly important to acknowledge distinctively Western conceptions of rule by consent and how they are rooted in the medieval experience, with its unique dependence on contractual arrangements of various kinds. It is also true that these conceptions implied distinctive notions of participation in sovereignty which suggest a kind of active citizenship absent in ancient Rome. Yet it is no less important to recognize how such notions of consent, or ideas about participation in the feudal distribution of sovereignty, differed from ancient Greek notions of active citizenship and the civic community. A comparison between medieval and ancient conceptions should not disguise the ways in which medieval forms of parcellized sovereignty shifted political discourse away from what the Greeks in particular regarded as 'political', and away from citizenship as its principal subject. This was true, as we shall see, even in the urban republics of northern Italy, where the city commune was particularly strong.

In previous chapters, we explored the conditions in which political theory emerged in ancient Greece. We saw that the civic sphere of the polis, where the citizen was the essential political agent and political relations were relations among citizens, not between rulers and subjects, presupposed specific social conditions distinct from others in the ancient world. The democratic polis represented a case perhaps unique in pre-capitalist history in which a propertied class for various historic reasons had neither the military nor the political predominance required to sustain its property and powers of appropriation. Unable to impose an unambiguous dominance, it depended on political accommodations with subordinate classes. The reforms of Solon and Cleisthenes, as we saw, were designed to manage class relations in the absence of a clear class dominance, creating a civic order where appropriators and producers confronted one another directly as individuals and as classes, as landlords and peasants, not primarily as rulers and subjects. This also created an unprecedented juxtaposition of, and new tensions between, economic inequality and civic equality.

In the new civic sphere, deep social divisions played themselves out in political terms, not simply in overt struggles for power but in the deliberations and debates of assemblies and juries. This was the setting in which the theory and practice of active citizenship emerged, as a means of comprehending and negotiating a very specific configuration of social power and the very specific conflicts it engendered. While the classics of ancient Greek political theory were written by philosophers who had no great love for the civic unity of rich and poor, their ideas were inevitably shaped by it. Even an antidemocratic thinker like Aristotle, in his philosophical reflections, followed in the tradition of Solon and Cleisthenes by considering what kind of civic accommodation between classes could save the polis from the social conflicts that threatened to destroy it.

The constitutive social relations of feudalism precluded the kind of civic accommodation that underlay the ancient polis and political theory. Relations between landlord and peasant depended on precisely the kind of juridical inequality ruled out by ancient Greek citizenship – or, indeed, Roman republicanism, for all its oligarchic limitations on the civic role of lesser citizens. The economic power of feudal landed aristocracies, their access to the labour of peasants, was inseparable from their extra-economic status and privilege, their political, military and jurisdictional powers. Lordship was economic and political at once. This meant that a civic identity uniting the appropriating and producing classes in one political community in the way landlords and peasants, as well as craftsmen, were united in the ancient polis – or even in republican Rome – would, by definition, have been the end of feudalism.

Theories of government in the medieval West, then, did not concern themselves with a civic relation between landlords and peasants; but nor was their principal theme a relation between rulers and producers. The constitution of relations between feudal lords and peasants as essentially a nexus of rulers and producers was taken as given, and the relation between classes ceased to be the central subject of political discourse. The questions addressed by political theory revolved around the nature and location of rule itself, together with relations among the various competing and overlapping claims to rule. Even when the ultimate power was said to derive from 'the people', this principle was invoked to support the claims of one ruling power – kingly, imperial or papal – against another. Conceptions of consent or popular participation in sovereignty could be mobilized as instruments of rule by those who claimed their own authority on the grounds of popular consent; but they could also be employed even more ingeniously – not to say cynically – to challenge the legitimacy of a competing power by questioning its consensual authority, as we saw in the case of Pope Gregory's challenge to European kings and Holy Roman emperors.

Even to the extent that feudal relations were relations among equals, they were not political transactions among citizens but the contractual agreements among, so to speak, fragments of the state, the bonds of mutual obligation that organized parcellized sovereignty. It is certainly true that various corporate entities, from guilds to civic communes, might practise self-government within their particular spheres; but it cannot be said that the internal transactions of corporate bodies, even the deliberative practices of the civic commune, were the principal subject of political philosophy. We may accept that questioning the right to rule and making it dependent on some form of consent represented, in principle, an advance in the development of accountable government; but the fact remains that the emphasis here was not on active citizenship but on the right to rule.

Ideas of active citizenship as conceived in classical antiquity would, later in the development of Western political theory, be replaced by conceptions of passive, indeed tacit, consent. In their more benign forms, these notions of consent simply extended the principles of medieval corporations, grounded in Roman law, according to which the corporate whole could be bound by the decisions of the few who represented it. But the early modern idea of consent, whether corporate or individual, could be compatible even with absolute monarchy (most notably in the work of Thomas Hobbes), and with notions of sovereignty deriving from 'the people' in which the people, however narrowly conceived, played no effective part at all. Such notions of consent and sovereignty owed more to medieval (and, indeed, imperial Roman) conceptions of rule than to ancient ideas of active citizenship. People whose political role was as passive as this might just have been accepted as 'citizens' by, say Augustine; but, by Aristotle's standards, they would have been 'conditions', not 'parts', of the polis.

How far removed medieval political discourse was from the classical vocabulary of political theory is nicely illustrated by a mistranslation of Aristotle in the first complete translation of the *Politics*. William of Moerbeke (c.1215–86), apparently at the instigation of Thomas Aquinas, translated the whole of Aristotle's works into Latin, including, in about 1260, the *Politics*. His mistranslation of one important passage would be taken up with significant consequences by St Thomas himself, among others. It is significant not simply because it exemplifies the contingent effects of one man's ambiguous translation but rather because it expresses the medieval understanding of politics itself.

We have alluded in previous chapters to Aristotle's distinction among different forms of rule. There is, for instance, the kind of rule exercised over men in servile conditions; but there is also a 'political' kind of rule among free men, in which political equals govern and are governed in turn. What makes this form of rule 'political' is that it occurs in, and only in, a civic community, a community of citizens of intrinsically equal status, all of them entitled to participate in rule. There is a certain ambiguity in Aristotle's conception of 'political' rule and whether it can apply to all forms of polity, from democracy to monarchy – whether, in particular, a monarchy can be 'political'; but what is clear is that rule can be political only among men who are free and equal, in principle capable of ruling as well as being ruled. In Aristotle's ideal polis, where the civic community is limited to the rich and well born and where that community rules over subordinate producing classes excluded from citizenship – that is, a polis that distinguishes between the 'parts' of a civic community and the 'conditions' necessary to, yet always governed by, the citizen body – the relation between conditions and parts, rulers and ruled, is not 'political'.

Aristotle, like Plato before him, was undoubtedly keen to reinforce the division between ruler and ruled; but he confronted the issue in the terms imposed by the experience and discourse of Athenian democracy. Because the civic community was so central to Athenian political practice and theory, in outlining his ideal polis he defined the relation between ruler and ruled as a relation between the civic community and those outside it. The civic community consists of citizens, the 'parts' of the polis, who are qualified to rule and who are therefore in a position to rule and to be ruled in turn. This is not to say that ruling and being ruled occur, for Aristotle, simultaneously; but it is the essence of a truly *political* community that its citizens are, in principle, fit for political praxis.

In Moerbeke's translation, 'in turn' becomes 'in part', and Aristotle's reference to ruling and being ruled 'in turn' no longer applies to a civic community whose members are all entitled to rule but rather to a ruler who is 'in part' both ruler and ruled. Whatever Moerbeke's intention may have been, for Thomas Aquinas, as we shall see, rule is 'political' to the extent that the ruler himself, like his subjects, is bound by laws. The 'political' sphere as a relation among civic equals altogether disappears. It is, indeed, far from clear that the category of citizenship as Aristotle understood it was meaningful at all in medieval terms. People might enjoy rights by virtue of lordship, or as members of a guild or corporation with a charter of freedom; but the complex hierarchical structure of feudal lordship and corporate entities that constituted the medieval order was something very different from the ancient Greek community of citizens.

This is not to deny that medieval philosophers reflected on the whole range of political forms from imperial or monarchical rule to popular government; and some, including Thomas Aquinas, even acknowledged the benefits of rule by popular consent. But the medieval distinction between 'regal' or 'kingly' rule and 'political' rule reflects not only a political order very different from the ancient Greek polis but also a preoccupation with causes of disorder and conflict very different from those that dominated Aristotle's political thought. The conflicts between rich and poor, which for Aristotle were the ultimate source of *stasis* in the polis, the conflicts that most required political solution, played no such central role in medieval philosophy. Such conflicts, needless to say, certainly existed; but they were replaced at the core of political thinking by disorders produced by overlapping and competing powers of rule. The political relations at issue were neither relations among citizens nor between a community of citizens and those outside it, and the questions addressed by political theory did not implicate the civic community or citizenship in the way that they did in ancient Greece.

The forms in which these questions posed themselves varied according to the diverse configurations of power in different parts of medieval Europe, the specific forms and relative strength of competing claims to temporal authority and the intensity of the contestations among them. In jurisdictional contests among landlords, kings, popes and emperors, lordly power was stronger and monarchy weaker in some kingdoms than in others, just as emperors or popes were greater threats to some kings than to others. France and England, for instance, differed from each other in all these respects, not least because in France corporate entities were stronger than in England, where the relative weakness of corporate powers in relation to the monarchy gave greater prominence both to a unified central state and to the private individual, or to relations between private rights and public sovereignty. These differences, as we shall see, expressed themselves in theory no less than in practice. Nevertheless, in neither case was the political domain defined by a civic community.

Italy was different again. In the north, where landlordly power was relatively weak and, instead, an autonomous civic commune exercised a kind of corporate, collective lordship over the *contado*, we might expect to see the civic community reinstated at the core of political discourse. Yet here too competing autonomous powers and conflicting jurisdictions were the dominant preoccupations of political philosophy. While lawyers and rhetoricians no doubt had much to say about civic life and citizenship, the relations that figured most prominently in major philosophical reflections on government were neither the relations among citizens as equals in a civic community nor the conflicts

– which were often intense – between the dominant urban oligarchies and forces beneath them.

The geographic proximity of papal power and the immediacy of its temporal pretensions represented a very particular challenge to the governing classes of Italy, as did imperial claims in those parts of Italy more vulnerable to intrusions from German kings in their capacity as Holy Roman emperors. In the relatively small civic republics of the north, where the material interests of urban elites were heavily invested in the commune – not only in its power over the *contado* but more particularly in its commercial strength and the profits of civic office – support by one or another of the greater powers, papal or imperial, could be critical to the dominance of this or that civic faction and its access to wealth. Although conflict between urban elites and those beneath them was always a central fact of civic life, it is not surprising that politics in the republics typically took the form of factional struggles within the urban patriciate, often with external support, for control over the lucrative resources of the commune. Even, indeed especially, Marsilius's *Defensor Pacis*, for many commentators the quintessence of medieval republicanism, has less to do, as we shall see, with active citizenship in a civic community than with the struggle between pope and emperor.

It is worth keeping in mind that, if these Italian cities represented any direct continuity with Greco-Roman antiquity, it was with the municipal system of Roman imperial rule, not the civic community of the polis or even the Roman Republic. Even when the civic community takes centre stage in medieval political philosophy, it is typically as a player in the conflicts among contesting powers. The civic commune might assert itself against signorial rule, or against intrusions from papal or imperial power; or, on the contrary, it might (as we shall see in our discussion of Marsilius of Padua) be invoked to support one or another of these antagonistic powers. But the principal subject of political philosophy was not the civic life of citizens in a self-governing community.[20] The fact that, in practice, there was a vibrant civic life in these medieval urban communes, and that there is a rich body of documentation

---

20 The continuities in political thought from medieval Italy to the Renaissance can be misleading. We might, for example, be inclined to include Machiavelli in a discussion of medieval Italian political theory, on the grounds that he represents the culmination of a tradition rooted in the medieval urban communes. But there is a significant difference between the role of the civic community in medieval political philosophy and the reflections on republican autonomy and civic life which emerge in Renaissance Italy, when the main threats to civic autonomy come not from popes and Holy Roman emperors but post-feudal monarchical states.

testifying to its deliberative activities, only serves to emphasize the distinctive preoccupations of medieval political philosophy.

Medieval political theory involved a particularly complex relation to the legacy of classical antiquity. It was complicated not only by relations between secular and ecclesiastical authority but also by the ever-changing scope of secular state power and ever-present tensions between the processes of state centralization and the forces of parcellization. The legacy of empire, together with its classical inheritance, continued to structure the parcellized sovereignty of feudalism, both in practice and in theory. It survived both in the theological doctrines of Christian universalism and in the institutional hierarchy of the Church; but these were always in tension with the particularities of plural kingdoms, lordly jurisdiction and autonomous corporations of various kinds. At the same time, political philosophy had to adapt to the absence of a neatly defined political terrain, not a civic community such as the polis but a particularly convoluted network of secular and ecclesiastical institutions, together with the unity of property and jurisdiction.

Medieval Political Thought?

Much of this chapter has been devoted to medieval reflections on authority and jurisdiction in the absence of a clearly defined *political* sphere. It has been suggested that political theory as a specific mode of thought was not ideally suited to the distinctive conditions of medieval governance. *The Cambridge History of Medieval Political Thought* even begins with the proposition that 'The character of "medieval political thought" is problematic', suggesting among other things that, in the medieval context, modes of 'political' thinking appropriate to the experience of the classical polis or of 'the state' in the post-medieval Western world have little application.[21] Since 'few writers in that period can be meaningfully described as "political thinkers" at all; and very few indeed can be regarded as having made a major individual contribution to the subject', a history that proceeds by studying the work of outstanding figures 'can hardly fail to yield an imperfect and distorted picture of political ideas in the medieval centuries.'[22]

On these grounds, the *Cambridge History* chooses to adopt a thematic or conceptual approach instead of systematically discussing the ideas of each major thinker in turn. Given the peculiarities of

21 *Cambridge* History, *op. cit.*, p. 1.
22 *Ibid.*, p. 4.

medieval governance and the forms of theoretical reflection it produced, there is much to be said for this choice; but it may be useful nonetheless to look at a sample of outstanding figures to illustrate how the tradition of political theory inherited from antiquity was adapted to medieval conditions, and how adaptations varied in specific medieval contexts.

If any thinkers have a claim to 'political theory' in the medieval West, they belong to the later Middle Ages, at a time when more or less stable governments, in the form of monarchies and city-states, were on the rise, and while conflict between secular and ecclesiastical powers, or among kings, popes and emperors, was especially intense. This is also the time when the influence of classical political philosophy gathered momentum, especially with the translation into Latin of Aristotle's *Politics*. We can gain some insight into the particularities of political thinking in that period by looking at a few major figures who, while subject to similar intellectual influences and in varying degrees adopting the language of classical political thought and of Aristotle in particular, put them to work in different local contexts and in pursuit of different ends.

Thomas Aquinas (*c*.1225–74), Marsilius of Padua (1290–1342) and William of Ockham (*c*.1288–*c*.1348) were all in one way or another caught up in the characteristic conflicts of their time and responded to them philosophically, at varying degrees of conceptual distance from political events and power struggles. The most immediately engaged of the three was Marsilius, who was very intensely involved in the bitter struggle between Pope John XXII and the imperial aspirant, Ludwig of Bavaria, arguing the case, in his classic philosophical work, *Defensor Pacis*, for the emperor against the pope. The work of the other two was more substantially theological, although both of them were mobilized to fight the battle of the mendicant orders, Thomas on the side of the Dominicans and William of Ockham later on the side of the Franciscans – with all the implications this had not only for theology but for the temporal interests of the Church and the papacy. Both also had some more direct involvement in public life and the conflicts among various temporal powers. Aquinas not only dealt with the practical affairs of the Church, even as adviser to the pope on public matters, but also for a time advised Louis VIII of France (technically, King of the Franks and Count of Artois), to whom he was related. His ideas would be taken up and adapted by others more directly engaged in power struggles – for instance, by John of Paris (d. 1306), who, as we shall see, elaborated Thomistic doctrines to support King Philip IV of France in his conflict with Pope Boniface VIII. William of Ockham, like Marsilius, found himself caught up in the struggle between Pope John XXII and Ludwig of Bavaria when his own interventions on behalf of the Franciscans angered the pope. The philosopher sought refuge at Ludwig's court – an experience which, needless to say, was very much at the heart of his writings on the relation between secular and ecclesiastical power.

Whatever else may distinguish these thinkers from each other, it is worth considering the differences among the immediate contexts in which they confronted similar theoretical questions. While the contrasts among them are certainly not reducible to divergences in their respective contexts, there are some notable conformities between their ideas and the particular circumstances in which their philosophies were formulated. The differences between William of Ockham and the other two are particularly striking, in ways that reflect the specific conditions of medieval England. Before we explore the ideas of these three thinkers, then, let us briefly remind ourselves of the variations among the networks of power and politically constituted property in France, and more specifically Paris (where Aquinas was engaged not only in theological disputes but in both ecclesiastical and secular politics), northern Italy (Marsilius's political terrain) and William of Ockham's England.

The feudal parcellization of sovereignty was still a major fact of life in thirteenth century France, where seigneurial rights and jurisdictions were very much in evidence – as they would continue to be until the rise of a strong central state in the form of an 'absolutist' monarchy in the sixteenth and seventeenth centuries, never to be completely eradicated until the revolution of the eighteenth century. At the same time, the monarchy had made important advances in its territorial ambitions, and by the late twelfth and thirteenth centuries was already working to establish Paris as a national centre, not only a seat of government but the fount of education and culture. The royal project was, however, in tension not only with seigneurial autonomy in the surrounding countryside but also with the claims of autonomous urban corporations. Even the government of Paris, by now a thriving commercial centre, was a complex network of royal and corporate institutions, much of its public life governed by powerful merchants and guilds. Beyond the kingdom's still unstable boundaries, there were challenges from the German princes of the Holy Roman Empire, whose authority the French refused to recognize, and bitter conflicts between the royal power and the papacy, culminating in the struggle between King Philip IV and Pope Boniface VIII.

Earlier in this chapter, we considered the ways in which the city-states of northern Italy and the kingdoms of England both before and after the Norman Conquest diverged from the feudal pattern of parcellized sovereignty exemplified by France. For our purposes here, it suffices to recall the complex organization of the Italian urban communes: their autonomy and relative independence from centralizing powers of one kind or another, and, at the same time, their internal fragmentation, the semi-autonomous powers and corporations within them, the pressures exerted on them by emperors and popes, together with internal factions associated with one or the other superior power. The corporate principles on which the city-states were organized – both the civic corporation itself and the corporate entities within it – would be particularly significant in the development of political theory emanating from the civic communes, as we shall see in the case of Marsilius.

The English differed from both these cases in ways that would have particularly important implications for political theory. Instead of parcellized sovereignty, in contrast to France, the English developed a precociously centralized state in tandem with uniquely exclusive individual property. In place of seigneurial jurisdiction, the English established a unitary state, while the common law increasingly recognized an individual 'interest' in property independent of any extra-economic claims, privileges or obligations. This was distinct from the right, also enjoyed by the French in the later Middle Ages, to defend individual property rights before the law. The latter, even before royal courts, could (as in France) exist where property was still held on feudal principles, with the attendant obligations, and where each seigneurie continued to have its own system of law and its own autonomous jurisdiction. In England, the individual right of property itself was far more independent of feudal obligations and seigneurial jurisdiction.

In contrast to both France and Italy, where corporate principles were stronger and where the constituent units of political order were corporate entities, the English state was increasingly constituted as a collection of free individuals, subject to no lord except the king (notwithstanding the private powers of manorial lords). These differences would be reflected in the English system of representation, giving rise very early to a unitary parliament, conceived as representing not corporate bodies (as the French estates represented corporate entities) but the whole national community, composed of individual free men and propertyholders. Parliament would also exercise legislative powers far earlier than French representative bodies, the powers of propertied classes not as possessors of feudal jurisdiction but as participants in the centralized state.

Thomas Aquinas, John of Paris, Marsilius of Padua and William of Ockham all in their various ways made use of classical political theory and of Aristotle in particular. No doubt each thinker possessed his own distinctive genius. No doubt, too, they differed in purpose and political commitment. Yet their adaptations of, and departures from, their classical antecedents vary in significant ways that are unmistakably related to their contextual differences.

Thomas Aquinas

Thomas Aquinas was born, probably but not certainly in 1225, into an aristocratic family – his father was Count Landulf, while his mother was related to the Hohenstaufen dynasty of Holy Roman emperors – in Seccarocca, between Naples and Rome. Belonging to a prominent landed family in the Kingdom of Sicily, at a time of bitter conflict between its king, Frederick II, and Pope Gregory IX, Aquinas learned very early and at close hand about the struggles between ecclesiastical and secular power. His formal education began in the Benedictine monastery where his uncle was abbot, and continued at the University of Naples, where, against the strong wishes of his family, he fell under the influence of the new Dominican Order. This was a time of intellectual and religious ferment, with new universities playing an increasingly prominent role, not least to satisfy a growing need for an educated clergy, and purveying the 'new learning' profoundly influenced by classical sources. As a doctor of philosophy, Aquinas went on to teach in various Italian cities; but it was in Paris that he engaged most intensely in theological disputes and debates on the mendicant orders. It is reasonable to assume that it was in Paris, too, in his management of church affairs and as adviser to the king, that he found himself most personally engaged at the intersection of ecclesiastical and secular power.

The implications of political events and conflicts for Thomas's work are not immediately apparent. His case for the Dominican conception of property certainly had, as we have seen, practical implications for the temporal affairs of the Church; but unlike Marsilius or even William of Ockham, he is not, in his philosophy, taking obvious sides in the power struggles of his day – unless it is to support, in general principle, monarchical power such as that of his relative Louis VIII. We should perhaps concentrate our attention on another, broader sense in which Aquinas's political philosophy, and his adaptation of Aristotle, reflect the conditions and preoccupations of his time.

It was suggested earlier in this chapter that Aristotle's political theory was ill-suited to the realities of medieval governance. A system of thought grounded in the civic life of the ancient polis could be made to fit medieval conditions only by means of significant conceptual leaps. Yet there was one essential function that Aristotelian political philosophy was well designed to perform. With certain adjustments, which Aquinas accomplished, it provided a conceptual framework for situating secular government in a larger cosmic order in a way that neatly met the temporal needs of medieval Christians.

This may seem an odd proposition. On the face of it, the political theory of a pagan philosopher like Aristotle may seem far more adaptable to the study of medieval government in its mundane operations than to theological reflections on humanity's place in a Christian universe. Yet it is precisely in the elaboration of such theological reflections that Aristotle played a crucial role. Medieval Christian philosophers like Aquinas continued to be deeply influenced by early Christian Neoplatonism, particularly in its Augustinian form; but their needs were different from those of earlier Christians. The other-worldliness of Neoplatonism, with its devaluation of earthly existence in favour of spirituality and mystical release from the material realm, served Christians reasonably well in the later Roman Empire. Where the civic community had given way decisively to imperial rule, there was no need for Christian subjects to concern themselves with the intricacies of secular governance. It was enough for theologians like Augustine to underwrite the division of labour between Caesar and God; and good Christians, while rendering obedience to Caesar, could get on with minding their own spiritual business. But something different was required to explain the preoccupation of medieval Christians with the complexities of feudal (and post-feudal) governance, not least their obsession with the conflicts among various claims to temporal power. Aristotle's theory of politics, and the place he accords it in his philosophical system, provided a conceptual framework for Christian thinkers to acknowledge the supremacy of the spiritual realm while treating temporal and even secular government as the highest of Christian concerns in this world.

Let us consider, first, the essential Aristotelian principles adopted by Aquinas, in very simple outline. We can then go on to explore his departures from Aristotle, as he responded both to the requirements of Christian theology and to the realities of medieval governance. The argument of Aristotle's *Politics*, as we have seen, proceeds from his general theory of nature. In his effort to explain the principles of order that remain invariable in a natural world of constant motion, he emphasizes two principles: the purpose or *telos* towards which every process tends, and the intrinsic hierarchy of the natural order. Aristotle applies these principles to the polis by arguing that this form of human association is the highest form, and that it perfects human development;

that 'man is by nature a polis-animal', a creature intended to live in a polis, because it is only in the polis that he can fulfil his own *telos* as a rational and moral being. It is the polis, with its customs and laws, that habituates people to living in accordance with the principles of virtue and the good required for the happiness appropriate to human beings. As for what kind of polis is best, Aristotle proposes an ideal form, in which the basic hierarchical principle of nature, the division between ruling elements and ruled, is clearly reproduced in the division between 'conditions' and 'parts' of the polis; but he suggests that the 'best practicable polis' is one that combines elements of oligarchic and democratic forms, to reduce the disorder generated especially by the conflicts between rich and poor and their divergent conceptions of justice.

Aquinas's Aristotelianism, spelled out above all in his *Summa Theologica*, begins with the treatment of humanity as part of the natural order, in which each part is directed toward its own proper natural *telos*. Human beings are uniquely endowed with reason, and, as rational creatures, have a unique cognitive access to reality, which includes a natural capacity to understand the fundamental moral principles required to achieve the happiness specific to humanity. The human *telos* is to realize those rational capacities, in pursuit of the good, which is accessible to natural reason.

The cognitive capacity to understand the nature of things is, for Aquinas as for Aristotle, extended by practical reason, enabling human beings to make rational judgments not only about how things really are but also about right actions. While the principles of goodness are accessible to reason, human goodness in practice is a function of feelings directed by reason. It is a matter of training and habituation, which produce a disposition not only to pursue the good but to love it; and, like Aristotle, Aquinas argues that life in a 'political' community trains people to moral principles and habituates them to loving the good for humanity. For this reason, human beings are by nature 'political' animals, in the sense that the natural *telos* of humanity is best achieved in 'political' communities governed by law. The highest virtue is justice: affording to people that which is due to them; and this can probably best be achieved in some kind of 'mixed constitution'.

The 'naturalization' of man, virtue, justice and the 'political' community in the manner of Aquinas is a major departure from earlier Christian doctrines, and in this respect he differs substantially from Augustine. Aquinas's account of life in this world is very different from his great predecessor's treatment of human history in this sinful earthly existence. For Aquinas history is not just a tragic spectacle, in which no harmony, no just or rightful order, can prevail: in such a world the best that can be hoped for is a certain degree of security and material comfort, as long as subjects, including Christians, obey Caesar, while seeking release in the spiritual realm. This is not to say that the Fall and sin have no bearing on Aquinas's theology, but political association for him is not just a necessary evil to deal with a fallen humanity. Since political order is natural, it must have existed before the Fall, even if the tendency of human beings to sin has required coercion to maintain peace and order in a way that it did not in the prelapsarian condition. The Fall has not meant the loss of natural reason; and, while human beings are capable of choosing not to follow the principles of reason, their distinctive rational capacities allow them to understand and follow natural law. They can achieve happiness or fulfilment (*beatitudo*) in this world by living in accordance with the principles of reason and morality. The temporal political order, directed towards a common good, is the means to accomplish that end. It is worth adding here that such a conception of temporal power would have been all but indispensable to a Christian defence of monarchical secular power.

Commentators may differ about the degree to which, or even whether, complete and ultimate fulfilment for Aquinas can be achieved only after death, in a world beyond this one (as commentators differ about Aristotle's views on the relative value of *praxis* as against the contemplative life); but, just as even the most extreme reading of Aristotle's commitment to a life of contemplation cannot deny the importance he attaches to the polis, there can be no mistaking the value for Aquinas of the *beatitudo* available in the here and now to human beings living in 'political' communities. It is also clear, although he never systematically elaborates his views on the relation between spiritual and temporal powers, that he grants a substantial degree of independence to the secular political community, the *civitas*. There certainly remains a vital function for the spiritual community and the Church that represents it, in preparation for eternal life; but this does not detract from, or even subordinate, the function of secular associations, whether families or states, in their pursuit of earthly happiness. Nevertheless, Aquinas is, after all, a devout Christian; and to accommodate the doctrines of Christianity required some adjustments in Aristotle's cosmos.

Aristotle's conception of the *telos*, as we saw in a previous chapter, includes 'final causes', the ultimate condition 'for the sake of which' natural processes of growth and development take place. These are immanent in objects themselves (as the potentiality of the oak is immanent in the acorn), requiring no deliberate purpose, no control from without, and no divine mind. His idea of the 'unmoved mover', the first cause of motion which is not itself set in motion by any prior cause, does not suggest divine intelligence or purpose. It is simply a way of stating the principle that, in a cosmos where motion is constant and eternal, there must exist some moving principle that sets things in motion without itself being moved, or else we must suppose an infinite regress of movers, which for him is an impossibility. For Aristotle, in other words, the unmoved mover is a principle of physics, not theology. For Aquinas, needless to say, there must be something more than an unmoved mover in this sense. There must be a *creator*, and the cosmic order presupposes the purpose and intelligence of God.

For political theory, the most important implication of this view lies in the concept of law. Aquinas constructs a bridge between theology and the principles of earthly government by distinguishing among various kinds of law: divine, eternal, natural and human or positive. Divine law, directed to eternal life and humanity's relationship with God, is the subject of divine revelation in scripture. This is conceptually distinct from eternal law, which represents the principles of a cosmic order governed by God. To the extent that human reason has access to this cosmic order, we can speak of natural law. Natural law is that aspect of divine regulation accessible to human reason, establishing the basic principles of the good in human practice and legitimate government. This, in turn, should be embodied in the positive laws enacted by governments on earth.

Aquinas's concept of natural law represents a significant departure from Aristotle. There have been disputes among scholars about whether Aristotle himself has a theory of natural law. Yet, while he certainly believes standards of virtue exist not merely by convention but by nature, he never formulates these principles in terms of law (as the Stoics and Cicero would do later). However much he may have contributed to later conceptions of natural law with his naturalization of virtue and justice, there is certainly no sense of legislation and, even less, of an ultimate lawgiver, never mind some kind of punishment for breaches of the law. His 'natural' principles of virtue are not even absolute, rigorous rules discovered by reason but often appear to be little more than rules of thumb as embodied (almost tautologically, as we have seen) in the man of practical wisdom. Natural law for Aquinas, by contrast, is very clearly and indispensably understood as *law*, implying legislation and an ultimate lawgiver.

The transformation of Aristotle's unmoved mover into a divine creator and legislator has an obvious role in Aquinas's theology and his Christianization of Aristotle. But there is more to be said about the function of natural law in medieval political theory, which has as much to do with the realities of medieval governance as with the requirements of Christian theology. We have already observed that the concept was absent, for example, from Islamic philosophy; but it is not enough to say that the concept plays a unique role in Western political thought simply because the Roman legacy, including Cicero's theory of natural law, was more readily available to Latin Christians than it was to Arabs. We also have to take account of the theoretical needs that were met by the concept of natural law: needs that existed in Christianity, in the context of Western feudalism, as they did not in the Islamic world.

We have already commented on the difference between Christianity and both of the other monotheistic faiths on the subject of law, the uniquely Christian separation between a divinely revealed religious law and the civil law of everyday life. Yet it did not suffice for medieval Christians simply to imagine a divine lawgiver, who legislated from on high and punished those who strayed from his law. It is precisely because medieval Christianity was constantly obliged to negotiate the division between divine and civil law, just as it was always faced by the tensions between ecclesiastical and secular powers, that Christian philosophy needed a conceptual bridge between them. It needed a sphere of law that in a sense had one foot in each camp, without violating the integrity of either or challenging its authority. There had to be a law ultimately sanctioned by the divine lawgiver but accessible to ordinary mortals in ways that did not require divine revelation, even if divine revelation served to confirm the discoveries of natural reason. A Christian Aristotelian like Thomas Aquinas could not settle for a truly Averroist solution, which presupposed a single system of law; so, unless he was prepared to accept a 'double truth' relating to two completely separate worlds, natural law was an exceedingly useful idea.

Not the least of its functions is that it can both situate secular associations in a divinely ordered cosmos and at the same time grant the secular *civitas* its independence from spiritual authority by emphasizing that human reason, even without divine revelation, has substantial access to the good. Human convention can, indeed, supplement natural law, or perhaps even modify its secondary principles. For example, although all men are equal by nature, slavery, which exists by the *ius gentium*, can be justified in relation to natural law: while there is no principle of nature that dictates that one man should be a slave and another man not, the enslavement of one man by another may be natural in another sense – on the grounds of utility, which dictates that it may be useful, as Aristotle said, for the slave to be ruled by a wiser man.

The serviceability of natural law as conceived by Aquinas is nowhere better illustrated than in his conception of property. We have already seen how the Dominican argument on property responded to the critics of the Church and served to make its vast wealth consistent with the principles of the mendicant orders; but Aquinas, here as elsewhere, also strikes a neat balance between principles of Christian theology and the mundane requirements of secular life. God, he argues, has *dominium* over the nature of material things, but man has effective *dominium* over their use. There is no principle in nature that determines whether possession is, or should be, private or communal; but private property does exist by the *ius gentium*. While the material world was originally intended for the use of all humanity, the utility of private property has made it consistent with natural law. It even serves a higher purpose, contributing not only to the sustenance of families but also to relief of the poor and promotion of the common good.

There are in Aquinas's work severe moral strictures against such economic practices as usury or fraud, and commerce for him is not a particularly noble activity; but, although the idea of 'just price' is central to his ethical philosophy, he certainly accepts the benefits of trade – as one might expect of a philosopher so deeply rooted in a major medieval commercial centre like thirteenth-century Paris. If he perceives moral dangers in wealth and commerce, which require regulation of property and commercial activity by civil law and even princely rule, he clearly favours private property and wealth when used in accordance with reason.

The Displacement of Civic by Legal Relations

The duality of Western Christianity is, however, still not enough to explain the critical role played by natural law. We must also take into account the overwhelming importance of law in general to the medieval order. While Aristotle was certainly concerned with the role of *nomoi* in the polis, there is nothing like the same preoccupation with law as the constitutive principle of social order that characterizes the philosophy of Aquinas. This divergence reflects the difference between the civic community of the ancient polis and the complex network of legal and contractual relations, within and among various corporate entities, that constituted the medieval order. If Aristotle's political theory had to do with the civic accommodation between classes in a single civic community, medieval thinkers were more concerned with mapping out the spheres of authority among overlapping and competing jurisdictions and negotiating interactions among multiple communities. It was not for nothing that the theorization of medieval governance was dominated by lawyers, civil and canonical. The concept of natural law, already imbued with ancient Roman legalism, neatly extended the legalistic conception of order to the cosmos as a whole.

The displacement of civic by legal relations runs very deep in medieval political philosophy. It is, for instance, visible in Moerbeke's mistranslation of Aristotle, in which the definition of the 'political', as we have seen, has less to do with relations among citizens than with the lawfulness, or otherwise, of rule. In Aquinas's commentary on the *Politics*, it is revealing that, although he follows Aristotle's discussion of citizenship, he renders the distinction between 'kingly' or 'regal' and 'political' regimes in the manner of Moerbeke. Just as the household is characterized by a twofold rule, domestic and despotic, the one over members of his family, the other over slaves, the city too 'is governed by a twofold rule, namely the political and the kingly. There is kingly rule when he who is set over the city has full power, whereas there is political rule when he who is set over the city exercises a power restricted by certain laws of the city.'[23] The immediately striking point about this passage is that it takes monarchical government for granted, distinguishing not between monarchy and other forms of polity but between lawful and unlawful forms of princely rule. There may even be grounds for doubting that Thomas unambiguously prefers 'political' monarchy – though he is so unclear about this that he has been called everything from an absolute monarchist to a forerunner of modern constitutionalism. The fundamental question here, however, concerns the criterion on which this distinction is made and how Aquinas redefines the 'political' in contrast to Aristotle.

It is certainly true that Aristotle distinguishes between lawful and unlawful rulers, or rulers who act in the common interest and rulers who act for themselves. But the defining characteristic of 'political' rule, by whomever it is exercised, is not simply that it is lawful but that it occurs within a community of citizens – not, it should be emphasized, just free men but citizens, who in principle are qualified for political participation. For St Thomas, by contrast, as for other medieval thinkers, the centre of political discourse shifts away from the community of citizens, as he adapts the 'political' to the conditions of the feudal order, its hierarchy of juridical status and corporate entities.

---

23 *Politics* I,1,13.

There are, to be sure, suggestions in Thomas's work that, even if he takes princely government for granted, rule in accordance with the common good entails some kind of consent on the part of those who are ruled that the relation between them and the ruler has something like the character of a covenant and that tyrannical rule – that is, rule in the interests of the ruler and not the common good – is a breach of the covenant which may perhaps produce an entitlement to depose or even kill the tyrant. [24] This is, however, not a private but a public right, nor is it a civic right belonging to individual citizens; and, while Aquinas is never precise on this question, it is likely that the public authority in which it resides is, for Aquinas as for his contemporaries in general, a function of feudal or corporate status.

The rational capacities of humanity, which enable individuals to judge the rectitude of law, seems to suggest that all of them are entitled to some share in sovereignty, residing in the whole community or in some representative entity; and this may mean that laws which do not conform to the principles of reason carry no absolute obligation to obedience. Disobedience may even be required when individuals are ordered to commit a sinful act. Yet even if we take these suggestions of consent and representation to the limits of interpretation, it is important to acknowledge the differences between these ideas and the ancient Greek conception of citizenship. We should acknowledge that, although we have become so accustomed in the modern world to thinking of civic participation in the terms of consent and representation, ideas such as those of Aquinas are very much rooted in the medieval order. Such notions of a share in sovereignty, as was suggested earlier in this chapter, have less to do with active citizenship in a civic community, or even the kind of civic participation still existing in the early Middle Ages in assemblies of free men, than with the distribution of sovereignty and jurisdiction in a complex organizational network, with a multiplicity of corporate communities, and the coexistence of various hierarchies, secular and ecclesiastical. The central 'political' agent in this medieval order is not the individual citizen of the classical polis, or the free man of the Carolingian era, but the possessor of some feudal jurisdiction or a corporate entity endowed with its own legal rights, a degree of autonomy, and probably a charter defining its relation to other corporations and superior powers.

It is perhaps in this light, too, that we can best understand Thomas's conception of, and apparent inclination towards, a 'mixed constitution',

---

24 See for example, *In Rom.* 13.1 V.6.

which combines monarchy with elements from other forms of polity. This idea may seem inconsistent with his unambiguous preference for princely rule, until we consider the realities of feudal monarchy, always balanced to some degree by autonomous lordly and corporate powers. Thomas may, if anything, lean further towards unchecked 'regal' monarchy than many of his contemporaries, and there may even be some justification for calling him an absolute monarchist *avant la lettre*; but in his time and place, an 'absolute' monarchy completely free of parcellized sovereignty was all but inconceivable.

Even Aquinas's conception of justice is shaped by these distinctive medieval realities, defined by its legalism and corporate organization. Justice, again, entails giving others their due. As a general principle of morality, it expresses the Christian rule of 'doing unto others as you would be done by'. Since it presupposes a concern with the good of others, its proper sphere is the community, the *civitas*, whose object is the common good where people learn to love the good of others as their own. Yet there is, as one commentator has nicely put it, 'a whiff of the feudal' in Aquinas's conception, together with a Ciceronian deference to rank and differential entitlements:[25] 'A thing is due', St Thomas writes, 'to an equal in one way, to a superior in another, and to an inferior in yet another; likewise there are differences between what is due from a contract, a promise, or a favour conferred.'[26] This is a reasonably clear departure from Aristotle. To characterize this departure, we could just point to the difference between Aquinas's conviction that 'what is due depends on the status of the recipient', and Aristotle's view 'that status is ideally a consequence of moral merit'.[27] Yet there is another way of looking at this difference, which perhaps tells us more about the divergences between the medieval order of Aquinas and Aristotle's polis.

It is certainly true that even Aristotle's notion of proportionate equality is not predicated on the principle that just deserts are determined by some clearly defined social status. It is, for example, compatible with a polis in which different classes share a civic status. Yet it surely cannot be said that social differences play no part in his conception of justice and what is due to any individual. In his discussion of the conflict between democratic and oligarchic conceptions of justice, the one committed to 'numerical' equality, the other to 'proportionate', Aristotle makes it very clear that both are incomplete, since they ignore the proper criteria

25 Coleman, *op. cit.*, p. 97.
26 Quoted in *ibid.*, pp. 97–8.
27 *Ibid.*, p. 97.

of equality and inequality, the qualities that properly dictate what, in true justice, is due to each man. It is wrong to assume, as the democrat does, that all free-born men are equal, and it is also wrong to treat wealth as the relevant criterion, in the oligarchic manner. The proper measure is the contribution men make to the fulfilment of the state's essential purpose, the truly good life. At the same time, the oligarchic commitment to proportionate equality, for Aristotle, most closely approximates the perfect form, while the democratic idea of justice as numerical equality is undoubtedly the worst. It is also clear that, for Aristotle, men of wealth and good birth are more likely to achieve the necessary virtues required for honours and offices. This means that, while some accommodation must be reached to avoid social conflict, the balance should never be tilted towards the democratic view of justice, or towards the participation of the demos in the civic life of the polis, more than is absolutely necessary to avoid *stasis*.

It would, then, be misleading to say that Aristotle's conception of justice is intrinsically more democratic than Aquinas's, or less concerned with social difference. In the polis, where classes share the same civic and legal status, proportionate equality and differential justice cannot be determined by legal status differences; but, if anything, Aristotle is more, rather than less, preoccupied with social difference, with class relations between rich and poor. His conception of moral virtue itself, as we have seen, is deeply influenced by social difference and even matters of style. It often appears that his principal moral standard is the aristocratic gentleman. In Aquinas's universe, by contrast, where class differences are inextricably bound up with 'extra-economic' powers and 'politically constituted property', the criteria of difference have less to do with simple distinctions of wealth and more to do with legal relations, juridically defined status differences, contractual networks and corporate hierarchies. Aristotle's conception of justice, in other words, reflects, yet again, his preoccupation with the civic accommodation between classes, while Aquinas is more concerned with the intricacies of medieval governance and jurisdiction, in a society where economic power is still closely tied to legal status, corporate identities and jurisdictional rights.

John of Paris

Although Aquinas may not have been so directly engaged in the power struggles of his day, his ideas would immediately be mobilized by other thinkers in more open defence of one temporal power against another. So, for instance, John of Paris, who probably studied with Aquinas and certainly used Thomistic arguments, in *On Royal and Papal Power* (*c*.1302) intervened in the debates generated by the conflict between King Philip IV of France and Pope Boniface VIII. Responding directly to the pope's *Unam sanctam*, John elaborated the Dominican conception of property, and the relation between *dominium* and *jurisdictio*, to make an argument not only about the relation of Church and state to property but also about the relation between ecclesiastical and secular power, as well as conflicts between kings and Holy Roman emperors.

In keeping with distinctively French preoccupations (to which Aquinas, in his Parisian involvements, was surely not indifferent), John had to strike a delicate balance: while the French king was in conflict with the pope, the kingdom did not accept the legitimacy of the empire and its German princes. This meant that an argument in favour of secular monarchy against papal supremacy could not be cast in terms that would strengthen imperial claims. John of Paris asserts the spiritual authority of the pope while denying his absolute *dominium* and hence his temporal supremacy. At the same time, he argues that the universality of the spiritual realm cannot apply to secular kingdoms, with their diverse conditions, which means there can be no universal empire.

John draws on Aquinas's theory of kingship and builds on his theory of property. The argument proceeds from a defence of private property, as against communal ownership, on the grounds that, if everything were held in common, it would be difficult to keep the peace. The common good can best be achieved by permitting individuals to put their property to fruitful use under supervision by some kind of secular power whose object is the common good. John, however, adds an important refinement to the Dominican distinction between ownership and administration. Defining *dominium* in narrow terms as *dominium in rebus* – that is, in material things – and not as lordship in a wider sense, he argues that individuals have inalienable rights in property deriving from their own labour and industry, which precede both secular and ecclesiastical institutions.

The secular state, then, has jurisdictional power to regulate the property of individuals and to arbitrate disputes among them, but it has no *dominium*. The fact that propertied individuals retain their rights and autonomy in relation to the powers of the state implies that the state is, in some sense, a fiduciary power whose authority is conditional on its pursuit of the common good. As for the Church, while the ecclesiastical corporation owns property collectively in material things, this property does not belong to the Church and its priests as vicars of Christ or apostolic successors but derives from concessions granted to them by pious rulers or laymen. This means that neither the state nor the papacy has absolute *dominium*; but it also emphasizes the temporal independence, even the priority, of secular kings in relation to the pope.

John of Paris's arguments on property, kingship and temporal authority clearly reflect the preoccupations of his time and place, not least the particularly complex French relations between the monarchy, the papacy, the empire and various lesser claims to the autonomy of property, whether from seigneurs or urban corporations. His emphasis on individuality and individual rights need not be understood as an anticipation of modern individualism or even modern constitutionalism. On the contrary, his argument on private property is inseparable from feudal principles and corporatism.

The right-bearing individuals of John's political thought are individual *propertyholders*, and much depends on how property itself is conceived. Even feudal property, however conditional it may be and whatever obligations it may entail, is vested in individuals; but these individuals are themselves defined by their juridical or corporate identity. They hold their property not simply as free men but as lords, or as landholders subject to feudal obligations and lordly jurisdiction. Perhaps even more fundamentally, John's view of private ownership coexists with a conception of the political community as constituted by corporate entities. If the state is in some sense accountable to individual propertyholders, this does not mean that it is constituted by a multitude of individuals. In medieval terms, it is much more likely to mean that the state is constituted by, and accountable to, the 'people' as a corporate entity, or even a collection of corporate bodies, whose representatives speak for them. Even the idea that the attribution of inalienable rights to individuals makes government in some sense a fiduciary power is not so much an anticipation of modern constitutionalism, as a residue of feudal parcellized sovereignty and claims to seigneurial or corporate autonomy against a centralizing state.

The idea that government derives its authority from the 'people' was widely accepted by medieval thinkers, and it was generally agreed that kings had a duty to protect the rights of their subjects. Yet these principles were compatible with a broad range of political commitments, including the conviction that monarchical power should be virtually unlimited. If anything, the 'people' – as a corporate entity – was more often invoked in support of monarchical authority than as a limitation on its power, let alone in favour of more democratic forms of government. Even when the 'people' were granted a right to depose kings who failed in their duty, that right was typically vested in a corporate entity or its representatives, not least in feudal magnates of one kind or another. For John of Paris, for instance, the rights of individuals do seem to constitute significant limits on government, even entailing a right to depose kings. Yet he invokes this right on behalf of feudal magnates and he does so primarily in order to deny that right to the pope, while the prince remains the arbiter of the common good.[28]

This is not to deny that feudal conceptions of the fiduciary relationship between kings and the people, however narrowly the 'people' was defined, could place severe restrictions on monarchical power. Nor is it to deny the profound influence that such medieval ideas would have on the development of modern constitutionalism, however misleading it may be to speak of them as anticipations of modernity. Precisely because they were predicated on the autonomous powers of magnates or corporate bodies, they could, indeed, be more restrictive than some later conceptions of individual consent, which (as in the case of Hobbes) could even underwrite absolute monarchy. The radical resistance theories of the sixteenth century in France, for example, would continue to be based on the autonomy of magnates and urban corporations.[29] There were also corporatist theories that challenged autocratic rule by invoking not only the autonomous powers of particular corporate entities but the superiority of a large, inclusive general corporation, on the principle that the ruler or pope might be superior to any lesser individual, but that he was inferior to the corporate entity constituted by the whole community. This doctrine – applied by John of Paris himself among others – was used against the pope, arguing that the general body of the Christian faithful, in the shape of a general council, was the ultimate ecclesiastical authority, which could even depose popes.

This idea would be developed in so-called conciliar theory, which flourished in the fourteenth and fifteenth centuries. By the mid-fourteenth century the papacy at Avignon had increasingly come under the influence of the French monarchy, and competing claimants to the papacy in Avignon and Rome were inevitably embroiled in inter-state rivalries between France and its European neighbours. In response to the growing conflicts within the Church, which eventually gave rise to

28 According to the *Cambridge History*, 'In France, the people's right to depose kings was normally discussed only in the context of rebutting papal claims to be able to do so.' (p. 517)

29 Huguenot resistance tracts like the *Vindiciae contra Tyrannos* asserted the 'people's' right to resist by invoking the independent powers of nobles and magistrates against the king.

the so-called Western Schism, conciliarists would elaborate the idea that it was not the pope but the corporate body of Christians in the form of a general Church council that held ultimate authority in spiritual matters. Although a resolution would emerge from a series of Councils, conciliarism would give way to a revived papal dominance, while surviving as a model for secular theories of consitutional government.

It is, nevertheless, important to keep in mind that conceptions of the social contract as a deliberate transaction between consenting individuals and a government whose only purpose is to protect their lives, liberties and property are grounded in conditions quite different from those assumed by John of Paris or Thomas Aquinas. Whether such conceptions are invoked in defence of absolute monarchy or to support some kind of limited, constitutional government, they presuppose, on the one hand, a centralized state not fragmented by parcellized sovereignty and, on the other, a political community of individuals detached from corporate identities. It is not insignificant that such an idea would first emerge clearly in England, where corporate principles were weaker and Parliament was conceived as both a representative body – representing a national community of free individuals – and a partner in the legislative functions of the central state, without whose consent the king could not govern.

Marsilius of Padua

Corporate principles, as we have seen, played an essential role in both France and Italy in ways that they did not in England; and this difference represented divergences not only in processes of state-formation but also in the nature of property. Corporate autonomy, like other forms of feudal power, belonged to the structure of parcellized sovereignty in opposition to a centralized state. Corporate liberties, privileges and powers, not unlike feudal lordship, were forms of politically constituted property, a fusion of public power and private appropriation, in contrast to appropriation independent of extra-economic status or jurisdictional powers.

The contrasts between Marsilius of Padua and William of Ockham nicely illustrate the effects of these contextual differences. Both philosophers argued the case against papal power, and both as a consequence sought refuge at the court of Ludwig of Bavaria, whose imperial claims had brought him into conflict with the pope. Yet their strategies of argumentation were quite different, and their differences cannot simply be put down to political or temperamental disagreements: the extremism of Marsilius's anti-papal arguments as against William's effort to strike a somewhat less one-sided balance between papacy and empire. The two thinkers proceed from divergent assumptions, and these divergences are strikingly congruent with the differences between Italian civic communes and the medieval English state.

Marsilius was born in Padua c.1275 into a family very much involved in the communal government, as civil lawyers, notaries and judges. Instead of following his family into the legal profession, he studied medicine, first in Padua and then in Paris, where he taught natural philosophy and, in 1313, became rector of the university. Although he was promised ecclesiastical preferment by Pope John XXII, his hopes were disappointed. Whether or not this disappointment had anything to do with his anti-papal venom, he went on to serve two of the great lordly families of northern Italy, the della Scala of Verona and the Visconti of Milan, both of whom, as was typical among the landed nobility, had strongly imperial (Ghibelline) loyalties, at a time when Padua was under papal (Guelf) lordship.

In his famous anti-papal treatise, the *Defensor pacis*, completed in 1324, Marsilius would single out for special praise Matteo Visconti, who ruled Milan as *podestà* or 'imperial vicar' and effectively destroyed communal government. It will be important to keep this in mind when we consider conflicting interpretations of the *Defensor pacis* as either a republican tract or a strong defence of imperial power. In any case, once its authorship was attributed to Marsilius, who had at first circulated it anonymously, he was forced to seek refuge with Ludwig of Bavaria; and he went on to give Ludwig his unambiguous support against the pope, even accompanying the king in his invasion of Italy. Marsilius's imperial connections may be more clearly reflected in his last work, the *Defensor minor*, than in his major work; but it remains for us to consider whether there are, in the *Defensor pacis*, indeed contradictions between the republican and an imperialist Marsilius of Padua.

Let us first examine his anti-papal argument. Marsilius regards the papacy as the main threat to peace in Europe, and he attacks the very foundations of the pope's claims to a plenitude of power, indeed the very notion that the pope and the clergy in general have a claim to temporal authority at all. His argument is not that there are separate spheres of jurisdiction, ecclesiastical and secular, but rather that the very idea of jurisdiction does not belong in the spiritual realm. He pursues his argument on two fronts, first by examining the origin, nature and purpose of the civic community, more or less in the manner of Aristotelian naturalism, and then by constructing a theological case and a historical argument which recounts the history of the Church after the Fall and traces papal claims to power back to their Roman imperial roots in the conversion of Constantine, the first Christian emperor.

The purpose of the civil community, as Marsilius already suggests in the first paragraph of the *Defensor pacis*, is to create the conditions of peace and tranquillity required to achieve 'the greatest of all human goods . . . the sufficiency of life.' Tranquillity in the city or realm means that each of its parts can perform its proper function according to reason and prevailing custom, in an organic harmony. This requires the imposition of law, and Marsilius's conception of law is significant for two principal reasons.

First, he emphasizes its coercive function, as a means of achieving peace and not, in the Aristotelian or Thomistic manner, as a means of habituating citizens to virtue. This emphasis, as he elaborates his argument, places jurisdiction firmly in the hands of secular authority and rules out ecclesiastical jurisdiction in the temporal sphere. Civil peace and tranquillity are the responsibility of secular powers, while the Church has no coercive function. The rewards and punishments promised by Christianity await the afterlife, since the benevolence of Christ allows repentance till the end. The priestly function is certainly an integral part of the civil order, as are military and judicial functions; but Marsilius makes it clear that the Church remains subordinate to secular power in the temporal domain. This does not mean, however, that his view of the state prefigures a modern secular state. His argument remains, in this respect as in others, firmly rooted in the medieval order, not only because of the importance he attaches to the priestly function but because, as we shall see in a moment, his challenge to the temporal authority of the Church is mounted on behalf of other unmistakeably medieval claims to temporal power.

Second, the law emanates from a human legislator, whom Marsilius identifies with the whole civic corporation, 'the universal body of citizens' (*universitas civium*). The ultimate authority of civil government derives from the whole corporation of citizens and requires its ongoing consent. This is where we confront the question of the philosopher's republicanism, and certain immediate problems arise. We have already remarked that there was nothing unusual in medieval political thought about the conviction that civil authority derived from the 'people'; and we have also observed that this proposition was perfectly compatible, and indeed commonly associated, with the defence of powers that were far from democratic, up to and including unlimited monarchy. Marsilius himself makes it clear that the corporation of citizens is represented and governed by a ruling part (*pars principans*), which may consist of many, few or even one. More significantly, he always qualifies his references to the universal body of citizens with 'or its prevailing part' (*valentior pars*, sometimes translated as the 'weightier part'), which apparently can be very limited in numbers. Not only the power to elect (or depose) the ruling or executive part but even the legislative function and the ultimate power of consent could, then, reside in a very small number.

Nevertheless, Marsilius does go substantially further than other medieval thinkers in his ascription of sovereignty to the corporation of citizens. His theory, writes one historian of medieval political thought, 'is medieval corporation theory with a vengeance', placing great confidence in the capacity of the corporate body (as distinct from any individual wise man or men) – both as the *unversitas civium* and as a community of faith, the *congretatio fidelis* or *universitas fidelium* – to judge and enact the laws most conducive to the sufficient life.[30] His theory is also distinctive in its insistence on the unity of jurisdiction, placing the legislative power entirely in the hands of the civic corporation. He denies the force, indeed the existence, of canon law, and this is certainly decisive in the attack on papal power. Yet there remains the question – to which we shall return – of how, or whether, these principles can be squared with a defence of imperial power or, for that matter, support for the kind of signorial power enjoyed by the Visconti.

The argument about the origin and purpose of the civil order is buttressed in the second discourse of *Defensor pacis* with theological arguments, interpretations of scripture and of various canonical sources on ecclesiastical authority, together with a complex historical argument about the origin of papal power. Marsilius uses scripture and the example of Christ, his poverty and his benevolence, to demonstrate that the Church has no role in temporal affairs or in coercive governance. The historical argument is intended to demonstrate that the history of the Church is, to quote one commentator, 'a history of gradual, papally inspired perversion', driven by 'greed for temporal possessions and ambition for secular *dominium*', as a consequence of which modern priests are antithetical to the example of Christ and his apostles.[31]

This process of corruption, according to Marsilius, began paradoxically with the conversion of Constantine. Before the conversion there

30 Coleman, *op. cit.*, p. 137.

31 George Garnett, *Marsilius of Padua and 'The Truth of History'* (Oxford: Oxford University Press, 2006), p. 146.

was a clear distinction between the Church and the human legislator, who was an infidel. This meant that the church and the bishop of Rome were obliged to assume a kind of institutional pre-eminence, acting on behalf of the Christian community, which could not freely assemble to deliberate on matters of faith. Once Constantine's conversion made it possible for Christians to gather and regulate questions of ritual and faith, it was no longer necessary for the Church or the pope to act on their behalf. Yet it was precisely then that the bishops of Rome asserted their pre-eminence over other bishops and priests. They did so on the basis of the so-called donation of Constantine, an edict that was supposed to have granted jurisdictional superiority to the Roman pontiff, St Sylvester. Although the authenticity of the donation was always in question, Marsilius chooses to accept it as historical fact, and argues that, while Constantine was simply and with good intentions following the practice of the early Church under infidel emperors, the circumstances had radically changed and the consequences would prove to be disastrous. Now that the human legislator was a believer, a new kind of division opened up between the Christian human legislator and the institutions of the Church. As the *universitas fidelium* and the *universitas civium* were united and the human legislator was perfected by Christianity, the institutions of the Church and the priesthood were gradually corrupted by temporal ambitions, the benefits of ecclesiastical office and property.

How the Holy Roman Empire figures in this argument is not immediately obvious. Although Marsilius suggests that human law can best achieve its purpose in creating the conditions of peace, tranquillity and the sufficient life when Church and civic community are one, he also allows for a diverse multitude of self-governing civic communities, such as Italian city-states. He does not, on the face of it, advocate a universal empire uniting the spiritual community of Christians with a coextensive temporal *imperium*. It has, however, been persuasively argued that, in this respect, Marsilius has much more in common than is commonly supposed with the poet Dante, who did, in his *De Monarchia*, make an unambiguous case for a single universal ruler (who turns out to be the Roman emperor).[32] While Dante accepts the need for different laws for different conditions, he insists that, in matters common to the whole of

---

32 The argument that follows here and in the next paragraph is outlined by Garnett, *op. cit.*, especially pp. 160–4. For a different view of Marsilius, see Cary Nederman, *Community and Consent: The Secular Political Theory of Marsiglio of Padua's Defensor Pacis* (Lanham: Rowman & Littlefield, 1995).

humanity, there should be one supreme prince. Marsilius does not go so far, indeed appears to deny any such a necessity. Yet his argument is not that a universal ruler is unnecessary to keep the peace among the faithful. It is rather that the need for one universal coercive judge has not yet been demonstrated 'as necessary to eternal salvation'; and he goes on to say that 'there seems to be a greater necessity among the faithful for this than for one universal bishop, in that a universal prince is more able to preserve the faithful in unity than a universal bishop.'[33]

If a universal prince would serve a useful purpose in maintaining peace among the faithful, and if unity among the faithful for the sake of salvation cannot be achieved without unity for the sake of peace, a case can certainly be made for some such universal ruler or coercive judge. Marsilius suggests several times in the *Defensor pacis* that, while various provinces or cities have their own legislators, they must be subordinate to the supreme human legislator of the Roman Empire, to avoid precisely the state of war that now exists within the Holy Roman Empire, where the pope has usurped the universal human legislator's role. This conception of a universal prince may not have quite the geographic reach of Dante's world empire, but it does suggest that the emperor has an essential role in reversing the papal usurpation which has destroyed the peace within the existing boundaries of the Holy Roman Empire. Marsilius's later work and his service to Ludwig of Bavaria are perfectly in keeping with this argument.

Can this reading of Marsilius be squared with the republicanism that is commonly attributed to him? If he was indeed a republican, do we have to accept that his republican leanings in the *Defensor pacis* were modified by his experience in Ludwig's court, making the *Defensor minor* more clearly imperialist? To put it another way, must we choose between imperialist and republican readings of Marsilius? Some commentators have pointed out, quite reasonably, that, given the realities of the Italian city-states, we need make no such choice, since even self-governing communes with an active civic corporation could exist under the lordship of the Holy Roman Empire (even if imperial power typically supported signorial rather than communal government). Yet something more needs to be said. What is striking about Marsilius's argument is that his call for unitary jurisdiction, which is so distinctive among medieval thinkers, applies only to the division between the Church and secular government. He makes no such argument against the feudal powers of *signori* and seems completely unconcerned by the

---

33 *DP* II.28.15. ed. and transl. Annabel Brett.

threat they pose to civil peace – a threat that certainly did not escape his contemporaries – in stark contrast to his apocalyptic vision of the danger posed by the papacy. Having established a single, apparently unified civic corporation, he leaves intact – indeed, in practice actively supports – one of the principal challenges to civic unity and unitary jurisdiction.

There is, perhaps, an explanation that can accommodate all the complexities in Marsilius's political theory. It would be perfectly reasonable to argue simply that, in his genuine horror at the threats posed to European peace by papal pretensions, he felt obliged, despite his deeply felt republicanism, to defend signorial supporters of imperial power. Let us, however, suppose for a moment that the reverse may be true: that he truly believed in the likes of Matteo Visconti and that his anti-papal argument was at least to some extent inspired by such signorial allegiance. Might there be a way in which his apparently republican ideas could serve that cause?

In the specific conditions of Italian city-states and especially his native Padua, which had experienced dramatic shifts between Guelf and Ghibelline dominance, his argument could readily be mobilized in support of a civic commune dominated by a seigneurial Ghibelline faction under imperial protection. Indeed, it is hard to imagine a more effective way of making the Ghibelline case in the context of Italian civic corporations, the case for something like the Visconti of Milan against the Guelfs of Padua. It is certainly possible, even likely, that Marsilius's support for the Visconti was tempered by sentiments in favour of more communal government than was practised by his signorial masters, even if the civic body in question might be a restricted oligarchy – though even signorial rule could maintain the forms of communal self-government. The least that can be said is that even the most republican reading of the *Defensor pacis* does not rule out oligarchy, while Marsilius's support for the lordship of the Holy Roman Empire tends toward the oligarchic dominance of feudal nobles like the Visconti.

It is significant that when Marsilius characterizes the 'parts' of the city or civic corporation, he does so in a way that accords a privileged status to precisely the military function conventionally associated with the feudal aristocracy. Of the various offices or parts of the city – following Aristotle, he says, these include 'agriculture, manufacture, the military, the financial, the priesthood and the judicial or councillor' – only the priesthood, the military and the judicial 'are parts of the city in an unqualified sense, and in civil communities they are usually called the notables [*honorabilitas*].'[34]

34 *DP* I.5.1.

The 'plebeian' multitude belong to the parts of the city only 'in a broad sense', because they service its needs. Those engaged in production or trade – and this presumably includes the commercial patriciate – belong, it appears, to something like Aristotle's category of 'conditions', while *signori* would be truly 'parts'. Even Marsilius's emphasis on the coercive function of the law seems to reinforce this point: '[G]iven that the sentences of judges on internal miscreants and rebels must be carried out by means of coercive force,' he writes, 'it was necessary to institute within the city a military or defensive part, to which many of the mechanical arts also minister.'[35]

The very argument that lies at the heart of Marsilius's 'republicanism', his elevation of the civic corporation, can be understood as playing a critical role in support of signorial interests. How persuasive would it be, after all, to argue the Ghibelline case against Guelf dominance and papal lordship by blatantly attacking communal self-government in favour of a ruthless *signoria* in the hands of an aristocratic family? Typically, the powers of mercantile anti-signorial factions resided in semi-autonomous, self-governing guilds and corporations. It would therefore surely be much more effective to begin by trumping the autonomous authority of lesser corporations, invoking the more general and inclusive corporation of the civic commune – corporatism indeed with a vengeance. An analogous strategy would later be adopted by absolutist monarchs, who claimed to represent the general will of an inclusive corporate entity, something like the nation, against the particular interests of feudal aristocrats, autonomous municipal authorities and other lesser corporations. Marsilius's conception of the civic corporation could then be buttressed by challenging the papal authority that supported anti-signorial corporate interests, and then defending the imperial powers that sustained aristocratic 'imperial vicars' like the della Scala and Visconti dynasties.

William of Ockham

Even a moment's reflection should make it clear how inconceivable such arguments would be in a different social context, such as the England of William of Ockham. Whatever other reasons an English thinker, reflecting on English conditions, might have for defending imperial against papal authority, the uniquely Italian civic conflicts between factions supporting, and supported by, one or another of these greater powers would not be among them. More fundamentally, even if we reject such

---

35 *DP* I.8.5.

a partisan reading of Marsilius and give his republicanism the benefit of
every doubt, his reliance on corporatist arguments would have nothing
like the same force in England that it did in northern Italy.

To accommodate English conditions, it would, at the very least, be
necessary to redefine the corporation. This is precisely what William
of Ockham does. The starting point of his arguments – epistemological,
theological and political – is emphatically the individual; and even his
conception of the corporation denies the very first premise of medieval
corporatism as conceived, most notably, by Marsilius: the idea that a
corporate body can assume a personality, with a corporate will,
separate from, and entitled to represent, the individuals who compose
it. While it would be foolish to ascribe Ockham's philosophical
individualism to purely contextual determinations, it would be no less
foolish to disregard the fact that his formative experience and education
took place in England, where a particular relation between state,
property and individual assigned a very different, and weaker, role to
corporations than was the case elsewhere in Europe.

William of Ockham was born in the 1280s in Surrey and was
educated at Oxford in theology and philosophy, continuing his studies
and going on to teach as a member of the Franciscan order. There is
some dispute about when and how he first came into conflict with the
papacy, but the most common view is that he was summoned to
Avignon to defend his theological and philosophical work before a
papal commission for some suspected heresy and then found himself
drawn into the dispute on apostolic poverty. John XXII's papal bull,
Quia vir reprobus, was, as we saw, the most powerful challenge to the
Franciscan position; and in his response, Ockham came to believe that
the pope himself was guilty of heresy.

Although Ockham was never formally excommunicated, he fled to
the court of Ludwig in the year that the king became Holy Roman
Emperor. Like Marsilius, he supported Ludwig in his conflict with the
pope, continuing to defend the doctrine of apostolic poverty and attacking
papal claims to a plenitude of power, which compelled him to elaborate
his view on the relation between secular and spiritual jurisdictions. He
never produced a systematic political theory, and what he did say is
subject to conflicting interpretations; but a theory of politics can be
reconstructed from various works.[36] Whatever else can be said about his

---

36 See, for example, *Contra Benedictum*, *Tractatus* against John XXII, parts of the
Dialogus, the *Breviloquium de potestate tyrannica* (*A short discourse on the tyrannical
government over things divine and human*), and *De imperatorum et pontificum potestate*
(*On Imperial and Pontifical Power*).

political ideas, there is no question about the originality and significance of his reflections on corporations and individual rights.

There is an unmistakeable congruence between Ockham's redefinition of the corporation and his individualist approach to philosophical questions in general, especially his theory of cognition. It might, therefore, be tempting simply to say that the former followed neatly from the latter without the intervention of contextual factors. Yet, while it would clearly be too strong to claim that his philosophy is entirely a by-product of English conditions, his theory of rights and corporations is so strikingly congruent with the realities of English law, property and governance that a failure to take note of the connections and correspondences would surely be a careless oversight.

Ockham starts from the premise that there is nothing in this world but individuals, and that no universals or essences exist except as abstractions constructed by the mind from reflection on particulars. Knowledge derives from individual cognition, which is by definition particular and contingent, and universal concepts do not reflect an external reality but rather the operations of the human mind. Universal concepts are names or signs human beings ascribe to particular things in the effort to find commonalities among them; and it is these linguistic creations, not the substance of things, that constitute the objects of knowledge.

Ockham's views on society and government start from analogous premises. The body politic, too, is a world constituted by individuals and nothing else. Collective opinion can never be more than a product of individual opinions, and no collectivity is ever more than the sum of its parts. This means that there can be no collective body with a corporate personality or will of its own, distinct from the sum of individual personalities and wills that compose it. Individuals do not, of course, exist in isolation from each other. They congregate for social, political and religious reasons; but they do so as free and autonomous beings, and the body politic does not exist as a sphere separate from the multitude of individuals that constitute it. There is no legally created imaginary persona which can claim to represent them. The collectivity or corporation is never anything other than a collection of autonomous rational individuals. Individual wills cannot be represented by a corporate entity, nor can individuals alienate their autonomy, their rights or their responsibilities.

It is, however, true, according to Ockham, that the Fall made secular authority necessary, since individuals could no longer rule themselves by their reason alone. Ockham not only allows for secular authorities that can impose their coercive powers on free individuals but even accepts the possibility of governments that stand above the law. Governments are established by the universal consent of individuals who will be governed by them; but thereafter circumstances will dictate whether the ruler will, or should, act in accordance with positive law. There is no need for repeated acts of consent by the governed. They have consented from the outset to government that will act and legislate in accordance with right reason, equity and the common good as demanded by particular circumstances. This may imply a right of resistance if and when that fundamental condition is not met, but there is no provision for continuous consent nor for any institutions to restrain the ruler. In the absence of any requirement for regular participation by the people or for institutional limits on government, William of Ockham's political stance has been described as 'absolutist'. At the same time, his is an absolutism firmly based on the principle that individuals cannot alienate their freedom and autonomy; and since no individual can claim absolute power over another, no such power exists for them to confer on anyone else. This insistence on the inalienability of human rights and freedoms has made it possible to invoke his doctrines to support the right of resistance and constitutional government.

What, then, of individual rights and especially the right of property? In the debate on apostolic poverty, Ockham explored the concept of *dominium*, distinguishing between conditions before and after the Fall. In the prelapsarian condition, humanity enjoyed a capacity to make use of all creation but not the ownership of property. Once Adam's sin transformed the human condition God provided the means of improving human life by giving humanity a capacity to appropriate temporal goods, in the form of individual property, and to protect their rights of property by instituting government. Ockham's immediate objective in the debate with the pope was to demonstrate that, since both property and government result from Adam's sin, they clearly belong in the temporal sphere, under the direction of secular authority, which means that the pope can claim no plenitude of power. His argument, however, has wider implications. Although property is a human creation, dependent on civil authority, the capacity to exercise *dominium* in its postlapsarian form was a gift from God. The utility of private property, recognized not only in civil law but in the *ius gentium*, suggests that it conforms to natural law, even if it does so in a different sense than did common possession before the Fall; and once acknowledged, it constitutes an inalienable right.

As a Franciscan defending apostolic poverty, Ockham opposed

Dominican doctrines on the unity of use and ownership, together with the separation of ownership and jurisdiction. But the principle that property was a civic institution had already been accepted by Dominicans like Thomas Aquinas and other medieval theologians. For Ockham's purposes, this doctrine had the advantage of undercutting the pope's authority by placing property squarely in the realm of secular authority. He also had in common with Aquinas a distinction between different forms of natural law and the suggestion that private property is, in its own way, consistent with natural law. But if Ockham's theory of property, despite his insistence on its civic institution, nevertheless brings us closer than do other medieval theories to the notion of private property as an irreducible natural right, inherent in the human individual independent of civic authority, it is because of the priority he gives the individual as the most fundamental constitutive unit of the social order, in contrast to the corporatism of other medieval theorists.

There are certainly ambiguities in Ockham's political doctrine. The practical implications of his views on individuals and corporations are probably clearer in relation to spiritual authority than to secular power, and, indeed, his innovative treatment of corporate principles was most immediately intended to deal with the question of spiritual power. Confronting the relation between spiritual and secular jurisdictions, he does not choose Marsilius's solution of simply subordinating one to the other. Yet again, he seeks his answer in the all-important individual. Individuals, he argues, are both spiritual and secular beings, so any resolution between the two jurisdictions must acknowledge that duality. As spiritual beings, individuals are governed by divine laws, while as secular beings they are subject to positive law. Since individuals are irreducibly free and autonomous, they are entitled to establish their own secular governments with their own systems of law.

Ockham may not go as far as Marsilius's outright subordination of Church to state, but his separation of the two jurisdictions represents a significant challenge to the temporal power of the Church and the papacy. At the same time, just as he denies the primacy of corporations in the secular sphere, he gives little credence to general councils of the Church. Some individual Christian, even a child or a woman, might come closer to the truth than a general Church council. Just as there is no secular corporation that is more than the sum of its individual parts, with a right to represent them, no spiritual collectivity has any superior standing. Unlike Marsilius and John of Paris, whose corporatism extended to general councils of the Church, granting them an infallibility that endowed them with a right to depose popes, Ockham had no such corporatist weapon available to him and was forced to rely on individual members of the Church to resist papal heresies and misdeeds.

William of Ockham's redefinition of the corporation was, then, a two-edged sword. There is no question that his doctrine of individual autonomy and rights could be adopted in support of constitutional limits on government. Once the representative can no longer be identified by definition with the collectivity it represents, the way is open to raise questions about the conformity of the representative's will to the desires of the individuals he claims to represent and therefore about the accountability of representatives to their constituents. No such questions arise, by contrast, in Marsilius's theory of the corporation. The will expressed by the corporate body, in the person of its representatives, necessarily defines the common good, whatever any individuals may think or wish.

Yet medieval corporatism could and did provide a foundation for limiting state power, by asserting autonomous powers and rights independent of the central state. Ockham's rejection of corporatism as understood by his contemporaries denies him some of the most powerful weapons available to medieval thinkers for checking the powers of monarchs and popes. Although some of his ideas would be adopted by conciliarists, his views on general councils of the Church would seem to undercut conciliar doctrine fatally; and it is hard to see how any notion of corporate resistance to tyrannical authority, secular or ecclesiastical, could survive his redefinition of the corporation.

At the same time, there are, as we have seen in the case of Marsilius, ambiguities in corporatism too, especially when the corporation in question is coextensive with the whole civic community. A universal corporation – whether a general council of the Church or a secular body of citizens – could certainly be mobilized against a monarch or a pope, but autocratic rulers could also assert their superiority over lesser autonomous powers by claiming to represent a more general corporate interest.

Both corporatism and individualism were, then, compatible with a wide range of political options, from more or less absolute government to constitutionalism and a defence of civic liberties. In the following centuries there would be varying traditions of both absolutism and constitutionalism, not only in theory but also in practice; and these differences, which have their roots in medieval Europe, reflect significant divergences – notably between England and France – in the nature of the body politic and its constituent units.

Long after William of Ockham, another Englishmen, Sir Thomas Smith, then Queen Elizabeth's ambassador to France, in a treatise on the English body politic, would define a 'commonwealth' or 'societie civill' as 'a societie or common doing of a multitude of free men collected together and united by common accord and covenauntes among themselves, for the conservation of themselves aswell [sic] in peace as in warre.'[37] His contemporary, Jean Bodin, reflecting on French conditions, had a different conception of a commonwealth, as composed not of free individuals but of 'families, colleges or corporate bodies'.[38] The differences expressed in these two definitions were already well established in the thirteenth century, visibly present in systems of property, law and representation.

In England, as we have seen, the corollary of an unusually centralized state and a uniquely unified system of law was a distinctive type of 'free' man, subject only to the king and to no lesser lord. Landlords certainly enjoyed great local powers; but outside the manor, and in relation to free men, they acted as delegates of the Crown. While there remained a sharp distinction between freehold property and unfree tenures, subject to manorial lordship and with no access to the royal courts, the free Englishman was a unique formation, with an individual 'interest' in property, recognized in common law and independent of any extra-economic claims, privileges or obligations. In France, by contrast, free status was more ambiguous. Charters of freedom did not dissolve seigneurial obligation, and even peasants who owned land and had access to royal protection could still be subject to seigneurial jurisdiction and its attendant obligations, in a society governed, even at the height of absolutism, by hundreds of local law codes, customs, and fragmented jurisdictions.

The status of the free man in England entailed a distinctive political identity, without all the feudal and corporate mediations that stood between the state and individuals elsewhere in Europe. This relationship was reflected in a new conception of representation. When knights of the shire were elected to represent their counties in the Parliament of 1254, they were representing counties not as feudal entities but as administrative units under the Crown; and they were elected by county courts, which were assemblies of free men, the same kind of free

---

37 Sir Thomas Smith, *De Republica Anglorum*, ed. Mary Dewar (Cambridge: Cambridge University Press, 1982), p. 57.

38 Jean Bodin, *Six Books of the Commonwealth*, ed. M.J. Tooley (Oxford: Basil Blackwell, 1967), p. 7.

individuals who constituted the English jury. Englishmen, to be sure, were no less inclined than other Europeans to speak of the commonwealth as if it were a corporation. Yet, when, for example, the Chief Justice of England declared in 1365 that 'Parliament represents the body of all the realm', that 'body' was no longer the kind of corporate entity imagined by Marsilius; nor was it a collection of corporate entities, such as Bodin's 'colleges and corporations' or the French estates. It was more a collection of individual free men like that conceived by William of Ockham.

It is important to acknowledge that these differences are not just theoretical. European thinkers certainly shared a rich philosophical and cultural tradition, as well as certain important commonalities in the development of property and state; but the legacies they drew upon in common only emphasize the significance of the divergences among them and the degree to which they reflect significant variations in social and political conditions, which produced different social conflicts and offered different practical options for their resolution. In the following centuries, there would be several divergent patterns of European state-formation and economic development, which would be expressed in diverse traditions of political thought.

CONCLUSION

Why, then, end this volume here, in the middle of the fourteenth century? Its subject is a social history of political theory from classical antiquity to the Middle Ages; but the 'medieval period, perhaps more than most, is subject to debate about its boundaries, and especially about when it properly ends. Histories of medieval political theory will often end a century later (or more) than this one does. The *Cambridge History*, for instance, spans roughly the years 350 to 1450, on the grounds that 'somewhere around the middle of the fifteenth century we can detect enough of a decisive shift in the patterns of intellectual life to justify the claim that the principal movements of "medieval political thought" . . . were drawing to a significant close.'[37] This is, of course, a difficult judgment to make, since there was, as there always is in historical processes, a continuity in change. Yet, the argument goes, while many medieval themes and 'traditions' of thought persist 'with considerable vitality into the later fifteenth century and beyond . . . they survive increasingly in a situation of co-existence with other, newer (and no doubt at the same time older) ways of thinking.' Renaissance 'humanism' coexisted, but came into conflict, with the 'scholasticism' of medieval philosophy, 'and just as the great institutions of medieval society – the papacy, the empire, the "feudal monarchies", the canon and civil lawyers – survived only in changed forms, so medieval political ideas survived to play a part in changed circumstances and were themselves changed in the process.'

This may not tell us much about epochal shifts, and readers may find it hard to imagine any moment in history that could not be described in similar terms, as a unity of change and continuity. It may,

---

37 *The Cambridge History of Medieval Political Thought: c.350–c.450* (Cambridge: Cambridge University Press, 1988), p. 652.

indeed, be impossible to formulate our temporal parameters much more decisively than this. Yet there is something more to be said. If we take seriously the concept of feudalism as laid out in the previous chapter, the boundaries may be just a bit less difficult to draw. If we focus our attention on feudalism, it is possible to situate some significant epochal moments in the mid-fourteenth century and beyond: a time of plague, demographic collapse, peasant revolts and the Hundred Years War. Taken together, these developments spell the crisis of parcellized sovereignty, and we can begin to speak of 'transitions' from feudalism.

From the middle of the fourteenth to the late fifteenth century, there is a period of canonical scarcity, which ends decisively with Machiavelli.[38] When the story of the Western canon resumes, we are in a European world shaped by different relations between property and state. In the rising absolutist state, particularly in France, the monarchy is seeking to co-opt the nobility by replacing its feudal autonomy with privileges and perquisites of office. In England, where an already well-established central state had developed in tandem with a powerful landed aristocracy, we can begin to see the rise of agrarian capitalism. The city-states of northern Italy, for all the continuities in their communal forms, are now no longer battle grounds for conflicts between popes and Holy Roman emperors but for wars between French and Spanish monarchical states.

It was with one eye on these neighbouring states, which posed a wholly new challenge to civic autonomy in Italy, that Machiavelli reflected on the history and politics of Florence. In France, Jean Bodin, in support of monarchical centralization, would engage in philosophical disputes with constitutionalist thinkers defending the declining autonomous powers of provincial nobles and corporate entities; while in England, Thomas More (who served and eventually fell victim to a

---

38 Nicolas of Cusa (1401–64), who falls within this period of canonical scarcity, is certainly an important figure, though his inconsistencies and changes of position make him hard to situate in the history of the canon. Identified by some commentators as a major theorist of conciliarism, he has also been accused of helping to destroy it, when he ended by siding with the pope against the council of the Church. It is, in any case, arguable that his story, like that of conciliar theory in general, belongs to the crisis of parcellized sovereignty and the process of state-centralization, which will be left for another volume. Conciliarism flourished in a period when divisions in the Church, leading to a major schism, were aggravated and even generated by rising secular states, and especially the French monarchy, which bolstered their own power by aligning themselves with this or that pope.

powerful monarch) observed – and participated in – the dispossession of small producers by enclosure as, in his own words, 'sheep devoured men'.

These various 'transitions' from feudalism, and the diverse traditions of political theory that accompanied them, are the subject of another book. But if we can speak of a crisis – or crises – of feudalism, the mid-fourteenth century seems a natural place to end the medieval period. At the same time, we should keep in mind that the transitions which followed bore the marks of what preceded them. This is so not only in the sense that later developments in Western political thought inherited a powerful legacy but, more fundamentally, in the sense that the whole canonical tradition, in all its national variations, would continue to be shaped by the autonomy of property and distinctive tensions between property and state, which would play themselves out in all the various transitions.

The canon of Western political theory, while it includes some notably radical thinkers, is largely the work of members or clients of dominant classes. Popular voices are seldom heard in the canonical tradition. Yet it has been shaped by a complex three-way interaction between the state, appropriating classes and producers. Propertied classes have depended on the state to protect their property and dominance against the challenge from below, yet they have also been in conflict with the state and its intrusions from above. They have, in other words, always been compelled to fight on two fronts. This has also meant that challenge to political authority has come not only from resistance by subordinate classes to oppression by their overlords, but also from the overlords themselves in opposition to the state.

These complex interactions between the state and propertied classes have certainly sustained the traditions of Western political theory, raising fundamental questions about authority, legitimacy and obedience even when popular voices have been muted in their opposition to oppression. But this has generated certain ambiguities and paradoxes, which remain deeply ingrained in Western political theory and practice. It is, for example, significant that constitutional and even democratic doctrines in the West owe as much to the defence of aristocratic power and property as they do to popular struggles. The constitutive principles of Western liberal democracy, its ideas of limited and accountable government, have more to do with medieval lordship and its claims to autonomous power than with rule by the demos as conceived in ancient Athens.

It is not just that tensions have always existed between the idea of civic equality and the realities of class inequality. What is most ambiguous and paradoxical in the Western tradition of political theory, which was born in the civic community of ancient Greece, is that its foundational ideas of citizenship and civic equality have almost since the beginning been adapted to serve the cause of inequality and domination. We have seen, for example, how the idea of citizenship was used by the Romans as a hegemonic instrument of oligarchy and imperialism. Not only did the imperial idea of Roman citizenship replace civic agency with passive obedience, but even a republican thinker like Cicero found ways to finesse egalitarian ideas, turning democratic principles against themselves, by relegating equality to an abstract moral sphere beyond the inequalities of daily life and oligarchic rule.

Christian doctrine, too, would assert the equality of all human beings before God, while condoning profound inequality, oppression and even slavery in the mundane reality of life in this world. Early modern political theorists would declare that human beings (or at least men) were free and equal in the state of nature, and go on to construct arguments in favour of absolute monarchy (Hobbes) or rule by the propertied classes (Locke), not in opposition to but on the basis of natural equality, by applying the very elastic idea of consent. An emerging capitalist 'economy', with its purely 'economic' modes of class domination, would perfect the paradox, making it possible to relegate democracy to a formally separate 'political' sphere, while leaving intact the vast disparities of power between capital and labour in the market and the workplace and putting much of human life beyond the reach of democratic accountability, to be governed by market imperatives.

What is at issue here is not the familiar human inclination to profess one thing and do another. It is rather that such paradoxes lie at the very heart of Western political theory and practice. Ideas of limited and even democratic government have enjoyed a long and vigorous life in the Western tradition, not least because a particular formation of property, class and state power has made it possible for them to be adopted as ruling ideas, and not only expressions of popular power or resistance to dominant classes. But whatever this may have done for the longevity and vigour of such ideas, it has also restricted our conceptions of democracy. A more generous vision of human emancipation requires us to go beyond ruling ideas to a richer tradition of emancipatory struggle, in action and thought; but we can best reveal the limits of prevailing orthodoxies if we understand the canonical tradition and the historical experience in which it is rooted.

INDEX